Nietzsche on Epistemology and Metaphysics

To the memory of my mother, Marie J. Doyle

Nietzsche on Epistemology and Metaphysics

The World in View

Tsarina Doyle

Edinburgh University Press

© Tsarina Doyle, 2009

Edinburgh University Press Ltd
22 George Square, Edinburgh

www.euppublishing.com

Typeset in 10.5/13 Sabon
by Servis Filmsetting Ltd, Stockport, Cheshire, and
printed and bound in Great Britain by
CPI Antony Rowe, Chippenham and Eastbourne

A CIP record for this book is available from the British Library

ISBN 978 0 7486 2807 0 (hardback)

The right of Tsarina Doyle
to be identified as author of this work
has been asserted in accordance with
the Copyright, Designs and Patents Act 1988.

Contents

Acknowledgements

I would like to thank the Irish Research Council for the Humanities and Social Sciences for a postdoctoral fellowship 2004–6, during which time my research into the Kantian background to Nietzsche's metaphysics began to take shape. Thanks are due to Brian O'Connor who supported this research. I am particularly indebted to Peter Poellner for discussions that have played a decisive role in my thinking on Nietzsche. Thanks are also due to Tom Bailey with whom, at various times, I have discussed aspects of the arguments presented in the book. My family, especially my sister Ericka, have been a source of support to me throughout. Above all, I would like to thank John O'Reilly for his patience, unfailing support and lively philosophical conversation.

I have cited from *Beyond Good and Evil* by Friedrich Nietzsche, edited and translated Marion Faber (1998). By permission of Oxford University Press.

I have cited From *The Will to Power* by Friedrich Nietzsche, edited R. J. Hollingdale, translated Walter Kaufmann, © 1967 by Walter Kaufmann. Used by permission of Random House, Inc.

Introduction

In *Beyond Good and Evil* Nietzsche emphasises the organic interrelatedness of all concepts, arguing that every concept emerges in a specific historical context, an appreciation of which is necessary to understand the concept.[1] In light of this view it is incumbent on any interpreter of Nietzsche's writings to attempt to understand those writings in the historical context in which they emerged and developed. Writing in a letter dated 1866, 'Kant, Schopenhauer and this book by Lange – I do not need anything else', Nietzsche tells us quite clearly that the historical soil and climate in which his own ideas are given birth and nourished are those of modern philosophy, with the writings of Immanuel Kant at the top of the list.[2]

In the course of the present study I seek to engage in an issue-led investigation of Nietzsche's writings, viewing them in terms of their interaction with and response to the philosophy of Kant. Our aim here is to disclose philosophical issues that were of concern to Nietzsche, using Kant 'as a strong magnifying glass with which one can make visible a general but furtive state of distress which is hard to get hold of'.[3] Allowing Nietzsche's engagement with Kant to light the way, the study excavates the specifically philosophical side of Nietzsche, the side of him that celebrates a '*basic will* of knowledge which commands from deep within . . . something ever more precise', a characteristic which, Nietzsche claims, 'alone is fitting for a philosopher'.[4] Despite the fact that Nietzsche employs a notoriously unsystematic writing style, which enacts his views, for example, on the need to 'read slowly, deeply looking cautiously before and aft', he nonetheless warns us that this does not warrant the conclusion that systematic arguments are lacking in his writings.[5] In 'Assorted Opinions and Maxims' he writes, '*Against the shortsighted.* – Do you think this work must be fragmentary because I give it to you (and have to give it to you) in fragments?'[6] Therefore, the present study offers a methodical reading of Nietzsche, stressing the coherence and consistence of his arguments. The principal objective is to make sense of two of Nietzsche's principal ideas: his perspectivism and the will to power. The study appeals to a Kantian influence to these aspects of Nietzsche's thought on the basis of what he actually writes rather than by appealing to a list of his readings, demonstrating how much of what Nietzsche has to say with regard to the perspectival character of human knowledge and the will to power can be fruitfully understood as a response to Kant. The historical component of the study, then, is employed as a device to focus our attention on Nietzsche's arguments with regard to these topics. The goal is to show that Nietzsche's views on the perspectival direction of our knowledge and his metaphysics of the will to power are compatible, and that his metaphysics derives from his perspectivism. The study contends that, looked at in this way, the much maligned metaphysics of the will to power is supported by what Nietzsche thinks are good reasons, and that these reasons, although emerging in a specifically historical and Kantian context, are ones that might still be worthy of our consideration. This study examines these reasons, highlighting both the Kantian context in which they were formulated and how they may be deemed intelligible and coherent in their own right. The Kantian optic that sets the parameters of the study and provides a narrative thread as we navigate our way through Nietzsche's writings demands that we seek the intelligible structure informing his thought, speculating, in those instances where it is not entirely visible to the naked eye, where this structure might be found. Given the nature of such a project the arguments presented throughout the book are deliberately selective; I do not attempt to offer a comprehensive overview of all the themes Nietzsche addresses in his writings but rather examine Nietzsche as responding to a specific philosophical issue inherited from Kant: the epistemological and metaphysical relationship between self and world.

Bringing this philosophical issue into focus with his approval of Kant's project to reconcile 'knowledge and metaphysics',[7] Nietzsche applauds the anthropocentric turn of Kant's Copernican revolution as a welcome methodological rejection of dogmatism, overcoming the presupposition that we can access fundamental truths about reality directly by stepping outside our specifically human point of view.[8] However, Nietzsche's approval is less than total. He argues that Kant ultimately fails to execute his task and is responsible for inducing an epistemic gap between self and world. This gap ensues, Nietzsche contends, from both Kant's constitutive account of knowledge that reduces the object of knowledge to mind-dependent objects of our awareness and his reference to the thing-in-itself, which although mind-independent is radically divorced from the possibility of our knowing it. By focusing on both Nietzsche's perspectivism and will to power thesis, I argue that he overcomes the epistemic division of self and world by putting forward an anthropocentric conception of knowledge that nonetheless can be objective. According to Nietzsche, objective knowledge is impossible if reality, like Kant's thing-in-itself, is external to the conditions under which we come to know. Therefore, naturalising the knowing intellect, rendering it a participator rather than a spectator, Nietzsche argues that our perspectives are always perspectives *in* rather than *on* the world, having reality in view to varying degrees. Thus reality, Nietzsche argues, is metaphysically independent of but epistemically accessible to human knowledge. According to Nietzsche, our perspectives do not divorce us from reality but rather mark the seal of our essential and unavoidable engagement with it. His claim that our knowledge is perspectival is therefore an enabling rather than a limiting thesis.[9] Although our perspectives are sometimes simplifications of the complexity of reality, we can, Nietzsche suggests, through careful and rigorous analysis, strive towards achieving more refined accounts of the nature of things. This is because, for Nietzsche, human knowers, although part of the natural world, also have the capacity to reflect on and make intelligible sense of their experiences, to justify their claims to knowledge. This study does not address how one can make normative claims from within a naturalist setting, but rather begins on the basis that, for Nietzsche, the human world is *prima facie* characterised by reflection and the ability to give reasons. Since our knowledge is unavoidably and necessarily human, our investigation into the relationship between self and world must take place within the sphere of seeking reasons and justifications. To do anything else, Nietzsche tells us, constitutes a dogmatic attempt to 'look around our own corner'.[10]

The argument that our knowledge is perspectival yet objective culminates in Nietzsche's naturalisation of Kantian synthesis in his will to power metaphysics, transferring the ordering principle of reality from human minds to the world. Putting forward an account of intentionally directed reality informed by an intrinsic inner nature, Nietzsche maintains that the fundamental constituents of reality are ordered from within rather than by human minds. This interpretation differs considerably from the predominant anti-essentialist readings of Nietzsche to date,[11] which contend that Nietzsche rejects the idea of intrinsic natures, acceptance of which, it is claimed, would place his will to power in tension with his explicit rejection of substantialist metaphysics.[12] One of the problems with substantialist metaphysics, according to Nietzsche, is its view that empirical reality is grounded in a non-empirical and static substance. Nietzsche's will to power metaphysics, in contrast, puts forward the view that empirical reality is intrinsically constituted from within, requiring no external substrate, mental or otherwise, in which to subsist. Domesticating the will to power, bringing it safely within the sphere of empirical reality available to but metaphysically independent of human knowledge, the present study offers a distinctive interpretation of Nietzsche's metaphysics, viewing this metaphysics as emanating from Nietzsche's desire to overcome the dualisms that, in his view, beset Kant's efforts to reconcile self and world. Although Nietzsche contends that will to power manifests itself differently in the human and the non-human world, that the human world is demarcated from the non-human by virtue of its being a reflective world of beliefs, his claim that '*This world is the will to power – and nothing besides! And you yourselves are also this will to power – and nothing besides*'[13] nonetheless holds that human knowers, far from being epistemically and metaphysically divorced from a static, unknowable and non-empirical thing-in-itself, in fact have the world in view from within their immersion in its intrinsically constituted but dynamic and empirical nature.

A recent attempt to formulate the role of the will to power in Nietzsche's naturalisation of Kant contends that whilst Nietzsche allows that empirical objects are independent of human minds he holds they are ultimately dependent on non-human minds or the interrelations between mentalistic forces. Arguing that Nietzsche's will to power proposes a pan-psychism of force where everything is both a perceiver and perceived, this recent interpretation maintains that Nietzsche denies that an object (microscopic powers) can have characteristics that obtain independently of all observers.[14] This Berkeleian interpretation construes forces as existentially dependent on other forces, rendering them ideal rather than real. However, the present study holds that deeper penetration of Nietzsche's engagement with Kant, particularly on the concept of force and causality, shows that Nietzsche's naturalisation of Kant requires the reality rather than ideality of empirical powers and that this requirement can be met only by rejecting the idea of mind-dependency in all its forms.

Thus whilst the present study is indebted to several earlier commentaries that address the historical context of Nietzsche's writings in addition to those that emphasise epistemological and metaphysical themes in Nietzsche,[15] it is nevertheless distinctive both in its effort to see Nietzsche's epistemology and metaphysics as inextricably linked and in its pushing Nietzsche's naturalisation of Kant further than any other commentary to date. This study holds that not only is Nietzsche's perspectivism, as a thesis about the parameters of our knowledge, compatible with his metaphysics, but also that the former precedes the latter, ensuring that all metaphysical claims are non-dogmatic and informed by considered justification.[16] Moreover, highlighting the distinguishing nature of Nietzsche's metaphysical conclusions and the manner in which they are not just of historical interest but feed into contemporary metaphysical debates, this study revitalises Nietzsche's philosophical arguments. Counteracting the predominant idea that his conception of the nature of things is alienating, I argue instead that Nietzsche's world in view, far from amounting to a fairytale or fairground metaphysics, is in fact informed by both historically and conceptually intelligible reasons.

OUTLINE OF THE ARGUMENT

The Kantian background to Nietzsche's reconciliation of self and world is examined in two parts addressing both his perspectival epistemology and his metaphysics of the will to power. Nietzsche's praise for the anthropocentric and perspectival direction of Kant's Copernican turn provides the thematic focus of Part I, examining Nietzsche's appropriation and modification of Kant's epistemology. However, Nietzsche's perspectivism, as a thesis about the extent and limits of human knowledge, also provides the justificatory parameters within which he formulates his metaphysics. Thus, in Part II we investigate Nietzsche's view that reality is ordered intrinsically independently of human minds in his will to power thesis. Appropriating the concept of force in his account of causal connection, Nietzsche sides with Kant against Schopenhauer in his identification of force with efficient causality, but ultimately rejects Kant's view that relational properties are grounded in a non-relational and unknowable substratum. Then, putting forward the idea of intrinsic relational properties contrary to both Kant and Schopenhauer who, according to Nietzsche, take the view that intrinsicality is instantiated at the non-empirical and non-relational level of things-in-themselves, Nietzsche brings to fruition his envisaged reconciliation of self and world through a naturalisation of Kant's account of synthesis. This naturalisation of Kantian synthesis amounts to the claim that the world is constituted independently of human minds, thus allowing for Nietzsche's view that although the human knower is immersed in the world, neither the world nor human knowers are ultimately reducible to one another.[17]

Chapter 1 initiates the investigation of the Kantian background to Nietzsche's epistemology, arguing that Nietzsche's project of reconciling self and world is intertwined with both his appraisal and reconfiguration of Kant's distinction between constitutive knowledge and regulative belief. The chapter argues that Kant's constitutive account of knowledge contains two components: a thesis about rational justification and a thesis about the nature of objects. Whilst Nietzsche praises Kant's efforts to save the rational justification of our beliefs contrary to Hume's challenge, he contends that Kant ultimately fails to demonstrate the objectivity of our beliefs due to his reduction of rational justification to a description of our psychology. Kant, according to Nietzsche, succumbs to the genetic fallacy in his efforts to demonstrate the justification of our beliefs. Nietzsche also contends that Kant's reconfiguration of what we mean by an object of knowledge reduces objects that are knowable by us to mind-dependent objects of our awareness. According to Nietzsche, the Kantian object of knowledge is narrowly anthropocentric and, when considered in opposition to things-in-themselves, dangerously sceptical. Thus Nietzsche argues that Kant is guilty of perpetuating the distinction between appearance and reality, which in its specific Kantian form holds that empirical knowledge is possible only if the objects of our knowledge conform to the *a priori* forms of human understanding. Otherwise, reality is accessible only to a God's Eye View that is beyond us.

Nietzsche's rejection of Kant's constitutive account of knowledge and his assimilation of it to the status of regulative belief overturns the appearance/reality distinction by naturalising the human knower and abandoning the Kantian oscillation between merely human knowledge, on the one hand, and a God's Eye View on the other. Nietzsche contends that the knowing self, as a physiological rather than transcendental self, is not divorced from reality but in fact participates in reality. The forms of our knowledge are not imposed on reality from without but emerge and evolve in the context of the self's immersion in reality. As such, reality is neither a mind-dependent object nor an unknowable thing-in-itself but something that is in principle available to our knowledge.

Having examined Nietzsche's arguments for the non-constitutive character of our knowledge and thus the mind-independent status of reality in Chapter 1, Chapter 2 investigates how we can have objective knowledge of mind-independent reality without violating the anthropocentric conditions of our knowledge. Taking up Nietzsche's specific arguments in favour of the objectivity of human knowledge, the chapter examines his perspectivism as a rejection of 'metaphysical realism', a term I use to describe the general Kantian view that there is a non-empirical thing-in-itself. Nietzsche underlines two specific matters for concern with regard to metaphysical realism: first, the thing-in-itself, although mind-independent, is unknowable to human knowers; and second, as a result, it gives rise to a sceptical gap between self and world. Thus, although metaphysical realism, the thesis that reality is metaphysically independent of our knowledge, does not by definition entail scepticism, Nietzsche contends that the two ideas have been historically connected. Nietzsche's reasons for rejecting this scepticism are examined, focusing on his arguments in the later writings from *Human, All Too Human*. Fundamental to Nietzsche's disagreement with metaphysical realism in its historical guise is its dissociation of truth and justification. According to Nietzsche's metaphysical realist, our best justified beliefs may be in error because they may conceivably be divorced from how things are in themselves. Nietzsche's perspectivism plays a key role in his overcoming of this sceptical dissociation of our knowledge from how things are in themselves by demonstrating the incoherence of the thing-in-itself and the God's Eye View of knowledge that supports it. Adopting a contextualist account of justification, Nietzsche argues our truths are always justified from within a particular point of view, concluding that once the idea of extra-perspectival truth has been shown to be unintelligible there is no longer any reason to consider our perspectival truths as anything but objective. Pivotal to Nietzsche's argument from perspectivism is its rejection of the anti-empirical tendency of metaphysical realism. According to Nietzsche, the empirical world plays a role in the justification of our epistemic claims without acting as an epistemological foundation for those claims. Internal realism, the term I employ to describe Nietzsche's anti-metaphysical realist position, entails a theory-internal view of truth and justification, holding that our perspectives are rooted in the world and constrained internally from within our practices of contextually seeking out the best reasons for and against our epistemic claims.

Chapter 3 turns to Nietzsche's early writings, arguing that his later views regarding the perspectival yet objective character of our knowledge are present in an embryonic form in his early thought, but that these views struggle to emerge in the midst of his early immersion in the philosophical frameworks of both Kant and Schopenhauer. Kant's and Schopenhauer's view that empirical reality although knowable by us is mind-dependent, coupled with their reference to the unknowable but mind-independent thing-in-itself, prevents, in Nietzsche's view, a possible reconciliation of self and world. This chapter, examining Nietzsche's early arguments thematically rather than chronologically, argues that in 'On Truth and Lies in a Nonmoral Sense' (1873) Nietzsche remains trapped within the appearance/reality distinction, but in the even earlier *The Birth of Tragedy* (1872) he has at his disposal the conceptual resources to overcome it. In 'On Truth and Lies' Nietzsche adopts a constitutive account of knowledge, contending that our knowledge is of a mind-dependent empirical world, divorced from the, in principle, unknowable thing-in-itself. Nevertheless, by appealing to the reciprocal rather than oppositional relationship between the Apolline and the Dionysiac in his first published book, *The Birth of Tragedy*, and the notion of the instinctive intellect in the unpublished notes other than 'On Truth and Lies', Nietzsche sows the seeds for overcoming the separation of self and world. The instinctive intellect, Nietzsche argues, is a non-constitutive naturalised intellect immersed within reality rather than constituting it from without. Although he appeals to the idea of a non-human primordial intellect, which projects both the instinctive intellect and the empirical world as an appearance, Nietzsche denies he is committed to things-in-themselves or that he has transgressed the perspectival parameters of justifiable knowledge. Rather, he argues that both the instinctive and primordial intellect share the same experiences and that we arrive at this explanation of things as a regulative hypothesis drawn analogously to our own experience. In light of Nietzsche's rejection of the charge that both the primordial intellect and our experience of the empirical world constitute two worlds, this chapter charitably interprets the primordial intellect as a not wholly successful effort on Nietzsche's part to capture the inner nature of appearances, concluding that this somewhat obscure metaphysics is intended to safeguard rather than undermine the objectivity of human knowledge. Although Nietzsche later abandons this quasi-divine metaphysics, it nonetheless points to the metaphysics of the will to power and its attempt to reconcile at the level of empirical reality the relational character of things with their intrinsic natures in addition to prefiguring his later view that all metaphysical claims must derive from our perspectival epistemology if they are to be justifiable.

Nietzsche's perspectivism as a rejection of the possibility of disinterested knowledge from no particular point of view has been well documented in the secondary literature. However, understood as a rejection of absolute truth, it has long been thought incompatible with the possibility of metaphysics. That is, Nietzsche's perspectivism is generally thought to be incompatible with attempts to capture the true nature of reality. As a result, his status as a metaphysical thinker has been a matter of considerable dispute. Appealing to his many criticisms of the philosophical tradition, some commentators have gone to considerable lengths to dilute Nietzsche's will to power thesis of all metaphysical import, interpreting it predominantly as a psychological thesis.[18] Martin Heidegger's claim that the will to power is a traditional metaphysical thesis about the essence of things is a notable exception to such efforts.[19] He contends on the basis of an historically sensitive examination that Nietzsche's metaphysics represents the logical conclusion of the metaphysical tradition of the West. Tracing how the will to power emerges from a synthesis of Kant's identification of Being with conditions of representation and Leibniz's notion of Being as effectiveness, Heidegger contends that Nietzsche's metaphysics perpetuates the Western tradition's humanisation of Being by construing Being as evaluative. In so doing, Nietzsche, who sets himself up as the critic of the philosophical tradition *par excellence,* according to Heidegger, in fact represents the culmination of this tradition's forgetfulness of the question of Being. Whether or not we agree with Heidegger's evaluation of the philosophical tradition, he succeeds in both taking Nietzsche's metaphysics seriously and demonstrating its rootedness in the philosophical tradition, which in turn provides the key to understanding the compatibility of Nietzsche's perspectivism with his will to power thesis. For an examination of the specifically Kantian-informed methodology that lies at the heart of Nietzsche's approach to epistemology and metaphysics enables us to reconcile these two aspects of Nietzsche's thought.

Part II begins by demonstrating that Nietzsche's proposal of the metaphysics of the will to power complies with the anthropocentricism of his perspectival view of knowledge which in Part I we see emerges out of his praise for the anti-dogmatic aims of Kant's philosophy. Unlike Heidegger, however, who interprets Nietzsche's views on truth and knowledge as grounded in the metaphysics of the will to power, Part II argues that Nietzsche's will to power emerges from his perspectival views on truth and knowledge.[20] Then, having examined the status of the will to power as a comprehensive perspective that has explanatory scope across both the physical and anthropological sciences, Part II demonstrates that Nietzsche's metaphysics develops in the context of his critical engagement with both Kant's constitutive-regulative distinction at the level of epistemology and his treatment of force and efficient causality at the level of metaphysics. These investigations conclude that the coherence of Nietzsche's will to power thesis resides in its espousal, contrary to both Kant and Schopenhauer, of the idea of intrinsic relational properties.

Chapter 4 commences the investigation into Nietzsche's metaphysics by addressing his justification of the will to power. Contrary to what I label the 'textual' and the 'philosophical' arguments against understanding Nietzsche as a metaphysical thinker, the chapter demonstrates that the attribution of a metaphysics to Nietzsche is both textually and philosophically defensible. Its philosophical defence resides in the fact that the will to power derives from Nietzsche's perspectivism. Rather than constituting merely an expression of Nietzsche's own values or an extra-perspectival claim to knowledge, Nietzsche presents the will to power as a comprehensive perspective that is warranted in multiple perspectives. The will to power is thus intra-contextually warranted rather than justified outside all contexts. Incorporating the points of view of both the physical and the anthropological sciences, the will to power emerges in the context of Nietzsche's efforts to overcome the polarities of materialist atomism and subjective idealism. Contending both points of view are one-sided arguments that give priority to either physical science (the quantitative 'objective' view) or anthropological science (the qualitative 'subjective' view) Nietzsche argues that the will to power is a comprehensive perspective that unifies these opposing points of view rather than reducing all explanation to one of them. Appropriating Boscovich's concept of force and supplementing it with an inner will analogously to our own experience, Nietzsche undercuts the distinction between non-relational, 'objective' primary qualities and relational 'subjective' secondary qualities, arguing instead for the mind-independent reality of powers. Moreover, his appeal to an argument from analogy is different from his criticism of some forms of analogical reasoning in his mature thought, where he expresses disapproval of the idea that human consciousness can act as a transparent and immediately knowable foundation for our knowledge of the outer world.[21] Nietzsche's appeal to analogy in support of the will to power thesis does not presuppose privileged knowledge of our inner selves but rather derives an account of the nature of the self from an attempt to offer a comprehensive explanation of things. Nietzsche's conclusion that the self can be understood as will to power and hence that the self is something complicated and diverse is a far cry from the transparent unity which he criticises in the appeal to introspection. Nietzsche's use of an argument from analogy constitutes, therefore, not an appeal to introspective immediacy, but rather an acknowledgement that justification of the will to power thesis, overcoming the opacity of the physicist's account of force in addition to offering a non-atomistic account of the human self, must take place from within the sphere of human perspectives. His appeal to analogy is thus an acknowledgement that we cannot step outside our own skins and not an appeal to privileged knowledge. However, as Nietzsche's attribution of an inner nature to the physicist account of force is central to the success of the will to power as a comprehensive perspective, the feasibility of combining intrinsic and relational natures forms the focus of the final two chapters.

Examining Nietzsche's mediated engagement with Kant through Schopenhauer, Chapter 5 holds that for Nietzsche the fundamental constituents of reality are powers obtaining at the level of empirical reality rather than things-in-themselves. Tracing how both Nietzsche's early and late writings engage not only with Kant's 'critical' thought but also with his 'pre-critical' writings and their response to the *vis viva* debate waged by Descartes and Leibniz, the chapter examines Nietzsche's thesis that the empirical reality of powers can be secured only by demonstrating both the intrinsicality and relationality of powers. Nietzsche's argument in support of this thesis takes us through a two-pronged engagement with Kant. First, Nietzsche praises Kant's pre-critical attempt in *Universal Natural History and Theory of the Heavens* to combine under one empirical description the mechanical relationality of powers along with their intrinsicality, arguing, however, that this attempt ultimately succumbs to failure as a result of its physico-theology, dogmatically inferring the existence of a creator from observations of empirical order. Second, Nietzsche contends that although Kant's critical philosophy overcomes the problem of dogmatism, it gives up the project of reconciling intrinsicality and relationality within the empirical sphere by reducing knowable empirical reality to mind-dependent mechanical relations constituted by us and relegating intrinsic natures to mind-independent but unknowable things-in-themselves. Sharing Kant's aim to shun dogmatism but wanting to avoid the dissociation of intrinsicality and relationality, Nietzsche abandons Kant's constitutive account of knowledge, assimilating it to the status of regulative belief. Nietzsche contends that Kant deprives regulative belief of true cognitive status by rendering it parasitic upon constitutive knowledge. According to Nietzsche, once we realise that reality is mind-independent but in principle available to our knowledge and that we are entitled to make cognitive regulative judgements about the intrinsic nature of things we can secure the metaphysical reality of empirical powers.

Nonetheless, Nietzsche's proposal that the fundamental constituents of reality are both intrinsic and relational is a contentious metaphysical thesis. Chapter 6 examines the philosophical cogency of the proposal, defending it from attacks made from within the confines of Nietzsche studies and beyond. Informing the objection is the idea that powers are bare dispositions that can be real only if they are grounded in a non-relational and non-power substrate. Furthermore, it is argued that intrinsicality and relationality are incongruous because relationality, unlike intrinsicality, is existentially committed.

Examining both Nietzsche's bundle theory of objects and the role of resistance in bringing powers into relations, the chapter argues that, for

Nietzsche, powers do not logically imply other powers on which they are existentially dependent. Rather, when placed in the context of Nietzsche's rejection of an event model of causality that contends that a relational thing is an existentially committed thing and his acceptance of a power model of causality that maintains that the proper relata of a power is the manifestation of its own nature rather than another power that seeks to interpret it and to which it is ultimately reducible, the chapter holds the intrinsic nature of relational powers resides in their existential independence from other powers. Examining two contemporary attempts to save the reality and intrinsicality of powers, the chapter argues that the first, conditional analysis is unsuitable to Nietzsche's project but that the second, a position that bears strong parallels with Nietzsche's own argument from analogy, yields more fruitful consequences. This argument, proposing that intentionality is characteristic of both the physical and the mental world in conjunction with its rejection of an event model of causality, facilitates Nietzsche's argument in favour of the reality of causal powers. Finally, rejecting the objection that powers cannot be empirically instantiated because they are not spatially located and arguing instead that spatial location is an extrinsic property of objects, the chapter demonstrates the coherence of Nietzsche's metaphysics as the culmination of his response to Kant. By demonstrating the metaphysical reality of empirical powers Nietzsche dissolves the appearance/reality distinction, arguing that empirical reality, although knowable by us, is, by virtue of the intrinsic natures informing its relational constituents, irreducible to human minds.

The arguments presented in this study see Nietzsche not only as immersed within the philosophical tradition, modifying it from the inside but also as committed to both the possibility of knowledge and adequate metaphysical accounts of the nature of reality. However, it has been strenuously argued from some quarters that Nietzsche is more concerned with the issue of value rather than with traditional epistemological issues of justification and truth or with the possibility of metaphysics.[22] As a result, it has been claimed that Nietzsche is more concerned with whether a belief enhances our life rather than with its epistemic status. Whilst I concur with the claim that Nietzsche is interested in the question of value, it is mistaken to think that he formulates his views on such matters independently of epistemological or metaphysical commitments.

That Nietzsche's philosophy of value is formulated against the background of such commitments can be discerned by reflecting on his existential project of replacing life negation with affirmation. Life denial rather than affirmation, according to Nietzsche, trades on the idea of a 'true' world in comparison with which the world of our experience is deemed false or illusory. He argues on the basis of genealogical investigation that, despite their appeal to the 'true world' to justify the denigration of the status of empirical reality, previous metaphysical systems in the guise of Plato's Forms and Kant's things-in-themselves have operated with a fictional conception of things. Nietzsche's genealogical argument aims to show that such metaphysical systems and the life-denying philosophy that ensues from them can be overcome only by discrediting such metaphysics. Nietzsche claims that intellectual honesty is necessary for this discrediting to take place. Moreover, intellectual honesty, he argues, leads to a more adequate account of reality. Nietzsche thus writes that nihilism or the realisation that the notion of a 'true world' is devoid of a metaphysical grounding emerges in the context of 'truthfulness',[23] which in turn begets knowledge. Defining the nihilist as one 'who judges of the world as it is that it ought *not* to be, and of the world as it ought to be that it does not exist',[24] Nietzsche argues that the conflict between our desires and reality leads to our coming to know the course of reality:

> it is only this desire 'thus it ought to be' that has called forth that other desire to know what *is*. For the knowledge of what is, is a consequence of that question: 'How? Is it possible? Why precisely so?' Wonder at the disagreement between our desires and the course of the world has led to our learning to know the course of the world.[25]

According to Nietzsche, our existentialist concerns are intertwined with epistemological and metaphysical ones. Therefore, just as the diagnosis of nihilism presupposes truthfulness and knowledge, so too does its overcoming; we must have knowledge of the nature of reality, Nietzsche suggests, if we are to properly affirm it:

> It is at this point and nowhere else that one must make a start if one is to understand what Zarathustra's intentions are: the species of man that he delineates delineates reality *as it is*, he is strong enough for it – he is not estranged from or entranced by it, he is *reality itself*, he still has all that is fearful and questionable in reality in him, *only thus can man possess greatness*.[26]

Nietzsche is of course aware that considerably more than this is required for a successful overcoming of nihilist metaphysics. To discredit it and formulate a more adequate account of reality is not enough. We must also investigate why such a world-view and its promise of a metaphysical other-world has been so attractive to us and how, confronted with its demise, we can motivate ourselves to act. Nietzsche engages in this type of investigation in both his psychological examination of the ascetic ideal and *ressentiment* in addition to his ultimately uncompleted project of a revaluation of values.[27] Although Nietzsche does not suggest that our transvalued human values and ideals are read off from reality, he argues that they are nonetheless expressions of our fundamental nature as will to power such that good becomes identified with strength, bad with weakness and happiness with 'The feeling that power *increases* – that a resistance is overcome'.[28] Thus whilst Gilles Deleuze's postmodernist interpretation, for example, is correct in its claim that Nietzsche is concerned with questions of value, Nietzsche construes value estimations as expressions of a metaphysical principle that presupposes, despite Deleuze's suggestions to the contrary, the possibility of adequate knowledge of reality. According to Deleuze, questions of adequacy, and so on, are inextricably linked to the dogmatic quest for transcendent truth, which, he correctly contends, Nietzsche abandons. Thus, whilst interpreting him as responding to the modern philosophical tradition of Kant and Hegel, Deleuze sees Nietzsche as abandoning the tradition outright. Writing, for example, that Nietzsche rejects the very notion of truth espoused by the philosophical tradition, Deleuze claims that Nietzsche replaces the disinterested quest for transcendent truth with a typology and symptomology of activity/nobility and reactivity/baseness. Deleuze writes:

> A new image of thought means primarily that truth is not the element of thought. The element of thought is sense and value. The categories of thought are not truth and falsity but the *noble* and the *base*, the *high* and the *low,* depending on the nature of the forces that take hold of thought itself.[29]

Deleuze's claim that Nietzsche reduces truth to an expression of value falters, however, with his further contention that value is an expression of the will to power.[30] This is because his appeal to the formative role of the will to power to questions of value arguably presupposes the veracity of the thesis, suggesting that, for Nietzsche, rejection of transcendent truth does not entail a denial of the possibility of knowledge altogether. Rather, according to Nietzsche, questions of value, such as that of life affirmation, rely on the possibility of knowledge. Nietzsche writes that 'this ultimate, joyfullest, boundlessly exuberant Yes to life is not only the highest insight, it is also the *profoundest,* the insight most strictly confirmed and maintained by truth and knowledge'.[31] A study of Nietzsche's epistemology and metaphysics, an account of how he arrives at and justifies the will to power thesis, is, therefore, a necessary prerequisite to a study of his philosophy of value. An examination of Nietzsche's epistemology and metaphysics, articulating the reasons informing his proposal of the will to power, can stand alone, whereas a study of his philosophy of value based on the will to power always presupposes that Nietzsche has intelligible reasons for putting forward the thesis in the first place.

Finally, there are two further possible objections to the project that must be addressed. The first relates to my decision to employ the term 'metaphysics' rather than 'ontology'. In *Nietzsche: Naturalism and Interpretation*, Christoph Cox has opted to employ the term 'ontology' rather than 'metaphysics'.[32] Cox argues that 'ontology' does not carry the other-worldly implications that Nietzsche vehemently rejects and associates with traditional metaphysics. However, my decision to employ the term 'metaphysics' rather than 'ontology' is motivated by the desire to capture the speculative and regulative character of Nietzsche's claims about the nature of reality.[33] These claims are speculative, not because they are unjustified, but rather because they are explanations with comprehensive scope and not merely empirical descriptions of reality. Rather, as I shall show, metaphysics constitutes, for Nietzsche, a research project guided by our interests and ultimately justified according to a strict methodology.[34] Thus, the use of the term 'metaphysics' is not intended to suggest that Nietzsche engages in any way in the other-worldly flights of fancy he castigates in Plato and Christianity.

The final issue that must be addressed before we proceed in earnest involves the status of those writings not published in Nietzsche's lifetime. There is a line of thought in contemporary Nietzsche studies that advocates restricting all analysis to Nietzsche's published writings.[35] Bernd Magnus, for example, has gone to considerable lengths to convince us that the collection of notes posthumously published as *The Will to Power* is not a book Nietzsche had intended for publication. Magnus provides evidence for his claim that whilst Nietzsche had seriously considered publishing a book with this title, he had by September 1888 abandoned the project altogether.[36] Magnus thus argues that we are not justified in formulating an understanding of Nietzsche's thought on the basis of the posthumously published notes. Magnus's argument obviously proves problematic for any study of Nietzsche's epistemological and metaphysical views. For Nietzsche's thoughts on these issues are given greater attention in the posthumous material. As Richard Schacht notes, the 'unpublished writings . . . contain much more of [Nietzsche's] expressed thinking on certain important matters than do his finished works'.[37] However, Schacht contends that Nietzsche's case is unusual and presents considerations that warrant a rethinking of the status of the unpublished notes. He argues that Nietzsche's illness was sudden and struck at a time when he had begun to publish with increasing frequency. Arguing that the notebooks were the workshop for Nietzsche's published writings, Schacht suggests the notes provide some clue to what would have been Nietzsche's future compositions.[38]

There is, however, a more philosophical reason that warrants the use of the posthumous material in formulating an interpretation of Nietzsche. This study, whilst acknowledging the concerns of Magnus and others, takes the view that any issue-led reading of Nietzsche is obliged to consider the posthumous writings in a serious and detailed way. The reasons for this centre on my contention that Nietzsche is primarily a philosopher who is concerned to address philosophical issues. In so doing, he attempts to get inside a philosophical problem, so to speak, addressing this particular problem by embodying multiple perspectives with regard to it. He writes:

> I am trying to be useful to those who are worthy of being seriously and opportunely introduced to philosophy. This attempt may or may not succeed. I am only too well aware that it can be surpassed and I wish nothing more than that I might be imitated and surpassed to the benefit of this philosophy.[39]

Nietzsche's writings are, by his own admission, very much the writings of a working philosopher. However, Nietzsche not only puts himself to work, he also makes his readers work through his unsystematic and aphoristic writing style, encouraging them to engage with philosophy by forcing them to occupy the various perspectives that he himself has occupied. Moreover, he forces his readers to organise these perspectival thoughts into a coherent structure. Thus Nietzsche's writings as a whole are a workshop for his interpreters, which, as Karl Jaspers points out, engage his readers in a creative and constructive fashion by encouraging them to philosophise themselves.[40] This being the case, it is difficult to formulate a convincing argument to demote the philosophical status of the posthumous material, which were arguably the contents of his own workshop. Furthermore, although questions of style are not insignificant in Nietzsche's writings, the style he adopts in the posthumous material is often more direct than that adopted in the published writings, making the unpublished notes a valuable source of possible clarification on issues that are sometimes deliberately obtusely formulated in the published writings.[41] Thus, even though Nietzsche had abandoned his plan to publish a book called *The Will to Power*, the unpublished notes, if treated with care and as a supplement to the published writings, provide a valuable insight into Nietzsche's epistemological and metaphysical arguments. For these reasons I shall use Nietzsche's unpublished notes as a source of clarification and supplementation of his published arguments regarding his response to Kant on the issue of the epistemological and metaphysical relation between self and world.

NOTES

1. Friedrich Nietzsche, *Beyond Good and Evil,* translated by Marion Faber (Oxford: Oxford University Press, 1998 [1886]), 20. Henceforth cited as *BGE.*
2. Letter to Mushacke, November 1866. See *Friedrich Nietzsche. Sämtliche Briefe. Kritische Studienausgabe,* edited by Giorgio Colli and Mazzino Montinari, 8 volumes (Munich: dtv; Berlin and New York: de Gruyter, 1986), 2, p. 184. I shall not address Nietzsche's relationship with Lange, which has already been given detailed consideration in the literature. Although Lange introduces Nietzsche to some points of contention in both the Kantian and Schopenhauerian systems, in addition to educating him in the natural sciences, Nietzsche remains true to his claim that 'One repays a teacher badly if one remains only a pupil' (Friedrich Nietzsche, *Thus Spoke Zarathustra,* translated by R. J. Hollingdale (London: Penguin, 1969 [1883–92], Part One, 'Of the Bestowing Virtue', 3), ultimately using what he learns from Lange to undermine the latter's idealism and scepticism, positions that Nietzsche argues originate in Kant. For discussions of Lange and Nietzsche see, for example, George J. Stack, *Lange and Nietzsche* (New York: de Gruyter, 1983); Claudia Crawford, *Nietzsche's Theory of Language* (New York: de Gruyter, 1988), chapter 6.
3. Friedrich Nietzsche, *Ecce Homo,* translated by R. J. Hollingdale (London: Penguin, 1992 [1908]), 'Why I am So Wise', 7. Henceforth cited as *EH.*
4. Friedrich Nietzsche, *On the Genealogy of Morality,* translated by Maudemarie Clark and Alan J. Swensen (Indianapolis, IN: Hackett, 1998 [1887]), Preface, 2. Henceforth cited as *GM.*
5. Friedrich Nietzsche, *Daybreak,* translated by R. J. Hollingdale (Cambridge: Cambridge University Press, 1993 [1881, new Preface 1886]), Preface, 5.
6. Friedrich Nietzsche, *Human, All Too Human,* translated by R. J. Hollingdale (Cambridge: Cambridge University Press, 1996 [1878–86, 'Assorted Opinions and Maxims' is the first sequel, 1879], Volume II, Part One, 128). Henceforth cited as *HAH.*
7. Friedrich Nietzsche, *The Will to Power,* edited by R. J. Hollingdale, translated by Walter Kaufmann (New York: Vintage Books, 1968 [1901]), 458. Henceforth cited as *WP.* Here Nietzsche criticises Kant for treating this issue as a purely theoretical one. However, that Nietzsche aims to reconcile knowledge and metaphysics can be seen from his praise of Schopenhauer's desire to reconcile 'knowledge and being'. Friedrich Nietzsche, 'Schopenhauer as Educator', 3 (1874) in *Untimely Meditations,* translated by R. J. Hollingdale (Cambridge: Cambridge University Press, 1994 [1873–76]).
8. Friedrich Nietzsche, *The Birth of Tragedy,* translated by Ronald Speirs (Cambridge: Cambridge University Press, 1999 [1872]), pp. 87–8 section 18. See also Nietzsche, *BGE,* Preface.
9. Bernd Magnus and Arthur Danto, for example, interpret Nietzsche's perspectivism as a limiting thesis. See Bernd Magnus, 'The Deification of the Commonplace', in Robert C. Solomon and Kathleen M. Higgins (eds), *Reading Nietzsche* (Oxford: Oxford University Press, 1988), pp. 152ff.; Arthur Danto, *Nietzsche as Philosopher* (New York: Columbia University Press, 1980 [1965]). For a critical discussion of the interpretation of perspectivism as a limiting

thesis, see Maudemarie Clark, *Nietzsche on Truth and Philosophy* (Cambridge: Cambridge University Press, 1990), chapter 5. See also Steven D. Hales and Rex Welshon, *Nietzsche's Perspectivism* (Urbana and Chicago, IL: University of Illinois Press, 2000), chapter 5; Bernard Reginster, *The Affirmation of Life: Nietzsche on Overcoming Nihilism* (Cambridge, MA: Harvard University Press, 2006), pp. 81–5.

10. Friedrich Nietzsche, *The Gay Science*, translated by Walter Kaufmann (New York: Vintage Books, 1974 [1882/1887]), 374; section 374 is from Book V, the second edition, dated 1887. Henceforth cited as GS. Michael Steven Green interprets Nietzsche's naturalism as a response to Afrikan Spir, arguing that Nietzsche's commitment to naturalism disallows the possibility of objectively valid judgement. Michael Steven Green, *Nietzsche and the Transcendental Tradition* (Urbana and Chicago, IL: University of Illinois Press, 2002). Maudemarie Clark and David Dudrick, in contrast, have recently argued that what Nietzsche learns from Spir is the importance of the distinction between causes and reasons, allowing Nietzsche to combine naturalism with the possibility of objectively valid belief. Maudemarie Clark and David Dudrick, 'The Naturalisms of *Beyond Good and Evil*', in Keith Ansell Pearson, *A Companion to Nietzsche* (Oxford: Blackwell, 2006). In GS, 374 from Book V, written immediately after *BGE*, Nietzsche entertains the possibility that normativity is characteristic of both the human and the non-human worlds, writing that we are not permitted to assume that interpretations are possible only within the human world. Although Nietzsche is reluctant to draw out the implications of this suggestion, commitment to it would lead to the idea that the natural world of causes is fraught with reasons. This conclusion arguably follows from Nietzsche's ascription of intrinsic natures to powers in his will to power thesis. However, since at times Nietzsche seems intent on clearly demarcating causes and reasons (Nietzsche, GM, III, 25), it is not necessary for us to pursue the issue any further. Suffice to say that for Nietzsche the human world is one that is characterised by reflection.

11. The most notable discussions of the issue of intrinsic natures in the context of Nietzsche's views on essentialism are Peter Poellner, *Nietzsche and Metaphysics* (Oxford: Oxford University Press, 1995); and Hales and Welshon, *Nietzsche's Perspectivism*. John Richardson attributes essentialism to Nietzsche. See his *Nietzsche's System* (Oxford: Oxford University Press, 1996).

12. See, for example, Nietzsche, *BGE*, 12. See also Nietzsche, *Twilight of the Idols*, included in *Twilight of the Idols/The Anti-Christ*, translated by R. J. Hollingdale (London: Penguin, 1990 [1889]), '"Reason" in Philosophy', 3, 5. Henceforth cited as *TI*.

13. Nietzsche, *WP*, 1067.

14. R. Kevin Hill, *Nietzsche's Critiques: The Kantian Foundations of His Thought* (Oxford: Clarendon Press, 2003), pp. 136ff.

15. Studies that focus on the historical context of Nietzsche's writings include Martin Heidegger, *Nietzsche*, translated by David Farrell Krell (San Francisco: HarperCollins, 1991 [1961]); Robin Small, *Nietzsche in Context* (Aldershot: Ashgate, 2001); Green, *Nietzsche and the Transcendental Tradition*; Hill, *Nietzsche's Critiques: The Kantian Foundations of His Thought*. Writers who emphasise epistemological and metaphysical themes in Nietzsche's writings include Richard Schacht, *Nietzsche* (London and New York: Routledge, 1995 [1983]); Clark, *Nietzsche on Truth and Philosophy*; Poellner, *Nietzsche and Metaphysics*; Hales and Welshon, *Nietzsche's Perspectivism*; Richardson, *Nietzsche's System*.

16. Mark T. Conard, 'Nietzsche's Kantianism', *International Studies in Philosophy*, Vol. 33, No. 3, 2001, and Peter Poellner, 'Perspectival Truth', in John

Richardson and Brian Leiter (eds), *Nietzsche* (Oxford: Oxford University Press, 2001) address the compatibility of Nietzsche's epistemology and metaphysics, arguing, however, that Nietzsche's epistemology derives from his metaphysics. See also Richardson's *Nietzsche's System*, p. 11. By emphasising the Kantian background to Nietzsche's thought, I argue, in contrast, that his epistemology is prioritised over the metaphysics.

17. See, for example, Nietzsche's description of the human as both natural and anti-natural in Nietzsche, *GS*, 354 and Nietzsche *GM*, III, 25.

18. Commentators who argue that Nietzsche's perspectivism does not entitle him to make metaphysical claims include Clark, *Nietzsche on Truth and Philosophy*, and Danto, *Nietzsche as Philosopher*. Walter Kaufmann argues that the will to power is compatible with Nietzsche's perspectivism by reducing the status of the will to power to that of an empirical theory in psychology, which he maintains is compatible with perspectivism in a similar manner to other empirical theories. Walter Kaufmann, *Nietzsche: Philosopher, Psychologist, Antichrist* (Princeton, NJ: Princeton University Press, 1974), p. 206.

19. Heidegger, *Nietzsche*, Volume 3.

20. According to Heidegger, Nietzsche accepts Kant's notion of truth as correctness but contends that correctness is a value estimation, in particular an expression of the conditions of preservation and growth as conditions of life. The biologism entailed in the appeal to conditions of life, Heidegger argues, is grounded in the metaphysics of the will to power. See Heidegger, *Nietzsche*, Volume 3, pp. 32–7.

21. Nietzsche, *GS*, 333, 355. See also Nietzsche, *TI*, 'The Four Great Errors', 3.

22. See, for example, Bernd Magnus, *Nietzsche's Existential Imperative* (London: Indiana University Press, 1978); Gilles Deleuze, *Nietzsche and Philosophy*, translated by Hugh Tomlinson (London: Athlone Press, 1992 [1962]); Ken Gemes, 'Nietzsche's Critique of Truth', in Richardson and Leiter (eds), *Nietzsche*; Reginster, *The Affirmation of Life: Nietzsche on Overcoming Nihilism*.

23. Nietzsche, *WP*, 3. Elsewhere he writes of the 'self-overcoming of morality through truthfulness' (Nietzsche, *EH*, 'Why I am a Destiny', 3). For further passages where Nietzsche argues for the importance of knowledge, see, for example, Nietzsche, *HAH*, Volume I, 'Tokens of Higher and Lower Culture', 252, 288, 292, and Nietzsche, *GS*, 14, 242, 249, 324, 343.

24. Nietzsche, *WP*, 585.

25. Ibid., 333.

26. Nietzsche, *EH*, 'Why I am a Destiny', 5.

27. Nietzsche's unpublished notes contain several outlines for a planned but never completed revaluation of values. *The Anti-Christ* is the first book of this revaluation.

28. Friedrich Nietzsche, *The Anti-Christ*, included in *Twilight of the Idols/The Anti-Christ*, translated by R. J. Hollingdale (London: Penguin, 1990 [1895]), 2. Henceforth cited as *AC*.

29. Ibid., p. 104. Deleuze argues that Nietzsche replaces Kant's transcendental critique with genealogy, fully realising the project of immanent critique attempted but ultimately unexecuted by Kant. According to Deleuze, Kant fails to realise this project because he 'lacked a method which permitted reason to be judged from the inside without giving it the task of being its own judge'. Deleuze maintains that Kant's conception of critique 'saw critique as a force which should be brought to bear on all claims to knowledge and truth, but not on knowledge and truth themselves'. Therefore, Kant's critique 'begins by believing in what it criticises'. Nietzsche's will to power, however, as a genetic and genealogical principle realises the project of immanent critique because it requires a genesis of reason

itself and the forces of reason. Deleuze, *Nietzsche and Philosophy*, pp. 89–94. Although Deleuze's immanentist interpretation is compelling, his juxtaposition of truth and value, reducing non-transcendent truths to expressions of value, is nevertheless guilty of committing Nietzsche to the very oppositional thinking that he aims to avoid.

30. Ibid., pp. 62–3.
31. Nietzsche, *EH*, 'The Birth of Tragedy', 2. At times Nietzsche argues that we need to create self-conscious fictions that are capable of motivating us to act. However, writing in *The Gay Science* that we choose fictions '*out of profundity*' (Nietzsche, *GS*, Preface, 4), Nietzsche argues that their self-conscious character presupposes truth and knowledge (see also Nietzsche, *BGE*, 39).
32. Christoph Cox, *Nietzsche: Naturalism and Interpretation* (London: University of California Press, 1999), pp. 6–7.
33. See John Wilcox, *Truth and Value in Nietzsche* (Ann Arbor, MI: The University of Michigan Press, 1974). Wilcox appropriately terms Nietzsche's metaphysics a 'speculative cosmology' or 'metaphysics in the empirical sense' (ibid., p. 120).
34. In *BGE*, 210 Nietzsche describes philosophy as an 'experiment' that incorporates both a strict methodology and high standards.
35. See Bernd Magnus, 'The Use and Abuse of *The Will to Power*', in Solomon and Higgins (eds), *Reading Nietzsche*, pp. 218–35. See also Wayne Klein, *Nietzsche and the Promise of Philosophy* (Albany, NY: SUNY Press, 1997), pp. 181–99; and Clark, *Nietzsche on Truth and Philosophy*, pp. 25–7.
36. Magnus, 'The Use and Abuse of *The Will to Power*', p. 225.
37. Schacht, *Nietzsche*, p. xii.
38. Richard Schacht, *Making Sense of Nietzsche: Reflections Timely and Untimely* (Chicago, IL: University of Illinois Press, 1995), pp. 118–19.
39. Friedrich Nietzsche, 'The Philosopher: Reflections on the Struggle between Art and Knowledge', paragraph 159 (1872), in *Philosophy and Truth: Selections from Nietzsche's Notebooks of the Early 1870's*, edited and translated by Daniel Breazeale (London: Humanities Press, 1993).
40. Karl Jaspers, *Nietzsche: An Introduction to the Understanding of his Philosophical Activity* (Baltimore, MD and London: Johns Hopkins University Press, 1997 [1936]), especially Introduction.
41. For Nietzsche's description of his style as 'esoteric', see Nietzsche, *BGE*, 30, 39, 43.

Part I
Epistemology

Chapter 1

Nietzsche's Appropriation of Kant

Throughout his writings Nietzsche highlights the dangers of oppositional thinking, which, in his view, has characterised the history of metaphysical thought. In *Human, All Too Human* he writes, 'Almost all the problems of philosophy once again pose the same form of question as they did two thousand years ago: how can something originate in its opposite.'[1] One such opposition that exercises Nietzsche is that between self and world. The difficulty centres on what Nietzsche sees as the 'opposition' between the world as it is known 'by us' and the world considered in itself and apart from human interpretations. Nietzsche contends that philosophical responses to this question have tended to oscillate between realism and idealism, appealing to a dogmatic God's Eye View on the one hand, or reducing the world to the forms of our knowledge on the other. He writes, 'Metaphysical philosophy has hitherto surmounted this difficulty by denying that the one originates in the other and assuming for the more highly valued thing a miraculous source in the very kernel and being of the "thing in itself"', or else, denying the human forms of our knowledge change and evolve 'some of them would have it that the whole world is spun from out of this faculty of cognition'.[2] Consequently, when Nietzsche writes in *The Gay Science* that 'We laugh as soon as we encounter the juxtaposition of "man *and* world," separated by the sublime presumption of the little word "and"', he highlights as an issue of philosophical importance the overcoming of this opposition.[3] In this chapter we see that Nietzsche's project of reconciling self and world is intertwined with both his appraisal and reworking of Kant's epistemology and that informing Nietzsche's response to Kant is his understanding and modification of Kant's distinction between constitutive knowledge and regulative belief.[4]

Central to Kant's constitutive account of knowledge, according to Nietzsche, are two components. The first is a thesis about rational justification; the second a thesis about the nature of objects. With regard to the first, Nietzsche points to Kant's aim of overcoming Hume's challenge regarding the rational justification of our beliefs. The second entails Kant's transcendental idealist claim that our rationally justified beliefs are objectively applicable to the empirical sphere that conforms to the conditions of our knowledge rather than to things as they are in themselves. In this way, Nietzsche contends, Kant promises to make the sphere of naturalistic phenomena an object of knowledge. However, Nietzsche argues that despite the merits of his response to Hume, Kant fails to execute either task successfully. Rather, Kant's philosophy, according to Nietzsche, perpetuates the distinction between appearances and things-in-themselves, oscillating between a position where the world is in view but only to the extent that it reduces to the transcendental and *a priori* forms of our knowledge and the claim that the world is not accessible to us but only to a God's Eye View that can never be ours.

Nietzsche's rejection of Kant's constitutive account of knowledge and his assimilation of it to the status of regulative belief aim to overcome this dichotomy by allowing for the possibility of objective human knowledge. That is, Nietzsche abandons the Kantian oscillation between a mere human point of view on the one hand, and a God's Eye View on the other. According to Nietzsche, once man has been returned to nature[5] and all our knowledge claims are justified regulatively rather than constitutively, it can be seen that the specifically human point of view is not divorced from reality but rather is in constant engagement with it, having the world in view to a greater or lesser extent. Our epistemic task then becomes that of adjudicating between these narrower and broader human perspectives on things.

Our examination in this chapter comprises two sections. The first examines both Nietzsche's understanding of and objections to Kant's constitutive account of our knowledge and the status of objects, whilst the second focuses on Nietzsche's appropriation and modification of Kant's epistemology. In so doing, we trace how Nietzsche's appeal to a naturalistic and regulative conception of knowledge rather than Kant's constitutive account makes possible objective human beliefs about the world.

NIETZSCHE *PRO* AND *CONTRA* KANT

In a revealing passage in *The Gay Science* Nietzsche explicitly links his own thought to Kant's where he praises Kant's response to Hume regarding the justifiable applicability of the concept of causality:

Let us recall ... *Kant's* tremendous question mark that he placed after the concept of 'causality' – without, like Hume, doubting its legitimacy altogether. Rather, Kant began cautiously to delimit the realm within which this concept makes sense (and to this day we are not done with this fixing of limits).[6]

What Nietzsche praises here is Kant's effort to save the rational justification of our beliefs in the midst of Hume's sceptical attacks. In *Beyond Good and Evil* Nietzsche praises Kant's attempt to overcome Humean scepticism by appealing to both a unified methodology and rigorous standards.[7] Hume had argued that although we do indeed possess the idea of causal connection, our employment of this concept in a judgement is not rationally justified. Kant aims to show, contrary to Hume, that such concepts are rationally justified in a judgement. Kant argues that it is necessary for us to justify the concepts of metaphysics for these concepts are the concepts of our cognition and so necessary for the possibility of rational thought.[8]

Informing Kant's response to Hume, according to Nietzsche, is his proposal of a Copernican revolution, which entails a reappraisal of how we are to construe the order of priority in the relation between subject and object. Central to this is his reappraisal of what constitutes an object of knowledge. Adopting what he calls a transcendental idealist stance, Kant argues that objects, if they are to be knowable by us, must be constituted by us. That is, our knowledge is of empirical objects that conform to the conditions of our knowledge rather than of things as they are constituted in themselves:

> Hitherto it has been assumed that all our knowledge must conform to objects. But all attempts to extend our knowledge of objects by establishing something in regard to them *a priori*, by means of concepts, have, on this assumption, ended in failure. We must therefore make trial whether we may not have more success in the tasks of metaphysics, if we suppose that objects must conform to our knowledge. This would agree better with what is desired, namely, that it should be possible to have knowledge of objects *a priori*, determining something in regard to them prior to them being given.[9]

In his earliest writing, *The Birth of Tragedy*, Nietzsche has the utmost praise for Kant's philosophical aims, which amount, in Nietzsche's view, to setting limits to conceptual and logical knowledge, thus curbing rationalist hubris. According to Nietzsche, Kant's Copernican turn and his views concerning the legitimate theoretical employment of the concepts of the Understanding aim to reject dogmatic metaphysics, denying pure conceptual access to how things are in themselves in favour of rendering the empirical realm an object of knowledge.

> The hardest-fought victory of all was won by the enormous courage and wisdom of *Kant* and *Schopenhauer*, a victory over the optimism which lies hidden in the nature of logic and which in turn is the hidden foundation of our culture. Whereas this optimism once believed in our ability to grasp and solve, with the help of the seemingly reliable *aeternae veritates*, all the puzzles of the universe, and treated space, time, and causality as entirely unconditional laws of the most general validity, Kant showed that these things actually only served to raise mere appearance, the work of maya, to the status of the sole and supreme reality . . . [10]

However, Nietzsche's claim in *The Gay Science* that Kant's project has not yet been completed indicates both that his own philosophical project is very much entwined with his estimation of the Kantian enterprise and that his praise for Kant comes with reservations.[11] These are threefold. First, Nietzsche contends that Kant commits the genetic fallacy by reducing rational justification to a description of our psychology. Second, Kant conflates the forms of our psychology with the constitution of objects resulting in a form of idealism whereby the objects of our knowledge are indistinguishable from our consciousness of them. Third, Kant's reference to an absolute point of view in the guise of the thing-in-itself poses a significant sceptical threat to the status of our human knowledge.

Nietzsche's first reservation is rooted in his response to Kant's project in the 'Transcendental Deduction' section of *Critique of Pure Reason* where Kant addresses the question of how synthetic *a priori* propositions are possible. The difficulty surrounding synthetic *a priori* propositions for Kant is that they state that the concept of the predicate is universally and necessarily connected with the subject concept despite the fact that the concept of the predicate is not 'contained in' the concept of the subject. With synthetic *a posteriori* claims both the subject term and the predicate term are connected by experience, but they lack the qualities of universality and necessity that are needed to avoid scepticism. Kant therefore argues that some additional factor is required to make this universal and necessary connection:

> The proof proceeds by showing that experience itself, and therefore the object of experience, would be impossible without a connection of this kind. Accordingly, the proof must also at the same time show the possibility of arriving synthetically and *a priori* at some knowledge of things which was not contained in the concepts of them.[12]

Nietzsche thinks (probably under the influence of Kuno Fischer) that the appeal to psychological faculties is central to Kant's response to how synthetic *a priori* propositions are possible.[13] As a result, his interpretation of Kant is primarily based on the 'A Deduction'.[14] This is made particularly evident in Nietzsche's description of Kant's project in *Beyond Good and Evil* where he writes:

> But let's think about it, it is high time. 'How are synthetic a priori judgements *possible?*' wondered Kant, and what did he answer? They are *facilitated by a faculty:* unfortunately, however, he did not say this in four words, but so cumbersomely, so venerably, and with such an expense of German profundity and ornateness that people misheard the comical *niaiserie allemande* in such an answer.[15]

Central to Kant's argument in the A Deduction is his account of synthesis, which is to be understood in the context of Kant's aim to establish a harmony between our *a priori* concepts and nature. Consequently, by synthesis Kant refers to the manner in which the multiplicity of the sensory manifold is combined or brought together for our intellectual comprehension. He writes, 'But if this manifold is to be known, the spontaneity of our thought requires that it be gone through in a certain way, taken up and connected. This act I name *synthesis.*'[16] Synthesis is intended by Kant to disallow the possibility that 'Objects may, therefore, appear to us without their being under the necessity of being related to the functions of understanding; and understanding need not, therefore, contain their *a priori* conditions.'[17] Nietzsche's claim that Kant appeals to a faculty to explain the possibility of synthetic *a priori* propositions can be seen in Kant's argument that synthesis of the manifold takes place in three stages, which are inseparably combined and each of which is attributed to a different faculty of the mind.[18] The three stages – apprehension of the representations in intuition, reproduction of them in imagination, and recognition of the reproduced representations in a concept – are performed by the faculties of Sensibility, Imagination and Understanding respectively.[19] Kant's appeal to faculties in his account of synthesis aims to establish the possibility of rational justification of our *a priori* concepts in a judgement in response to Hume's challenge. Hume had argued that reason, whilst affording us direct and certain knowledge of 'relations of ideas', cannot ground our beliefs about the world. He contends that although the imagination encourages our consent to beliefs, it functions independently of reason, thus depriving our beliefs of rational justification.[20] Kant's account of synthesis argues that our concepts are rationally justified because they have application in a judgement, entailing that the Imagination as the non-rational component of our cognition operates in accordance with the concepts of the Understanding.

The first stage of synthesis – apprehension in intuition – refers to the manner in which the knower interprets the 'given' of sense experience as ordered in space and time. However, Kant claims that the first stage of synthesis whereby the manifold 'must first be run through and held together' is intimately interconnected with the second, contending that 'The synthesis of apprehension is thus inseparably bound up with the synthesis of reproduction.'[21] He suggests that even to apprehend a manifold in intuition requires the transcendental activity of the reproductive imagination. He writes, 'There must then be something which, as the *a priori* ground of a necessary synthetic unity of appearances, makes their reproduction possible.'[22] We can understand what Kant means by reproduction here by taking his example of drawing a line in thought.[23] Kant uses the term drawing to describe the activity of representing something in space. He claims: 'To know anything in space (for instance, a line), I must *draw* it, and thus synthetically bring into being a determinate combination of the given manifold . . .'[24] The drawing of the line is divisible into stages, all of which need to be held together. This is the synthesis of apprehension in an intuition. As the line is drawn, however, the results of the earlier stages of the constructive process need to be both retained and continued. Kant calls this temporalising process the synthesis of reproduction.[25] In addition to the ability to cognise a series of representations, the knower must also be able to recognise what goes on at each later stage (of, say, drawing a line) as a continuation of the earlier activity. That is, the knower must be able to recognise the earlier and present stages of drawing a line in thought as a single, continuous activity. This is the third stage of synthesis, which Kant calls synthesis of recognition in a concept. The knower must be conscious of having begun to draw a line and of having proceeded through successive sequences in doing so.[26] This self-conscious activity Kant calls 'transcendental apperception'.[27] This unitary self-consciousness, according to Kant, is not a self that can be known through introspection but is what he describes in the 'B Deduction' as the 'I think' that must 'accompany all my representations'.[28] Self-consciousness as a condition of synthesis ensures that 'appearances have *a necessary relation to the understanding*'.[29] For, according to Kant:

> *The unity of apperception in relation to the synthesis of imagination* is the *understanding*. In the understanding there are then pure *a priori* modes of knowledge which contain the necessary unity of the pure synthesis of imagination in respect of all possible appearances. These are the *categories*, that is, the pure concepts of understanding.[30]

As a result of this account of synthesis, Kant argues, *contra* Hume, that we are justified in employing *a priori* concepts in a judgement. Such judgements are objective because they are subject to the constraints of *a priori* rules, distinguishing them from mere subjective associations of consciousness. Of Hume Kant writes: 'He thus confounds a principle of affinity, which has its seat in the understanding and affirms necessary connection, with a rule of association, which exists only in the imitative faculty of imagination, and which can exhibit only contingent, not objective, connections.'[31]

However, Nietzsche argues, pre-empting but also surpassing contemporary dissatisfaction with Kant's 'Subjective Deduction' that Kant's account of how synthetic *a priori* judgements are possible is guilty of a genetic fallacy by conflating the psychological origin of our beliefs with their proper justification.[32] Nietzsche writes: 'But the origin of a belief, of a strong conviction, is a psychological problem: and a *very* narrow and limited experience often produces such a belief!'[33] Nietzsche suggests that the fact that Kant is appealing to a transcendental grounding of synthesis here fails to defend him from the objection.[34] This is because Kant's appeal to the transcendental self that accompanies our representations rather than reducing to them in the manner of what he calls the empirical self still offers only a subjective rather than objective account of our knowledge.[35] Nietzsche maintains that as a result of Kant's appeal to synthesis, our human beliefs about reality are deemed to be *merely* human and the universality and necessity that Kant attributes to them are wholly relative to our specifically human point of view. That Nietzsche understands Kant in this way can be discerned from his claim that Kant's account of synthesis disallows the possibility of appealing to objective criteria to distinguish the truth or falsity of our beliefs. Responding to Kant in the form of a question – 'What distinguishes the true from the false belief?' – Nietzsche argues that we must be able to establish the objectivity, or not, of our judgements from within our immersion in the empirical world.[36] Although Nietzsche argues that psychology is the queen of the sciences and the key to the basic issues, he means this in a different sense from Kant.[37] In particular, Nietzsche appeals here to a naturalistic psychology, arguing that our human knowledge is not subject to merely subjective constraints, but rather is always rooted in and pertains to reality which is both independent of but available to our knowledge. He argues that we need to understand the human naturalistically, mastering through disciplined investigation 'the many conceited and gushing interpretations' of the relation between self and world.[38] According to Nietzsche, we can deem our beliefs true or false not by appealing to subjective psychological constraints, but rather by distinguishing between narrower and broader perspectives within the world as it shows up for us. That the possibility of such a distinction is lacking in Kant, Nietzsche maintains, results from the latter's second reservation regarding Kant's project. In addition to reducing rational justification to a description of our psychological faculties, Nietzsche argues that Kant's account of synthesis reduces objects of our knowledge to the status of mental representations.

According to Nietzsche, Kant's account of synthesis runs together the fact that our human cognition is constituted by our faculties with the argument that objects must be *a priori* so constituted as to harmonise with our cognitive constitution. This is suggested by Kant himself in the A Deduction when he writes: 'The *a priori* conditions of a possible experience in general are at the same time conditions of the possibility of objects of experience.'[39] Nietzsche contends that Kant renders the object of knowledge coextensive with our cognition by emphasising the constitutive role of the Understanding over the role of empirical content in his account of synthesis. That Nietzsche understands Kant's account of synthesis in terms of a form/content distinction is evident from his description of Kant's synthetic *a priori* judgements. He describes such judgements in terms of the capacity of the human mind to 'make connections' by 'giving form' to sensory content.[40] According to Kant, as we have seen, the pure concepts of the Understanding inform cognition of an object right from its apprehension in intuition to its recognition in a concept. The Understanding guided by the transcendental unity of Apperception is responsible for the taking up of the given of sense-experience and its construction into an object that is knowable by us.[41] This entails that an object that is knowable must be constituted by us in the specific sense of conforming to the conditions of our cognition.[42] For Kant, according to Nietzsche, our concepts fit empirical reality (the empirical object of knowledge) because our concepts form that reality. As a result, Nietzsche maintains that Kant construes the object of knowledge as a mental representation that is dependent on our consciousness of it. Kant describes our knowledge of the object in such terms when he writes:

> That nature should direct itself according to our subjective ground of apperception, and should indeed depend upon it is absurd. But when we consider that this nature is not a thing in itself but is merely an aggregate of appearances, so many representations of the mind, we shall not be surprised that we can discover it only in the radical faculty of all our knowledge, namely, in transcendental apperception, in that unity on account of which alone it can be entitled object of all possible experience, that is, nature. Nor shall we be surprised that just for this very reason this unity can be known *a priori*, and therefore as necessary.[43]

By construing the object as an 'object of representations' and as the product of the synthesising activity of the human mind, Nietzsche contends that Kant, rather than answering how synthetic *a priori* propositions are possible, merely repeats the question.[44] Nietzsche argues that Kant's account of how synthetic *a priori* propositions are possible, emphasising the constitutive status of the categories, concludes that an object of knowledge is one that is defined and constituted by our cognitive machinery. Anything that cannot be registered, interpreted or synthetically processed by this machinery cannot be called an object. Thus Nietzsche argues that the universality and necessity that Kant attributes to our synthetic *a priori* propositions is relativised to our psychological perspective or point of view. The point here is that anything that can be called an 'object' that is knowable by us is predefined and determined by our cognitive faculties such that any attempted explanation of that object must reduce to a description of the features that we have put there. Accordingly, Nietzsche argues that Kant's account of synthesis presents us with a narrowly anthropocentric conception of an object of knowledge, giving rise to a third difficulty, which is that of the sceptical dissociation of our knowledge from how things are in themselves. Rather than rendering the empirical world an object of knowledge, according to Nietzsche, Kant reduces it to the status of 'mere appearance' or mental representation that is divorced from how things are in themselves. Consequently, Nietzsche writes in 'Schopenhauer as Educator', 'If Kant ever should begin to exercise any wide influence we shall be aware of it in the form of a gnawing and disintegrating scepticism and relativism . . .'.[45]

According to Nietzsche, Kant's reference to unknowable things-in-themselves, stemming directly from his constitutive account of knowledge and its identification of the forms of our psychology with the nature of objects of knowledge, reopens the possibility of an absolute point of view that can never be ours. Consequently, Nietzsche argues that Kant's Copernican turn initiates a project that Kant himself does not complete. Nietzsche writes that Kant

> had obtained the 'thing in itself' by *stealth* . . . and was punished for this when the 'categorical imperative' crept stealthily into his heart and led him *astray – back* to 'God,' 'soul,' 'freedom,' and 'immortality,' like a fox who loses his way and goes astray back into his cage. Yet it had been *his* strength and cleverness that had *broken open* the cage![46]

Kant's project, he suggests, promised to remove the appearance/reality divide, thus elevating the realm of appearance to the status of reality. However, Kant's reference to the thing-in-itself as a ploy to facilitate faith and morality, Nietzsche argues, reinstates this dichotomy and threatens to lock our empirical claims to knowledge within a strict anthropo-morphism that has no connection to reality. The reference to things-in-themselves, therefore, opens up the possibility that our best justified beliefs are, unbeknown to us, radically in error. Nietzsche maintains that the concept of the thing-in-itself as an unconditioned and unknowable thing renders the world with which we are experientially acquainted a realm of possible illusion and falsehood. Thus Nietzsche maintains that the concept of the thing-in-itself as the concept of an unconditioned thing does not even feature in the realm of appearance:

> more rigorous logicians, having clearly identified the concept of the meta-physical as that of the unconditioned, consequently also unconditioning, have disputed any connection between the unconditioned (the metaphysi-cal world) and the world we know: so that what appears in appearance is precisely *not* the thing in itself, and no conclusion can be drawn from the former as to the nature of the latter.[47]

Here Nietzsche argues that the thing-in-itself cannot serve as the standard by which we distinguish true from false beliefs because Kant's conception of the thing-in-itself evokes the idea of a God's Eye View transcending our specifically human capacity for knowledge. Furthermore, the appearance/reality distinction passes judgement on the realm of appearance by con-sidering it less valuable than that of an inaccessible 'true' realm. However, Nietzsche argues that Kant's initial transcendental project of restricting our knowledge to appearances renders any appeal to a thing-in-itself ille-gitimate and conceptually incoherent:

> The sore spot of Kant's critical philosophy has gradually become visible even to dull eyes: Kant no longer has a right to his distinction 'appearance' and 'thing-in-itself' – he had deprived himself of the right to go on distinguish-ing in this old familiar way, in so far as he rejected as impermissible making inferences from phenomena to a cause of phenomena – in accordance with his conception of causality and its purely intra-phenomenal validity –[48]

Nietzsche attributes to Kant the view that things-in-themselves 'cause' us to have sensations which are then synthesised by the constitutive character of the Understanding to formulate an 'appearance' or empiri-cal object of knowledge. Things-in-themselves are understood by this reading to relate to appearances in terms of the affection of the former on our Sensibility. However, Nietzsche maintains that Kant is not justified in holding such a view because the critical limits that Kant has established with regard to our knowledge entails that the concept of causality is legitimately employed only within the realm of possible experience which is the realm of appearance. The thing-in-itself as situated outside these parameters cannot, therefore, be known to act as the cause of our appearances.[49] The thing-in-itself cannot be the cause of our sensations because the thing-in-itself is not, properly speaking, an object for Kant. An object for Kant is the product of the synthesising activity of the mind whereby the faculties of Understanding and Sensibility '*are employed in conjunction*'.[50] The thing-in-itself cannot be an object because 'the question . . . whether in addition to the empirical employment of the understanding – to its employment even in the Newtonian account of the structure of the universe – there is likewise possible a transcendental employment, which has to do with the noumenon as an object' must, according to Kant, be 'answered in the negative'.[51] However, Kant complicates the issue by suggesting in his *Prolegomena to Any Future Metaphysics* that the thing-in-itself is responsible for our sensations, writing: 'I say that things as objects of our senses existing outside us are given, but we know nothing of what they may be in themselves, knowing only their appearances, i.e., the representations which they cause in us by affecting our senses.'[52] And again in *Critique of Pure Reason*, Kant states: 'How things may be in themselves, apart from the representations through which they affect us, is entirely outside our sphere of knowledge.'[53]

Nietzsche receives his particular historically rooted interpretation of Kant and the problem of the thing-in-itself from Schopenhauer. According to Schopenhauer, Kant's appeal to the thing-in-itself is either a self-contradiction or a misnomer.[54] Its contradictory nature can be detected, in Schopenhauer's view, by examining the very notion of a thing-in-itself. If the thing-in-itself is to be properly called a thing, then it must be a possible object of experience and so stand under the category of causality and exhibit the characteristics of spatiality and temporality. However, this is incompatible with maintaining, according to Schopenhauer, that the thing exists in itself. This would entail that it is unknowable and thus that it is not causally active, lacking the characteristics of the forms of our Sensibility. Schopenhauer states:

> if a thing-in-itself is to be assumed, it cannot be an object at all, which, however, he always assumes it to be; but such a thing-in-itself would have to lie in a sphere *toto genere* different from the representation (from knowing and being known), and therefore could least of all be inferred according to the laws of the connexion of objects among themselves.[55]

Equally, Schopenhauer maintains that if the Kantian thing-in-itself is not self-contradictory, then it must be understood as a misnomer for a material object, which Kant calls appearances.[56] However, if Kant were to claim that the object that affects Sensibility is an appearance or empirical object, he would be led into a circular argument whereby 'appearance' would be both the cause and the result of affection. These difficulties surrounding the cogency of the concept of the thing-in-itself throw Kant's realist pretensions into disarray. According to Kant, the thing-in-itself is required as an object of thought to put at bay the threat of idealism. He argues that it must be possible to think the thing-in-itself to ensure that 'we have *experience* and not merely *imagination* of outer things'.[57] However, if we can only think the thing-in-itself rather than know it, then it seems the thing-in-itself cannot put at bay the threat of both idealism and scepticism.

Nietzsche argues that Kant's attempt to reconcile self and world is incompatible with his retention of the thing-in-itself that transcends the boundaries of our possible cognition. He contends that the very reference to an extra-empirical realm casts doubt on the epistemic status of our ordinary empirical claims to knowledge.[58] It is for this reason that Nietzsche suggests that what Kant considers to be empirical 'knowledge' cannot properly be accredited with epistemic status. Nietzsche claims that Kantian empirical 'knowledge' is devoid of epistemic weight, writing that for Kant, 'judgment is a belief that something is thus and thus! And *not* knowledge!'[59] Nietzsche thus articulates his view that Kant does not give us knowledge at all but only beliefs that are cut off from the world. Defining the concepts of the Understanding as 'provisional assumptions' Nietzsche argues, in contrast to Kant, that the forms of our knowledge are tools of inquiry and the perspectival lens through which we view the world.[60] He claims the forms of our knowledge direct our inquiry into the world, which in turn limits our attempts at finding our interests instantiated there. Denying that our concepts 'constitute' the empirical world, divorcing it from things-in-themselves, Nietzsche contends that 'knowledge' properly understood entails a process of mutual interaction between self and world. Thus Nietzsche writes:

> Coming to know means 'to place oneself in a conditional relation to something'; to feel oneself conditioned by something and oneself to condition it – it is therefore under all circumstances establishing, denoting, and making-conscious of conditions (not forthcoming entities, things, what is 'in-itself').[61]

Nietzsche argues, contrary to Kant, that as the world is neither reducible to the forms of our knowledge nor inaccessible to them in principle, our beliefs can be objective. He writes: 'There is *only* a perspectival seeing, *only* a perspectival "knowing"; and *the more* affects we allow to speak about a matter . . . that much more complete will our "concept" of this matter, our "objectivity" be.'[62]

In the next section and throughout the book we shall take up Nietzsche's appeal to perspectival and objective knowledge in greater detail. In the present chapter, we shall see that Nietzsche's project entails, not a rejection of Kant but rather a modification of him. This is manifest in Nietzsche's claim that we should abandon Kant's constitutive view of knowledge in favour of a regulative account. Nietzsche argues that the three difficulties in Kant's system whereby his explanation of rational justification reduces to a description of our psychology and objects of our knowledge reduce to mental representations divorced from how things are in themselves result from Kant's constitutive view of knowledge. Nietzsche contends that these difficulties can be remedied by assimilating the constitutive account to the status of regulative beliefs. Specifically, this entails for Nietzsche construing Kant's appeal to psychology and the human point of view naturalistically whilst denying that objects are mind-dependent and reducible to our psychology. What constitutes 'objectivity' for Nietzsche is reconfigured such that it stands not for a unified judgement subject to conceptual/psychological constraints but rather beliefs that, although originating in our psychological interests, are nonetheless adequate to reality.

NIETZSCHE'S APPROPRIATION AND MODIFICATION OF KANT

Nietzsche contends that Kant's appeal to subjective (in the sense of *merely* human) transcendental conditions on the one hand, and things-in-themselves on the other, cuts off our knowledge from the world. In response, he argues that the question regarding synthetic *a priori* judgements should be rephrased to ask not after their 'possibility' but rather to explain why they are necessary.[63] They are necessary, according to Nietzsche, because such judgements reflect our psychological interests. However, writing that 'man is not necessarily the "measure of all things"',[64] the objectivity and justifiability of our beliefs, he argues, reside not in a description of our psychology but rather in the extent to which they adequately capture the nature of the world which, whilst available to, is nonetheless metaphysically independent of, our knowledge. Thus Nietzsche contends that although 'inventing' should precede 'finding' the former must be constrained by the latter.[65] Describing the proper methodology of philosophy as that of seeking reasons to support one's philosophical 'experiments' he points to the need, as he sees it, to secure the proper objective justification of our judgements if the appearance/

reality distinction is to be overcome.[66] Central to the successful implementation of this task for Nietzsche is his rejection of Kant's constitutive account of knowledge in favour of a regulative and naturalistic conception of our knowledge.

That Nietzsche rejects Kant's constitutive account of knowledge can be discerned from his claim that Kant's categories should be properly construed as regulative beliefs:

> The basic laws of logic, the law of identity and the law of contradiction, are forms of pure knowledge, because they precede all experience."– *But these are not forms of knowledge at all! They are regulative articles of belief.* (my emphasis)[67]

Kant introduces regulative ideas in the 'Appendix to the Transcendental Dialectic' in *Critique of Pure Reason* and the two introductions to *Critique of Judgement.*[68] His distinction between constitutive and regulative principles divides *Critique of Pure Reason* into approximately two halves, the first dealing with the constitutive principles of knowledge and the second with regulative ideas of Reason. The latter are introduced by Kant to supplement the former.[69] Briefly put, constitutive principles are said to ascertain what *is* rather than what *ought to be*. Constitutive principles are those that derive from the concepts of the Understanding and are instantiated within our sensible experience in space and time. As such, they 'record' rather than 'explain' our experience.[70] Regulative principles, on the other hand, are said to transcend what immediate experience can verify. They are guided by ideas of Reason, such as the idea of a systematically unified and complete science. Regulative principles guide our experience and attempt to 'explain' that experience 'by way of a never actually completed sequence of approximations, toward an ideal state of completion'.[71] Regulative ideas are, in Kant's view, principles of research that *seek* systematic unity in nature. He states: 'this regulative capacity . . . goes far beyond what experience or observation can verify; and though not itself determining anything, yet serves to mark out the path towards systematic unity.'[72] As such, regulative ideas are 'heuristic' rather than 'ostensive' concepts.[73] Constitutive principles, according to Kant, furnish us with experience or what he also refers to as 'nature',[74] whilst regulative principles supplement such furnishings by ordering 'nature' into a systematic unity.[75] Thus Kant maintains that just as the Understanding works on and synthesises the offerings of Sensibility, Reason works on and orders the deliverances of Understanding. He states:

> Reason presupposes the knowledge which is obtained by the understanding and which stands in immediate relation to experience, and seeks for the

unity of this knowledge in accordance with ideas which go far beyond all possible experience.[76]

According to Kant, Reason's interest in systematic unity is necessary for the 'coherent employment of the understanding'.[77] Regulative ideas are not object concepts but rather principles that guide the Understanding towards its 'greatest [possible] unity combined with the greatest [possible] extension'.[78] As such Kant contends that the 'schema of reason does not yield knowledge of the object itself (as is the case in the application of categories to their sensible schemata) but only a rule or principle for the systematic unity of all employment of the understanding'.[79] Since regulative principles are not constitutive of objects and so not instantiated in space and time, they are, according to Kant, 'subjective principles which are derived, not from the constitution of an object but from the interest of reason in respect of a certain possible perfection of the knowledge of the object . . .'[80] To the extent that regulative principles do not constitute objects they are said to function as heuristic research maxims serving a purely methodological and 'subjective' role in relation to the Understanding. Kant writes that 'such a principle does not prescribe any law for objects, and does not contain any general ground of the possibility of knowing or of determining objects as such'.[81] According to Kant, regulative principles can be deemed to have objective validity only to the extent that they supplement the operations of the Understanding. Considered in this way they have 'objective but indeterminate validity'.[82] Kant writes:

> The unity of reason is the unity of system; and this systematic unity does not serve objectively as a principle that extends the application of reason to objects, but subjectively as a maxim that extends its application to all possible empirical knowledge of objects. Nonetheless, since the systematic connection which reason can give to the empirical employment of the understanding not only furthers its extension, but also guarantees its correctness, the principle of such systematic unity is so far also objective, but in an indeterminate manner.[83]

Whilst Nietzsche contends that Kant ultimately fails to deliver on his promise to make the empirical world an object of knowledge due to both its mind-dependent status and its separation from mind-independent things-in-themselves, he argues that Kant's regulative maxims, if subject to some modification, offer a glimmer of hope in overcoming the detrimental consequences of his constitutive account of knowledge. Nietzsche's appropriation of Kant's appeal to regulative ideas can be discerned from as early as 'On Teleology' (1868) where he argues that our concepts must be treated as regulative ideas rather than constitutive ones:

> One can only comprehend the mathematical completely (that is the formal view). In all else man stands before the unknown. In order to overcome this man invents concepts, which only gather together a sum of appearing characteristics, which, however, do not get hold of the thing. Therein belong force, matter, individual, law, organism, atom, final cause. These are not constitutive (*constitutiven*) but only reflective (*reflektirende*) judgements.[84]

Although Kant appeals to regulative maxims, their role as construed by him, according to Nietzsche, is parasitic on that of constitutive principles, with the consequence that regulative principles are relegated to that of mere 'as if' (*als ob*) principles devoid of objective status.[85] However, Nietzsche argues that if employed in a way that is non-parasitic on constitutive principles, regulative ideas provide an avenue by which to overcome the narrowly anthropocentric object of knowledge that stands between us and reality, without, however, collapsing into dogmatism and claiming a God's Eye perspective on things. Understood non-parasitically, regulative principles, for Nietzsche, are no longer 'transcendental', extra-historical and extra-natural principles, and as non-constitutive the objects of our knowledge are irreducible to them.[86] Nietzsche is critical of Kant's claim that unless our concepts 'constitute objects' they are denied objective cognitive status. He contends that the status of regulative principles can be redeemed if we deny that our concepts constitute objects, allowing only that they frame the context and parameters of our naturalistic and interest-directed research into nature. Consequently, Nietzsche suggests that our beliefs can be justified regulatively rather than constitutively. In this way, he thinks that he can overcome the narrowly anthropocentric and mind-dependent character of the Kantian object of knowledge. This can be illustrated by briefly contrasting the status of human knowledge in Kant and Nietzsche.

We have seen that, according to Kant, the object of knowledge is composed of *a priori* concepts and intuitions. An intuition is the manner in which we immediately relate to objects as sensed. Concepts are said to relate mediately to objects through their application to intuitions. Appealing to these two sources, Kant contends that our knowledge is conditioned by the specifically human forms of our cognition. Moreover, objects that are knowable by us are conditioned and determined by these forms. Kant writes:

> It is therefore, solely from the human standpoint that we can speak of space, of extended things, etc. If we depart from the subjective condition under

which alone we can have outer intuition, namely, liability to be affected by objects, the representation of space stands for nothing whatsoever.[87]

That such knowledge is *merely* human rather than properly objective is highlighted by Kant's contrast between our mode of knowledge and other possible, non-human ways of knowing. Kant entertains the possibility that there are other modes of knowing and other types of objects to be known than the human. Since our mode of knowing objects is restricted to the human standpoint, Kant maintains that 'we cannot judge in regard to the intuitions of other thinking beings, whether they are bound by the same conditions as those which limit our intuition and which for us are universally valid'.[88] Nor can we explain why we must think of objects in the specifically human way that we do:

> This peculiarity of our understanding, that it can produce *a priori* unity of apperception solely by means of the categories, and only by such and so many, is as little capable of further explanation as why we have just these and no other functions of judgment, or why space and time are the only forms of our possible intuition.[89]

The difficulty is exacerbated by Kant's reference to the thing-in-itself as an absolute, outside viewpoint which is unavailable to our human sensible mode of intuition and which renders our knowledge narrowly anthropocentric:

> What we have meant to say is that all our intuition is nothing but the representation of appearance; that the things which we intuit are not in themselves what we intuit them as being, nor their relations . . . We know nothing but our mode of perceiving them . . .[90]

According to Nietzsche, Kant relativises the nature of objects knowable by us to the subjective forms of our cognition. In so doing, the objects that obtain relative to our specifically human point of view are radically different from those that obtain from an alternative, non-human point of view. Understood in this way, our knowledge, according to Nietzsche, is devoid of real objectivity. However, in claiming that Kant's categories should be given regulative rather than constitutive status, Nietzsche distinguishes between points of view and objects. He contends that although all our knowledge is directed by our points of view, they do not constitute objects. Objects knowable by us, according to him, are neither reducible to nor determined by our point of view. Moreover, Nietzsche contends that Kant paradoxically paves the way for such an undertaking.

Nietzsche argues that, viewed closely, we can see that Kant's account of transcendental apperception takes a step towards the collapse of his constitutive account of knowledge, a collapse which points to the need for an alternative, naturalistic account of synthesis that does not entail the mind-dependency of objects. By arguing that self-consciousness is attained through the self's awareness of itself as the source of unity of the object and thus that self-consciousness both emerges from and is dependent on the synthetic process, Kant paves the way for his rejection of rational psychology in the 'Paralogisms' in *Critique of Pure Reason*. By denying that transcendental apperception can be identified with the substantial and introspective self of rational psychology, Kant, Nietzsche maintains, takes, contrary to his aims, an important step towards diluting a constitutive and non-naturalistic grounding of our knowledge altogether. Nietzsche writes:

> In earlier times people believed in the 'soul' just as they believed in grammar and the grammatical subject. They said that 'I' is a condition, that 'think' is a predicate and thus conditioned: thinking is an activity for which a causal subject *must* be thought. And then, with admirable tenacity and cunning, people tried to see . . . whether perhaps the reverse was true: that 'think' was the condition, and 'I' the conditioned; 'I' would thus be a synthesis, which was *made* through the thinking itself. Basically, *Kant* wanted to prove that the subject could not be proved by means of the subject, nor could the object be proved either. Perhaps he was already familiar with the possibility of an *apparent existence* of the subject (that is, the soul), this thought that was once present on earth, tremendously powerful, in the philosophy of Vedanta.[91]

Nietzsche's argument is that Kant's dilution of the status of the self of rational psychology points to the ultimate dissolution of a non-naturalistic account of the self in general, undermining the distinction between transcendental subjects and objects constituted by them. Once this oppositional framework has been abandoned, Nietzsche claims that the distinction between mind-dependent 'appearances' and mind-independent but unknowable things-in-themselves disappears. It is a further and important step, according to Nietzsche, from here to the view that the ordering principle of reality is inherent in the structure of reality itself rather than in transcendental conditions of knowledge. Consequently, pre-empting his will to power thesis, which takes the ultimate constituents of reality to be powers rather than self-identical subjects and objects, Nietzsche writes:

> If we give up the effective subject, we also give up the object upon which effects are produced. Duration, identity with itself, being are inherent neither in that which is called subject nor in that which is called object: they are complexes of events apparently durable in comparison with other

complexes – e.g., through the difference in tempo of the event (rest – motion, form – loose: opposites that do not exist in themselves and that actually express only variations in degree that from a certain perspective appear to be opposites. There are no opposites: only from those of logic do we derive the concept of opposites – and falsely transfer it to things).[92]

A naturalised account of synthesis, according to Nietzsche, points to the need to understand reality, not in terms of subjects and objects, but rather in terms of the will to power. In so doing, Nietzsche maintains that knowable reality is no longer construed as a 'representation' constituted by us but rather is 'a kind of instinctual life in which all the organic functions (self-regulation, adaptation, alimentation, elimination, metabolism) are synthetically linked to one another – as a *preliminary form* of life?'[93] This means that reality, for Nietzsche, is perspectival and that the self that has been properly returned to nature[94] is also a perspective immersed in the evolving whole that is reality construed along the lines of the will to power. We shall discuss the will to power thesis in considerably more detail in later chapters. In the present context, however, Nietzsche's appeal to the will to power as a naturalised synthesis has the important consequence that reality is neither a mind-dependent object that reduces to the forms of our knowledge nor a thing-in-itself that is inaccessible to our knowledge. In so denying us any constitutive role Nietzsche attempts to realign the metaphysical and the epistemological object. What he leaves us with is one metaphysical object, reality, with which we engage naturalistically and in an *interest*-focused manner.

It is in this context that we can best understand Nietzsche's ambiguous claim that our truths are errors. Such passages are often read as committing him to sceptical idealism with regard to human knowledge. The sceptical idealist interpretation argues that we are caught in a strict anthropocentric conception of knowledge that is not in touch with the real in any way. It claims that our human knowledge is perpetually vulnerable to the charge of radically falsifying reality. However, if we read Nietzsche's claim that our truths are errors in the light of his commitment to a naturalistic and regulative conception of knowledge rather than a constitutive one, we can see that he is making a more interesting philosophical point. This point stresses the non-constitutive nature of our knowledge and thus the genuine independence of the world that is the object of both metaphysical and epistemological inquiry. Consider the following passage from *Human, All Too Human*:

> The establishment of conclusions in science always unavoidably involves us in calculating with certain false magnitudes: but because these magnitudes

are at least *constant,* as for example are our sensations of time and space, the conclusions of science acquire a complete rigorousness and certainty in their coherence with one another; one can build on them – up to that final stage at which our erroneous basic assumptions, those constant errors, come to be incompatible with our conclusions, for example in the theory of atoms.[95]

In this passage Nietzsche plays with the notion of an 'idea'. In opposition to Kant he denies that knowable reality can be identified with mental representations. We may be acquainted with ideas, but such ideas are 'errors' in the sense that they are regulative. Their regulative character can be inferred from Nietzsche's emphasis on the results of scientific inquiry. Should the regulative ideas come into conflict with the results of empirical investigation they may have to be abandoned. However, it may be objected that Nietzsche, in reinstating the metaphysical object as the focus of epistemological inquiry, merely undoes the good work that Kant had established. In other words, it may be argued that Nietzsche merely reintroduces the problem with which Berkeley confronted Locke, that is, how to explain that the 'idea' conforms to the object if it is distinct from that object. However, Nietzsche's position arguably does not collapse back into this dichotomy because his ideas, unlike Berkeley's, are not first-order ideas to which the objects of our knowledge are metaphysically reducible. Rather, they are regulative principles of research that guide our investigation of nature. As such, Nietzschean ideas are second-order methodological tools. In this way Nietzsche in fact makes good Kant's epistemic turn which prioritises epistemology over metaphysics. But it is important that we recognise that Nietzsche's regulative ideas of research are not *just* methodological tools. They are also indicators of our immersed and *interest*-directed engagement with the world. Thus he puts forward an anthropocentric conception of knowledge. However, unlike Kant as interpreted by Nietzsche, this does not entail that our human knowledge is inadequate to reality. Nietzsche's aim here is to overcome what he sees as the Kantian oscillation between narrow anthropocentrism on the one hand, and a God's Eye View on the other. Nietzsche's point is that once we dismount from such an oscillation we abandon the idea that our knowledge is merely anthropocentric in favour of the view that our perspectives, which are rooted in our psychology, always capture the world. They do this, however selectively, because our perspectives are *in* the world rather than imposed on it from without. Our perspectives or points of view, according to Nietzsche, are in the world, but the world is not reducible to them.

However, there is a possible objection to this argument that we must consider. This objection claims that Nietzsche's employment of the notion of *Becoming* commits him to the Kantian conception of a realm or level of reality that is radically different from our beliefs about it. Proponents of this view argue that, for Nietzsche, reality as it is in itself, that is, as it is independently of our cognitive simplifications, is in radical flux. According to this view, our cognitive practices simplify the flux in a way that arbitrarily stabilises it and that is constitutive of 'objects'.[96] Thus this interpretation posits an epistemic gulf between our knowledge and the character of the world. In so doing, it commits Nietzsche to the very Kantian dualism that he wishes to avoid. This difficulty can be removed, however, if we interpret Nietzsche's views on Becoming as also applying to our cognitive apparatus. This entails considering Nietzsche's doctrine of Becoming as both an epistemic and metaphysical thesis without either being reducible to the other. This alternative interpretation proposes that Nietzsche's conception of Becoming applies to *both* our manner of knowing the world and the character of the world. Nietzsche suggests that the knowing self is immersed in the process of Becoming and consequently that our knowledge is not to be understood independently of this process. He thereby removes the epistemic gap that was opened up by Kant's constitutive account of knowledge. According to Nietzsche, the forms of our knowledge do not stand over and above a world of Becoming constituting it from without, but rather are provisional maxims subject to revision and enclosed within the world. Christoph Cox, who interprets Nietzsche's notion of Becoming in a similar way, supports his interpretation by glossing some of those passages that are often cited in defence of the claim that Nietzsche posits a realm of Becoming that is incommensurable with the realm of human knowing. I will cite one of these passages along with Cox's gloss in parenthesis:

> The character of the world of becoming as *unformulable*, as 'false,' as 'self-contradictory.' (We can never stabilize and totalize from without a world that is in constant transition and of which we ourselves are a part.) *Knowledge* and *Becoming* exclude one another. (Conceived as the totalizing comprehension of a world of being, knowledge will be confounded by the world of becoming in which we live.) *Consequently*, 'knowledge' must be something else: there must first of all be a will to make knowable, a kind of becoming must itself create the *deception of beings*. (If we want to maintain some notion of knowledge, we must conceive it differently. Instead of setting it over and against 'becoming,' we should see it as itself 'a kind of becoming,' as a process *within* becoming – as an active interpretation rather than a passive mirroring, as the will of living beings to select from, simplify, and stabilize their world so as to insure their self-preservation and/or -enhancement. Such a simplification and stabilization constitutes a

"deception" insofar as it is not uniquely correct, for there are other purposes toward the satisfaction of which one might construe the world differently; and there is no construal that conjoins all purposes.)[97]

By considering human knowledge as a 'process *within* becoming' Nietzsche highlights the perspectival and revisable character of our knowledge whilst emphasising that the knowing self is not divorced from reality. Our cognitive interests (what Kant's categories really are in Nietzsche's view) do not stand over and above the world playing a constitutive role. The question of what constitutes knowledge, according to Nietzsche, has only provisional answers adopted from within our immersion in a larger evolving whole. In this way Nietzsche considers that both his naturalisation of Kant's project and his assimilation of Kant's constitutive principles to the status of regulative maxims can make good Kant's initial aim of overcoming dogmatism whilst also making possible objectively justified beliefs about the world.

The following chapters investigate how Nietzsche realises these claims, examining how his appropriation of Kant informs both his perspectival epistemology and his will to power metaphysics in more detail. In Chapter 2 we shall examine Nietzsche's perspectivism in the particular context of his rejection of the thing-in-itself and what he sees as the 'metaphysical realist' dissociation of truth and justification.

NOTES

1. Friedrich Nietzsche, *Human, All Too Human,* translated by R. J. Hollingdale (Cambridge: Cambridge University Press, 1996 [1878–86], Volume I, 'Of First and Last Things'), 1. Henceforth cited as *HAH*. In *Beyond Good and Evil* Nietzsche proposes the dissolution of such oppositions, suggesting that 'It could even be possible that the value of those good and honoured things consists precisely in the fact that in an insidious way *they are related* to those bad, seemingly opposite things, linked, knit together, even identical perhaps' (Friedrich Nietzsche, *Beyond Good and Evil,* translated by Marion Faber (Oxford: Oxford University Press, 1998 [1886]), 2. Henceforth cited as *BGE*).
2. Nietzsche, *HAH*, Volume I, 'Of First and Last Things', 1–2.
3. Friedrich Nietzsche, *The Gay Science,* translated by Walter Kaufmann (New York: Vintage Books, 1974 [1882/1887]), 346. Henceforth cited as *GS*.
4. I do not distinguish between Nietzsche's mature and early writings in this chapter. However, Chapters 2 and 3 do address the developments of Nietzsche's arguments, in his mature and early writings respectively.
5. Nietzsche, *BGE*, 230.
6. Nietzsche, *GS*, 357. See also *BGE*, 209, 210 and 252. Note that in *GS*, 346 Nietzsche speaks of Hegel in approving terms suggesting perhaps that he thinks that Hegel's explanation of the relationship between self and world is more satisfactory than Kant's. However, Nietzsche finds neither the Kantian approach nor the Hegelian is ultimately satisfactory. Thus he writes, alluding to Hegel,

that 'We have become cold, hard, and tough in the realization that the way of the world is anything but divine; even by human standards it is not rational, merciful, or just' (Nietzsche, *GS*, 346).

7. Nietzsche, *BGE*, 210. In this passage Nietzsche juxtaposes the 'sceptic' and the 'critic'.

8. Immanuel Kant, *Critique of Pure Reason*, translated by Norman Kemp Smith (London: Macmillan, 1929 [1781/1787]), Preface, Avii–Aviii. Henceforth cited as *CPR*.

9. Ibid., Bxvi.

10. Friedrich Nietzsche, *The Birth of Tragedy*, translated by Ronald Speirs (Cambridge: Cambridge University Press, 1999 [1872]), pp. 87–8, section 18. Henceforth cited as *BT*.

11. For commentators who consider Nietzsche's relationship to Kant, see Martin Heidegger, *Nietzsche*, edited by David Farrell Krell (San Francisco: Harper & Row 1991 [1961]), Volume 3; Gilles Deleuze, *Nietzsche and Philosophy*, translated by Hugh Tomlinson (London: Athlone Press, 1992 [1962]); John Wilcox, *Truth and Value in Nietzsche* (Ann Arbor, MI: University of Michigan Press, 1974); Josef Simon, 'Die Krise des Wahrheitsbegriffs als Krise der Metaphysik: Nietzsche's Alethiologie auf dem Hintergrund der Kantischen Kritik', *Nietzsche-Studien*, Vol. 18, 1989, pp. 242–59; Olivier Reboul, *Nietzsche: Critique de Kant* (Paris: Presses universitaires de France, 1974); Michael Steven Green, *Nietzsche and the Transcendental Tradition* (Urbana and Chicago, IL: University of Illinois Press, 2002); R. Kevin Hill, *Nietzsche's Critiques: The Kantian Foundations of his Thought* (Oxford: Oxford University Press, 2003).

12. Kant, *CPR*, A783/B811.

13. Kuno Fischer thinks that Kant's account of rule-governed synthesis and rational psychology is important. He interprets synthesis as a process that guided by the Understanding produces the empirical world. Fischer interprets Kant as maintaining that the empirical world does not exist apart from our perception of it. See Hill, *Nietzsche's Critiques*, pp. 16–17.

14. The A Deduction is expressed in terms of cognitive faculties and their operations. In the B Deduction Kant articulates his argument by appealing to transcendental conditions.

15. Nietzsche, *BGE*, 11.

16. Kant, *CPR*, A77–8/B102–3.

17. Ibid., A89/B122.

18. Ibid., A102.

19. Ibid., A98–A110. Kant's account of synthesis appears to operate on two levels. That is, he seems to offer both an empirical and a transcendental account of synthesis without explicitly distinguishing between them. R. P. Wolff, drawing on Adickes', Kemp Smith's and Weldon's account of 'double affection' in Kant, explains that transcendental synthesis is responsible for the synthesis of both empirical objects and the empirical self by combining the manifold that results from the affection of things-in-themselves on the transcendental self. Empirical synthesis is said to occur when physical objects of the spatio-temporal world constituted by the transcendental self affect and are combined by the empirical self (Robert Paul Wolff, *Kant's Theory of Mental Activity* [Gloucester, MA: Peter Smith, 1973], p. 170). Kant explicitly appeals to transcendental synthesis in *CPR*, A118, where he contends that the former entails the productive rather than reproductive imagination and a pure rather than sensible manifold. Wolff explains that the two levels of synthesis are supposed to explain the mind-independent status of empirical objects and the mind-dependent status of perception (Wolff, *Kant's Theory of Mental Activity*, p. 169). However, Wolff

contends that this view renders problematic how a synthesis of perceptions can yield knowledge unless the objects are also products of a mental synthesis. He contends that Kant adopts the latter position, which, however, results in the incoherent view that appearances are both the cause and the result of affection (ibid., 168ff).

Nietzsche emphasises the role of transcendental psychology in Kant and does not explicitly distinguish between empirical and transcendental synthesis. This may be due to his contention that without a non-naturalist transcendental grounding idealism succumbs to incoherence, holding that the empirical self is both immersed in and the cause of the external world (Nietzsche, *BGE*, 15). However, with a transcendental grounding, Nietzsche argues, human knowledge is divorced from reality.

20. David Hume, *Enquiry Concerning Human Understanding* (Oxford: Clarendon Press, 1992 [1777]), sections IV and V.
21. Kant, *CPR*, A102.
22. Ibid., A101.
23. Ibid., A102.
24. Ibid., B137–8.
25. Ibid., A102.
26. Ibid., A107. See Jay F. Rosenberg's account of synthesis in *Accessing Kant* (Oxford: Clarendon Press, 2005). Rosenberg, however, interprets Kant's argument as a phenomenological one.
27. Kant, *CPR*, A103.
28. Ibid., B131.
29. Ibid., A119. There is considerable debate in the Kant literature regarding what Kant means when he claims to have established the objective validity of the categories at the end of the Deduction. Jonathan Bennett, for example, argues that Kant aims to establish a strong sense of the object but that he only manages to do this in the 'Analytic of Principles' and not in the Deduction. The strong notion of objectivity in the Principles entails distinguishing cognitively valid judgements from mere states of consciousness. The distinction between the two is elucidated in the *Prolegomena to Any Future Metaphysics* (sections 18–20) where Kant distinguishes between judgements of perception and judgements of experience. The 'former merely report the judger's sensory states, while the latter make claims about necessary connections amongst sensory states' (Jonathan Bennett, *Kant's Analytic* [Cambridge: Cambridge University Press, 1966], p. 132). In the Principles, according to Bennett, Kant shows that 'there could not be an intuitional sequence which was not experience of an objective realm.' (ibid., p. 132). In the Principles Kant holds, according to Bennett, 'that self-consciousness is possible only to a being who has experience of an objective realm such that not only does the *it* entail an *I*, but conversely, the *I* entails an *it*' (ibid., p. 130). However, Nietzsche does not seem to acknowledge a difference between the arguments of the Deduction and those of the Principles. This may account for his view that, for Kant, the objects of our cognition are mind-dependent.
30. Kant, *CPR*, A119.
31. Ibid., A766/B794–A767/B795.
32. Henry Allison, for example, contends that Kant would be guilty of such a fallacy if he were to confuse a 'genetic account of a belief or an empirical explanation of why we perceive things in a certain way' with an account of objective validity. However, Allison argues that by clearly distinguishing between epistemic and psychological conditions Kant avoids the difficulty. In so doing, Allison plays down the role of psychology in Kant (Henry Allison, *Kant's Transcendental Idealism: An Interpretation and Defense* [New Haven, CT and London: Yale

University Press, 1983], p. 11). Patricia Kitcher, in contrast, claims that Kant's project can be fully appreciated only in terms of transcendental psychology which, she argues, is not guilty of the strong psychologism just outlined. Kitcher contends that although Kant clearly thinks psychological facts are important to philosophical claims, his argument 'does not, for that reason, rest on a fallacy of confusing the normative with the factual' (Patricia Kitcher, *Kant's Transcendental Psychology* [Oxford: Oxford University Press, 1990], p. 2). This is because Kant first of all gives us an epistemic analysis that we must have a particular type of faculty if particular sorts of *a priori* knowledge are to be possible, and second, an analysis of empirical capacities, deriving from and depending on the epistemic analysis. Rather than arriving at normative claims on the basis of empirical facts, Kant, according to Kitcher, arrives at an empirical analysis of our cognitive faculties on the basis of normative claims. The epistemic analysis contains a normative component whilst the empirical analysis does not. There is no fallacy of psychologism because the empirical analysis only establishes the existence of the faculties or cognitive equipment on the basis of the epistemic analysis.

Nietzsche's view differs from both Allison and Kitcher. Nietzsche suggests that Kant's appeal to the transcendental self confuses an account of the specifically human origins of our knowledge with its objective validity. Kant is guilty of this charge, in Nietzsche's view, as a result of his contrast between human and non-human points of view.

33. Friedrich Nietzsche, *The Will to Power*, edited by R. J. Hollingdale, translated by Walter Kaufmann (New York: Vintage Books, 1968 [1901]), 530. Henceforth cited as *WP*. That Kant's transcendental account of our knowledge is concerned with origins can be seen from his claim that 'what can alone be entitled transcendental is the knowledge that these representations are not of empirical origin . . .' (Kant, *CPR*, A56/B81).

34. Kant indicates that his appeal to transcendental apperception as a logical condition of our knowledge is also a psychological condition. Logic and psychology are ultimately inseparable for Kant, as can be seen from his statement that 'the possibility of the logical form of all knowledge is necessarily conditioned by relation to this apperception *as a faculty*' (Kant, *CPR*, A118n).

35. Nietzsche's interpretation of Kant's account of synthesis as grounded in the transcendental self is most likely influenced by Kuno Fischer's non-naturalistic interpretation of Kant's appeal to transcendental spontaneity. However, Nietzsche's argument that the role of the self in knowledge should be understood naturalistically is arguably influenced by both Schopenhauer and Lange. See Hill's *Nietzsche's Critiques*, pp. 18ff. for a discussion of Nietzsche's appropriation of the respective interpretations of Kant. Despite the influence of Schopenhauer and Lange, Nietzsche denies that their combination of naturalism with idealism is a feasible option (Nietzsche, *BGE*, 15).

36. Nietzsche, *WP*, 530. In *BGE*, 11 Nietzsche argues that Kant must allow that our judgements could be false from within our human point of view and not by contrasting our judgements with the possibility of a non-human perspective.

37. Nietzsche, *BGE*, 23.

38. Ibid., 230.

39. Kant, *CPR*, A111.

40. Nietzsche, *WP*, 530. Sometimes Nietzsche suggests that Kant's emphasis of form over content results in the elimination of content altogether, claiming that Kant's account of synthesis is a precursor to the German Idealist appeal to intellectual intuition (Nietzsche, *BGE*, 11). Nevertheless, Nietzsche's view that for Kant the thing-in-itself is the source of affection suggests that Kant allows some role, however slight, to content.

41. This particular interpretation of Kant is an historically rooted one. One of Kant's earliest reviewer's, Christian Garve (1783), for example, ascribes to Kant a phenomenalistic idealism, which entails that outer objects are reducible to subjective representations (Christian Garve, 'The Garve Review', in Brigitte Sassen, *Kant's Early Critics* [Cambridge: Cambridge University Press, 2000], p. 76). However, this particular interpretation is not confined to Kant's contemporaries. P. F. Strawson, for example, argues that Kant's appeal to synthesis and faculties commits him to subjective idealism. Strawson writes: 'What really emerges here is that aspect of transcendental idealism which finally denies to the natural world any existence independent of our "representations" or perceptions, an aspect to which I have already referred in remarking that Kant is closer to Berkeley than he acknowledges' (P. F. Strawson, *The Bounds of Sense* [London: Routledge, 1966], p. 35). Nietzsche's interpretation was most likely influenced by Fischer, Schopenhauer and Lange, all of whom argue that Kantian objects are mind-dependent (See Hill, *Nietzsche's Critiques*, p. 16). However, this view is in contrast to the predominant 'analytic' reading, which claims that Kant is putting forward what have been called 'transcendental arguments', which are intended to have anti-sceptical import by revealing necessary conditions for knowledge. These arguments attempt to de-psychologise Kant and abstract his arguments from his talk of synthesis and faculties. Transcendental arguments begin with some undisputed fact about our experience (that we have experience, make judgements, and so on), followed by the claim that some disputed factor is necessary and must obtain if this fact of our experience is to be possible. Proponents of this reading of Kant's arguments tend to take the uncontroversial starting point to be that of self-consciousness and Kant's target to be the Cartesian sceptic. In such accounts the independent existence of objects is deemed to be a necessary condition of our experience of self-consciousness (see Strawson, *The Bounds of Sense*, pp. 26–7).
42. Kant, *CPR*, A114.
43. Ibid., A114. See also A104. Kant's claim that we introduce order into nature (ibid., A125) has given rise to a debate as to whether he includes particular empirical laws in this account. Gerd Buchdahl argues that Kant treats the issue of particular laws at the level of regulative research and discovery. Michael Friedman contends, in contrast, that particular empirical laws, the laws of Newtonian mathematical physics, are a necessary component of Kant's constitutive account of knowledge. See Gerd Buchdahl, 'The Kantian "Dynamic of Reason" with Special Reference to the Place of Causality in Kant's System', in Lewis White Beck (ed.), *Kant Studies Today* (La Salle, IL: Open Court, 1969); Gerd Buchdahl, *Metaphysics and the Philosophy of Science* (Oxford: Oxford University Press, 1969); Michael Friedman, 'Regulative and Constitutive', *The Southern Journal of Philosophy*, Vol. XXX, Supplement, 1991; Michael Friedman, *Kant and the Exact Sciences* (Cambridge, MA: Harvard University Press, 1992).
44. Nietzsche, *BGE*, 11. Nietzsche interprets Kant as reducing the empirical world to a mental representation from his earliest writings where he describes Kant's empirical object of knowledge crudely as a ball tossed about in the heads of men (Friedrich Nietzsche, 'The Philosopher: Reflections on the Struggle between Art and Knowledge', paragraph 106, in *Philosophy and Truth: Selections from Nietzsche's Notebooks of the Early 1870's*, edited and translated by Daniel Breazeale [London: Humanities Press, 1991]) to his later writings where he interprets Kant as putting forward a distinction between appearance and reality (Friedrich Nietzsche, *Twilight of the Idols*, included in *Twilight of the Idols/The Anti-Christ*, translated by R. J. Hollingdale [London: Penguin, 1990 (1889)], '"Reason" in Philosophy', 6. Henceforth cited as *TI*).
45. Friedrich Nietzsche, 'Schopenhauer as Educator', 3 (1874) in *Untimely*

Meditations, translated by R. J. Hollingdale (Cambridge: Cambridge University Press, 1994 [1873–76]).

46. Nietzsche, *GS*, 335.
47. Nietzsche, *HAH*, Volume I, 'Of First and Last Things', 16.
48. Nietzsche, *WP*, 553.
49. Gerd Buchdahl maintains that when Kant appeals to the *thing-in-itself*, the *transcendental object* and *appearances*, he is not appealing to different objects but to one epistemological object under different interpretations (Gerd Buchdahl, *Kant and the Dynamics of Reason, Essays on the Structure of Kant's Philosophy* [Oxford: Blackwell, 1992]). Borrowing from Husserl, Buchdahl argues that Kant engages in a dynamic 'reduction-realisation' process whereby his references to transcendental objects, things-in-themselves and appearances stand for different stages in the realisation of empirical objects. See also Nathan Rotenstreich, *Experience and its Systemization: Studies in Kant* (The Hague: Martinus Nijhoff, 1965).
50. Kant, *CPR*, A258/B314.
51. Ibid., A257/B313.
52. Immanuel Kant, *Prolegomena to Any Future Metaphysics*, translated by Paul Carus (Cambridge, MA: Hackett, 1977 [1783]), 13 remark II, p. 33.
53. Kant, *CPR*, A190/B235.
54. See Moltke Gram, 'Things in Themselves: The Historical Lessons', *Journal of the History of Philosophy*, Vol. 18, No. 4, October 1980, pp. 407–31, especially pp. 414ff.
55. Arthur Schopenhauer, *The World as Will and Representation*, Volume I, translated by E. F. J. Payne (New York: Dover, 1966 [1819]), Appendix, p. 503. Henceforth cited as *WWR*, I. See Nietzsche's rejection of the thing-in-itself in *BGE*, 16. For a discussion of this 'traditionalist' reading of Kant and why it might be incorrect, see Allison, *Kant's Transcendental Idealism*, Introduction.
56. Schopenhauer thinks that the concept of the thing-in-itself is meaningful to the extent that it can be intuited directly as *Will*. However, within a strictly Kantian framework it becomes, in Schopenhauer's view, a meaningless concept. (Arthur Schopenhauer, *The World as Will and Representation*, Volume II, translated by E. F. J. Payne [New York: Dover, 1966 (1844)], p. 196. Henceforth cited as *WWR*, II.)
57. Kant, *CPR*, B275.
58. See *HAH*, Volume I, 'Of First and Last Things', 16 where Nietzsche states there is no epistemic connection between things-in-themselves and the realm of appearances.
59. Nietzsche, *WP*, 530.
60. Ibid., 497.
61. Ibid., 555.
62. Friedrich Nietzsche, *On the Genealogy of Morality*, translated by Maudemarie Clark and Alan J. Swensen (Indianapolis, IN: Hackett, 1998 [1887]), III, 12. Henceforth cited as *GM*.
63. Nietzsche, *BGE*, 11.
64. Ibid., 3.
65. Ibid., 11, 12.
66. Ibid., 210.
67. Nietzsche, *WP*, 530. It is to be noted that in this passage Nietzsche does not recognise Kant's distinction between formal and transcendental logic.
68. Nietzsche was familiar with both texts. In 'On Teleology' [1867–8] he makes page references to Kant's *Critique of Judgement* (Friedrich Nietzsche, 'Zur Teleologie', in *Werke und Briefe. Historisch-Kritische Gesamtausgabe*, [München: C. H. Beck'sche Verlagsbuchhandlung, 1933–42], 3: 371–94). These

notes are translated by Claudia Crawford and included under the heading 'On Teleology' (*OT*) as an Appendix to her *The Beginning of Nietzsche's Theory of Language* (Berlin: de Gruyter, 1988)]. In *Philosophy in the Tragic Age of the Greeks* (1873), 15 Nietzsche cites *CPR* footnote on A37 (see *Sämtliche Werke. Kritische Studienausgabe*, edited by Giorgio Colli and Mazzino Montinari [Berlin/München: Walter de Gruyter and dtv, 1980], 1, pp. 799ff. The text is translated by Marianne Cowan [Washington: Regnery Publishing, 1962 (1873)]). *CPR* B xxx is quoted in *Daybreak*, 197, translated by R. J. Hollingdale (Cambridge: Cambridge University Press, 1993 [1881/1887]). *CPR* A319/B376 is cited in the preface to the second 1886 edition of *Daybreak*. For further details see Hill, *Nietzsche's Critiques*, p. 20n.

69. Kant states that the function of reason 'is to assist the understanding by means of ideas, in those cases in which the understanding cannot by itself establish rules . . .' (Kant, *CPR*, A648/B676).

70. See Susan Neiman, *Rereading Kant* (Oxford: Oxford University Press, 1994), p. 61.

71. Michael Friedman, 'Philosophy of Natural Science', in *The Cambridge Companion to Kant and Modern Philosophy* (Cambridge: Cambridge University Press, 2006), p. 326.

72. Kant, *CPR*, A668/B696.

73. Ibid., A671/B699.

74. Ibid., A114.

75. Kant contends that corresponding to the three logical laws of genera, species and affinity are the three transcendental laws of the '*homogeneity, specification,* and *continuity* of forms' (Kant, *CPR*, A658/B686) according to which Reason seeks the systematic unity of nature. He argues that these 'laws contemplate the parsimony of fundamental causes, the manifoldness of effects, and the consequent affinity of the parts of nature . . .' (ibid., A661/B689). However, Kant's argument that the logical principles of unity, as subjective heuristic maxims, presuppose transcendental objectively valid principles has been deemed incoherent by some commentators. See Norman Kemp Smith, *A Commentary to Kant's Critique of Pure Reason* (New York: Humanities Press, 1962 [1923]), and Jonathan Bennett, *Kant's Dialectic* (Cambridge: Cambridge University Press, 1974).

76. Kant, *CPR*, A662/B690.

77. Ibid., A651/B679.

78. Ibid., A644/B672.

79. Ibid., A665/B693.

80. Ibid., A666/B694.

81. Ibid., A306/B362.

82. Ibid., A663/B691.

83. Ibid., A680/B708.

84. Nietzsche, *OT*, p. 246. I have emended Crawford's translation of this passage slightly to include Nietzsche's reference to constitutive judgements, which is omitted from Crawford's translation.

85. Buchdahl points out that sometimes Kant conflates the constitutive with the regulative by suggesting that without the regulative idea of 'system' we cannot posit 'law-likeness' at all, and moreover, that without 'the regulative systematic activity of reason, the whole concept [of causal necessity] could not arise in the first place' (Buchdahl, *Metaphysics and the Philosophy of Science*, p. 518). Michael Friedman, who interprets Kant differently from Buchdahl (see note 43 above), contends that Kant's philosophical project ultimately demands principles that are both constitutive and regulative in order to overcome the 'gap' between pure *a priori* principles and the classification of empirical concepts.

Overcoming the gap requires a guarantee that 'the ideal complete natural science at which reflective judgement aims asymptotically will in fact contain the specifically Newtonian natural science grounded by the *Metaphysical Foundations*' (Friedman, 'Regulative and Constitutive', p. 95). Friedman contends that Kant addresses this need in the *Opus postumum*, where 'Although this demand proves ultimately an impossible one, there is nonetheless a moment, when, deeply impressed by the extraordinary success of the just completed chemical revolution, Kant thinks he has found a way to meet it' (Friedman, 'Regulative and Constitutive', p. 95).

86. Nietzsche's appeal to regulative principles with their emphasis on research thus entails the idea that our knowledge, contrary to Kant's constitutive account, is always subject to revision and alteration. It is noteworthy that Reichenbach distinguished two notions of the *a priori* in Kant. The first identifies the *a priori* with that which is necessary and unrevisable, whilst the second identifies it as constitutive of best scientific practice at a particular time. Reichenbach appropriates the second, contending, as Michael Friedman explains, that 'What Kant did not and could not see, rather, is that precisely such constitutive principles change and develop as empirical natural science progresses' (Friedman, 'Philosophy of Natural Science', p. 331). Had Kant not conflated the two aspects of the *a priori* in his account of constitutive knowledge, Nietzsche may have looked on this aspect of Kant's project more favourably as he is certainly of the view that our perspectives colour how we view the world but he denies that reality is reducible to those perspectives and that our perspectives are unrevisable.

87. Kant, *CPR*, A26/B42–43.

88. Ibid., A27. Nietzsche thinks that Kant has not justified his constitutive employment of the categories, arguing that philosophers have viewed concepts as if they were a dowry from some kind of wonderland (Nietzsche, *WP*, 409). See also *BGE*, 11 where Nietzsche argues that Kant is unable to 'explain' why we possess the specific categories that he attributes to human knowing.

89. Kant, *CPR*, B145–6.

90. Ibid., A42/B59. In *GS*, 374 Nietzsche argues that the question of whether there are possibly beings whose mode of cognition is radically different from ours is a nonsensical question for human knowers. Nonetheless, he contends that we should not therefore conclude that existence itself is non-interpretive, warning us, however, against improper assessments of what this means. He warns against an illegitimate deification of the world or other forms of 'human folly'. In his articulation of the will to power thesis in *BGE*, 36 he suggests that the interpretive structure of existence is not something divorced from human knowing but rather is a process within which human knowing is embedded.

91. Nietzsche, *BGE*, 54.

92. Nietzsche, *WP*, 552.

93. Nietzsche, *BGE*, 36.

94. Ibid., 230.

95. Nietzsche, *HAH*, Volume I, 'Of First and Last Things', 19.

96. Heidegger interprets Nietzsche this way in *Nietzsche*, Volume 3, pp. 68ff.

97. Christoph Cox, *Nietzsche: Naturalism and Interpretation* (London: University of California Press, 1999), pp. 145–6; Nietzsche *WP*, 517. According to Cox, Nietzsche's interpretive account of knowledge disallows the possibility of a unifying view of the world because, he maintains, Nietzschean perspectives are ultimately incommensurable with each other (Cox, *Nietzsche: Naturalism and Interpretation*, pp. 155–6). For my alternative conclusion, see Chapter 4.

Chapter 2
Nietzsche's Perspectival Theory of Knowledge

In Chapter 1 we saw that, according to Nietzsche, Kant's constitutive account of knowledge results in the sceptical idealism that Kant wants to avoid. Nietzsche thinks that this difficulty can be resolved by rejecting Kant's constitutive epistemology in favour of a regulative and interest-directed conception of knowledge. The resulting Nietzschean view is that knowledge is anthropocentric but realist; empirical reality, he claims, is mind-independent but knowable.

In this chapter I investigate Nietzsche's argument supporting the view that we can have objective knowledge of mind-independent reality by examining his perspectivism and interpreting it as a rejection of metaphysical realism, the general Kantian view that there is a thing-in-itself.[1] Nietzsche's concerns with metaphysical realism are twofold: first, Kant contends that the thing-in-itself, although mind-independent, is non-empirical and unknowable to beings with our specifically human cognitive constitution, and, second, if so, there is an epistemic gap that opens up between self and world, a gap that induces scepticism. Nietzsche rejects this scepticism and the metaphysical realism that provokes it. In this chapter we investigate his reasons for doing so, focusing on his later writings from *Human, All Too Human* onwards.

This investigation is divided into three sections. The first sets up the problem of metaphysical realism and outlines the requirements that Nietzsche must meet if he is to overcome it. The following two sections address the extent to which Nietzsche satisfies these requirements, concluding that his anti-metaphysical realist position, which I describe as internal realism, holds that our perspectives are rooted in empirical reality and constrained internally from within our practices of contextually seeking out the best reasons for and against our epistemic claims.

METAPHYSICAL REALISM

This section draws out the epistemological dimension of Nietzsche's dissatisfaction with metaphysical realism, focusing on the specifically extra-perspectival epistemology, which according to Nietzsche is historically inherent in metaphysical realism and which in its identification of reality with the non-empirical ultimately leads to a sceptical dissociation of truth and justification. The interconnection between extra-perspectival epistemology and metaphysical realism can be discerned from Nietzsche's claim that our philosophical heritage has left us with a dualistic metaphysical system that adopts what he terms the 'will to truth' as both a moral and epistemological imperative. Nietzsche construes the will to truth as a desire for disinterested truth expressed in the form of resentment against our instincts and the interests they embody. The will to truth is a form of asceticism that emphasises disinterested and objective truth purely for its own sake:

> For let us guard ourselves better from now on, gentlemen philosophers, against the dangerous old conceptual fabrication that posited a 'pure, will-less, painless, timeless subject of knowledge' . . . here it is always demanded that we think an eye that cannot possibly be thought, an eye that must not have any direction . . .[2]

Moreover, this 'priestly' form of thinking,[3] according to Nietzsche, demarcates the world of change and instincts from a 'true' or 'real' world that corresponds to the ascetic demand that the object of truth be unchanging and stable. Nietzsche describes the will to truth as 'Contempt, hatred against everything that perishes, changes, varies . . .', arguing that 'Obviously the will to truth is here merely the demand for a *world of the stable*'.[4] Consequently, Nietzsche contends that philosophers have operated within an appearance/reality dichotomy where reality is deemed to be an extra-empirical realm of truth whilst the empirical world of our experience is deemed to be a realm of deception and untruth. Nietzsche thus thinks that metaphysical realism, the doctrine that there is a world independent of our experience of it, has been coupled with both an extra-perspectival epistemology and extra-empirical ontology, ultimately divorcing our knowledge of the empirical world from how things are in themselves. At this point the objection may be raised that metaphysical realism is not by definition a sceptical position. However, Nietzsche maintains that scepticism emerges from the extra-perspectival epistemic thesis that has historically informed metaphysical realism. This epistemic thesis is articulated in metaphysical realism in two ways; we can characterise metaphysical realists, according to Nietzsche, as either cognitivists or non-cognitivists with regard to the knowability of the metaphysical 'real' world.[5] The cognitivist claims that reality is both accessible and knowable by extra-perspectival and non-empirical means whilst those metaphysical realists of the non-cognitivist persuasion argue that reality as it is in itself is inaccessible. Rationalist metaphysicians represent the former. The latter view arrives on the philosophical scene, according to Nietzsche, in the guise of Kant. This non-cognitivist form of meta-physical realism emerges following the demise of the cognitivist version. Kant's inaccessibility thesis, he contends, derives from the demise of the rationalist idea that we can have extra-perspectival knowledge of non-empirical reality.

Nietzsche argues that the cognitivist metaphysical realist claim to extra-perspectival knowledge has its roots in the rationalist appeal to *a priori* Reason as the source of knowledge of the 'real' world. According to Nietzsche, rationalist metaphysics claims to have unmediated con-ceptual access to an extra-empirical realm of reality as it is in itself. Its concepts are presented as something innate and certain as opposed to Nietzsche's view that they have evolved over a period of time:

> They put that which comes at the end . . . the 'highest concepts', that is to say the most general, emptiest concepts, the last fumes of evaporating reality, at the beginning *as* the beginning. . . . Moral: everything of the first rank must be *causa sui*. Origin in something else counts as an objection, as casting a doubt on value.[6]

However, of the cognitivist metaphysical realist model, Nietzsche writes that 'reality does not appear at all, not even as a problem'.[7] He argues that this particular interpretation of the world is 'fabricated solely from psychological needs'[8] and that once this has been revealed through genealogical and historical inquiry the dissolution of this metaphysical picture will be inevitable.[9] Genealogy inquires into the contingent origins of a belief, whilst historical inquiry traces the development of the belief. By examining the origin and historical development of a belief Nietzsche aims to expose the motivations that inform those beliefs. It is sufficient in his view to expose the suspect origins of a belief in order to question its reasonableness. However, Nietzsche is not guilty of the genetic fallacy here. He suggests that a belief that is shown to have emerged in a delib-erate attempt to distort reality (for example, to paint a 'moral' image of the world) will not have undergone a rigorous process of justifying its epistemic credentials by exposing itself to the public realm of agonistic debate whereby we give 'an account of the final and most certain reasons pro and con'.[10] On the basis of this Nietzsche claims that once the psychological and moral ulterior guiding motives informing the invention of metaphysical dualism are revealed, this dualism will be refuted. He writes: 'When one has disclosed these methods as the foundation of all extant religions and metaphysical systems, one has refuted them.'[11] Moreover, Nietzsche suggests that rationalism, motivated by the will to truth, ultimately performs this examination of itself. He writes:

> All great things perish through themselves, through an act of self-cancellation: thus the law of life wills it, the law of the *necessary* 'self-overcoming' in the essence of life – in the end the call always goes forth to the lawgiver himself: '*patere legem, quam ipse tulisti*' [submit to the law which you yourself have established].[12]

Metaphysical realism, in its cognitivist guise, becomes an untenable philosophical position, according to Nietzsche, once the will to truth undermines itself. The will to truth can no longer endorse the belief in the 'true' world once its origins in a reactive and ascetic morality that is not disinterested but motivated by a hatred of our drives and instincts has been revealed. He contends that the belief in a 'true' world, when subject to the demands of intellectual honesty, is exposed as a partial point of view 'implanted by centuries of moral interpretation' and therefore as a belief we are no longer 'allowed' to entertain.[13] The consequent collapse of the cognitivist version of metaphysical realism indicates, in Nietzsche's view, the untenability of the extra-perspectival conception of knowing inherent in the God's Eye View of knowledge. The motivations informing rationalist metaphysics turn out not to be disinterested but rather a distorted view on things. Although this is an important aspect of his complete rejection of metaphysical realism, Nietzsche argues that the revelation that Reason is not an objective and disinterested cognitive tool that facilitates access to the world as it is in itself does not result in the complete collapse of metaphysical realism. Rather, metaphysical realism merely adopts a non-cognitivist stance with regard to the 'real' world. In so doing, the possibility of extra-perspectival knowledge and its correspondent non-empirical object are upheld as ideals even though they are unattainable in practice.

In his outline of the history of philosophy in *Twilight of the Idols*, Nietzsche traces the progressive demise of the rationalist conception of reality and our knowledge of it:

How the 'Real World' at last Became a Myth

HISTORY OF AN ERROR

1. The real world, attainable to the wise, the pious, the virtuous man – he dwells in it, *he is it.*

(Oldest form of the idea, relatively sensible, simple, convincing. Transcription of the proposition: 'I, Plato, *am* the truth').

2. The real world, unattainable for the moment, but promised to the wise, the pious, the virtuous man ('to the sinner who repents').

   (Progress of the idea: it grows more refined, more enticing, more incomprehensible – *it becomes a woman*, it becomes Christian . . .)

3. The real world, unattainable, undemonstrable, cannot be promised, but even when merely thought of a consolation, a duty, an imperative.

   (Fundamentally the same old sun, but shining through mist and scepticism; the idea become sublime, pale, northerly, Königsbergian.)

4. The real world – unattainable? Unattained, at any rate. And if unattained also *unknown*. Consequently also no consolation, no redemption, no duty: how could we have a duty towards something unknown?

   (The grey of dawn. First yawnings of reason. Cock-crow of positivism.)

5. The 'real world' – an idea no longer of any use, not even a duty any longer – an idea grown useless, superfluous, *consequently* a refuted idea: let us abolish it!

   (Broad daylight; breakfast; return of cheerfulness and *bons sens*; Plato blushes for shame; all free spirits run riot.)

6. We have abolished the real world: what world is left? the apparent one, perhaps? — But no! *with the real world we have also abolished the apparent world!*

   (Mid-day; moment of the shortest shadow; end of the longest error; zenith of mankind; INCIPIT ZARATHUSTRA.)[14]

Nietzsche's complaint here centres on his belief that philosophy has operated within a dualistic, two-world model. According to this model, our knowledge can be adequate to reality only if we disengage ourselves from our particular anthropocentric interests. Stages 1 to 4 in Nietzsche's history of philosophy represent this two-world mode of thinking which has its origins in Platonism and Christianity. Nietzsche places Kant at stage 3, thus indicating he considers that Kant too operates within this two-world mode of thinking. According to Nietzsche, Kant retains the rationalist appeal to non-empirical reality in the guise of the inaccessible and unknowable thing-in-itself. In so doing Kant adopts, in Nietzsche's view, the non-cognitivist strain of metaphysical realism.

Nietzsche argues that Kant belongs to this metaphysical realist category because he retains the thing-in-itself as a metaphysical hangover from rationalist metaphysics. This hangover results, in Nietzsche's view, from Kant's acceptance of the demise of unmediated conceptual knowledge coupled with his retention of the idea that our human senses are unable to provide insight into the ultimate nature of reality. Nietzsche argues that Kant is caught within the philosophical tradition that thinks that empirical knowledge is deficient and captures only 'appearances' whilst conceptual knowledge refers to the 'real' world. With Kant's Copernican turn, however, comes the realisation that concepts do not hook onto 'reality' directly and that concepts, in conjunction with the senses, give us knowledge of the objects of the empirical world. Despite this realisation, however, Kant, according to Nietzsche, retains the rationalist idea of the thing-in-itself and attributes to it greater merit than the world of the senses, thus further instantiating a two-world view, which now, however, carries with it sceptical implications.

Kant's distinction between the thing-in-itself and appearances as a distinction between the 'real' and the merely 'apparent' world consequently gives rise, according to Nietzsche, to the further distinction between truth-in-itself and truth merely 'for us'. Truth-in-itself is a correspondence idea whereby reality is said to confer truth on our epistemic claims. Truth 'for us', however, is said to be merely perspectival, divorced from how things are in themselves. Thus Nietzsche contends that with Kant metaphysical independence and epistemic inaccessibility go hand in hand. It is metaphysical realism combined with this additional epistemic premise that Nietzsche rejects; he rejects the view that reality is constituted such that its ultimate nature is both non-empirical and inaccessible to beings whose mode of cognition is sensual and perspectival.

Nietzsche's main contention with metaphysical realism thus centres on the issue of the dissociation of truth and justification. Truth comprises, for the metaphysical realist in general, a correspondence between the way the world is in itself and our epistemic and normative assertions. With the demise of the cognitivist version, however, and its metamorphosis into the non-cognitivist version we witness what may be termed a decoupling[15] of truth and justification whereby our experience of the empirical world as the only world available to us and the justification of our epistemic claims are denied the title 'truth'. Thus according to this version, truth-in-itself and our actual practices of justification are radically divorced. In such a case we witness what Nietzsche terms a severing of theory from practice.[16] In theory, the non-cognitivist metaphysical realist adopts an extra-perspectival approach to the question of truth. However, in practice, given the cognitive inaccessibility of truth-in-itself, the non-cognitive metaphysical realist operates with possible falsehoods and illusions in the guise of beliefs that are lacking in epistemic worth. Nietzsche aims to overcome this underlying extra-perspectival and anti-empirical approach.

If Nietzsche is to succeed in this he must satisfy a number of demands. First, he must overcome the non-cognitivist version of metaphysical realism by recoupling truth and justification. He does this by adopting a contextualist argument claiming that our practices of justification determine truth. Second, if Nietzsche is to succeed in recoupling truth and justification he must also overcome the two-world view of metaphysical realism. In particular, he must overcome the anti-empirical tendency of this dualism. This anti-empirical tendency is evident in the insistence that the empirical arena of our lived experience cannot be an arena of truth but only of practical beliefs of doubtful epistemic status. If Nietzsche is to recouple truth and justification he must establish that the empirical arena of our lived experience is conducive to truth and not radically divorced from it. In sum, if truth is not to be divorced from justification, we must rid ourselves of the thing-in-itself.

The remainder of this chapter sets about demonstrating the manner in which Nietzsche meets the above demands. By examining Nietzsche's perspectivism and empiricism, we see that he adopts an internal realist response, arguing that our knowledge is immersed in the empirical world rather than divorced from it.

NIETZSCHE'S PERSPECTIVISM

The notion of perspective permeates the entire corpus of Nietzsche's writings, although its meaning is often rather fluid, operating on different occasions as a social, historical, epistemic and biological thesis. Appealing to a visual metaphor, he defines a cognitive perspective as influencing the 'look' or appearance of things, arguing that our perspectives comprise a specifically 'human contribution' to how things appear.[17] Moreover, he often identifies cognitive perspectives with the Kantian categories such as causality and substance but with an important difference.[18] Whereas the Kantian categories are constitutive extra-historical conditions of the possibility and limitation of our knowledge to appearances, Nietzsche argues that our perspectives are regulative tools of inquiry rooted in our interests and values.[19]

Nietzsche's perspectivism emerges in the context of his complaint that 'Lack of historical sense is the family failing of all philosophers'.[20] He argues that philosophy has traditionally ignored the fact that our social institutions, values and ways of thinking in general have developed over time in favour of the idea of a timeless rational human essence:

> many, without being aware of it, even take the most recent manifestation of man, such as has arisen under the impress of certain religions, even certain political events, as the fixed form from which one has to start out. They will not learn that man has become, that the faculty of knowledge has become;

while some of them would have it that the whole world is spun out of this faculty of cognition.[21]

Central to the development of an historical sense, according to Nietzsche, is the realisation that our social institutions and values are not instantiations of a timeless and purely rational 'ideal' but rather are expressions of psychological and physiological conditions. He argues that psychology provides the key to understanding the fundamental questions that concern us[22] and that human psychological inclinations must be understood in terms of physiological factors.[23] According to Nietzsche, human beings are organisms whose mode of knowing the world is rooted in their physiological drives and instincts. Appropriating various aspects of nineteenth-century biology, particularly that of the embryologist Wilhelm Roux's notion of the organism as an inner struggle between parts and the Anglo-German zoologist William Rolph's principle of insatiability, Nietzsche argues that we are intentional beings that seek out conditions for our growth.[24] Consequently, our relation to things other than ourselves, according to Nietzsche, is never disinterested but is always guided and informed by our instincts. He contends that our perspectives are rooted in these instincts, writing that knowledge is 'actually nothing but a *certain behaviour of the instincts toward one another*'.[25] He further writes:

> It is our needs that interpret the world; our drives and their For and Against. Every drive is a kind of lust to rule; each one has its perspective that it would like to compel all other drives to accept as a norm.[26]

As organisms made up of a multiplicity of instincts and drives, we are capable of viewing things from multiple points of view. As knowers we are a multiplicity of perspectives engaged in an inner struggle for dominance and temporally under the control of a dominating perspective. Arguing that our knowledge is always conditioned by our nature as biological and intentional beings, Nietzsche's perspectivism holds in contrast to the notion of epistemological disinterestedness historically fostered by metaphysical realism that our knowledge is contextual and empirical.

Contextualism denies the possibility of intrinsically credible beliefs from which other beliefs are inferred in favour of a locally holistic conception of justification.[27] Contextualism is thus a form of anti-foundationalist thought. Foundationalism takes two forms, both of which Nietzsche rejects. Structural foundationalism maintains that there is a certain structure to our knowledge such that it is founded on inferences from basic, intrinsically credible beliefs. Substantive foundationalism adds that these basic beliefs must be of a certain kind. Both forms adopt an atomistic conception of justification whereby intrinsic credibility entails that our basic beliefs are justified independently of the particular context of our inquiry. Although contextualism appeals to default justification whereby some beliefs are 'basic' because they frame the parameters of intelligibility for an inquiry, these basic beliefs nevertheless depend on a host of contextually variable factors such as the particular inquiry in which we are engaged or the current state of our knowledge.[28] By adopting a form of contextualism, Nietzsche aims to replace the metaphysical realist view *from nowhere* with the perspectivist view *from somewhere*. Defining a perspective as an 'interest of certain types of life',[29] he argues that our truths are irretrievably entwined with our interests. A perspective for Nietzsche, as we have seen, is a point of view that we take on a matter, the point of view being determined by our context and situation. Understood analogously to an optical perspective whereby the optical perspective influences how the object 'looks' to the perceiver, a cognitive perspective influences how we understand the world. Perspectivism thus aims to induce a form of epistemological modesty by claiming that we cannot acquire extra-perspectival knowledge. We cannot know the world from a God's Eye view or no point of view at all.

Extra-perspectival knowledge is conceivable, according to Nietzsche, only if we permit both the objectionable concept of the thing-in-itself or Platonic eternal verities and the necessary rationalist cognitive tools. We have seen from our discussion of the demise of the cognitivist form of metaphysical realism that genealogical and historical inquiry reveal, in Nietzsche's view, that what was considered extra-perspectival knowledge was in fact only a distorted perspective or point of view. Since the God's Eye View and the thing-in-itself are mutually dependent, according to Nietzsche, the demise of one must lead to the inevitable collapse of the other. Nietzsche argues that without the possibility of a God's Eye view the distinction between things-in-themselves and appearances dissolves and with it the basis for scepticism.

Thus, in keeping with his epistemic quarrel with metaphysical realism Nietzsche denies that reality is epistemically inaccessible to our cognitive constitution. He does this by arguing that the concept of the thing-in-itself or a metaphysical world that is inaccessible to our cognitive faculties is a contradiction in terms. Nietzsche argues that it is impossible to conceptualise such a notion. Any attempt to conceptualise it is a fruitless activity because, he argues, 'We cannot look around our own corner: it is a hopeless curiosity that wants to know what other kinds of intellects and perspectives there *might* be . . . .'[30] With this Nietzsche argues that the reach of our perspectives forms the boundary of both intelligibility and rational acceptability. The suggestion that we can intelligibly think the idea of a realm of reality that is radically divorced from our perspectives is incoherent, according to Nietzsche, because our perspectives provide the framework of human rational thought. He writes:

> *We cease to think when we refuse to do so under the constraint of language; we barely reach the doubt that sees this limitation as a limitation.*
>
> *Rational thought is interpretation according to a scheme we cannot throw off.*[31]

It may be objected that Nietzsche's perspectivist account of justification merely describes what we happen to do rather than that which we ought to do. However, Nietzsche rejects the idea that there is available to us some normative standard independent of our most conscientious practices of perspectival justification, arguing that appeals to such standards further manifest the metaphysical realist quest for objective knowledge from no point of view whatever. Any such appeal to normative standards independent of our perspectival practices of justification, according to Nietzsche, is an attempt to escape the parameters of human rational discourse. He contends that standards of justification only make sense within the parameters of human rationality conditioned by our affective perspectival take on the world. He claims that our affective perspectival take on the world is rationally informed, writing contrary to what he calls the 'misunderstanding of passion and reason' that the latter is not 'an independent entity' but 'rather a system of relations between various passions and desires'. According to Nietzsche, every passion possesses 'its quantum of reason'.[32] Thus perspectivism narrows our interest in truth to truth 'for us', as opposed to what he considers to be the implausible metaphysical realist notion of truth-in-itself. Moreover, according to Nietzsche, truth 'for us' is perspectival but objective:

> There is *only* a perspectival seeing, *only* a perspectival 'knowing'; and *the more* affects we allow to speak about a matter . . . that much more complete will our 'concept' of this matter, our 'objectivity' be.[33]

Arguing that our truths are always justified from a particular point of view and debunking the idea of extra-perspectival truth as incoherent, Nietzsche contends that there is no reason to castigate our perspectival truths as less than objective. They are objective, according to Nietzsche, because they must undergo a process of justification in the context in which they are entertained. With this refined account of what constitutes objectivity we no longer consider our best justified beliefs as radically divorced from reality.

We can shed further light on the logic of Nietzsche's argument here by appealing to Maudemarie Clark's understanding of Nietzsche's position as founded on a distinction between what she calls our cognitive interests and cognitive capacities. Clark captures Nietzsche's thinking when she defines metaphysical realism as the view that truth is independent of both our cognitive capacities and cognitive interests whilst Nietzsche's response entails the view that truth is independent of our cognitive capacities but dependent on our cognitive interests. Arguing that our standards of rational acceptability express the cognitively relevant properties that we want from a theory and defining our cognitive interests as that which is cognitively useful to us or that which 'we could ever want' from a theory, Clark argues that Nietzsche rejects the view that 'Truth is independent not simply of what we now want, but of what we could ever want, that is, of what we would want even under ideal conditions for inquiry for beings like ourselves'.[34] Clark maintains that for Nietzsche our ideal theory is true even though this would 'imply no guarantee that we have the capacity, even in principle, to acquire the information that would justify accepting the theory'.[35]

Although it is a little unclear from Clark's presentation what exactly constitutes 'greater cognitive capacities', there is some suggestion that it would entail privileged insight into reality that is in some way self-evident such that it is outside the sphere of justification or the giving of reasons.[36] This is why the metaphysical realist appeal to greater cognitive capacities entails truth that is also independent of our cognitive interests or the perspectival arena of justifying our beliefs. This certainly fits with Nietzsche's association of metaphysical realism with an extra-perspectival view of knowledge.[37] As a form of non-perspectival privileged insight, greater cognitive capacities refer to an ability to acquire information about the world that due to its extra-perspectival status would be unintelligible to beings whose mode of cognition is perspectival. A being with greater cognitive capacities than us, then, would be a being with enhanced abilities to acquire information. However, Nietzsche argues that such information can be recognised by us only if it is interpreted, that is, brought into the justificatory sphere of giving reasons and justifications for our beliefs. Since the metaphysical realist is guilty, according to Nietzsche, of conflating acquisition with justification, I therefore employ the distinction between cognitive capacities and cognitive interests as a distinction between the mere acquisition of information on the one hand, and the justification or interpretation of that information such that it can make a difference to our knowledge on the other.

The view that truth is independent of both our cognitive capacities and interests leaves open the possibility that our beliefs may be massively in error in a similar manner to Descartes' subject deceived by the demon, or the brain in a vat that is deceived by the master-scientist. Nietzsche's metaphysical realist thinks it intelligible that our beliefs about the world may be illusory, bearing no significant cognitive relation to how the world is in itself. It is possible, according to his metaphysical realist, that there are beings with a privileged insight into reality, an insight which, being beyond our arena of giving justifications, renders reality inaccessible to and unknowable by us. The situation depicted in the demon scenario transcends our capacities because it is beyond our detective abilities to discern whether the beliefs induced in us by the demon are adequate to the true nature of reality. It is independent of our interests implying that, without a divine guarantee, a theory that gave us all we could ever want from a theory might nevertheless be massively in error. Thus truth is independent of our cognitive interests if it is claimed that our cognitive engagement with the world may be radically false. In order to close the possibility of massive error Nietzsche, in contrast, must maintain that truth is dependent on our cognitive interests but independent of our cognitive capacities. It must be independent of our cognitive capacities in order to allow for the real possibility of increased observational abilities and discovery. However, it must be dependent on our cognitive interests in order that such discoveries are justified and intelligible to us. By emphasising that the acquisition of such new information must enter the justificatory arena Nietzsche rules out the possibility of such acquisitions casting our beliefs into massive error. Thus for Nietzsche truth is dependent on what we could ever want from a theory understood as that which is intelligible to cognitive subjects with our mode of rationality. This entails that a proposition or theory, which is supported by the best reasons we have for holding that particular view, cannot be radically in error. This is suggested by Nietzsche's association of our best reasons (the balancing of reasons for and against a view) with the quest for certainty:

> *the great majority of people* does not consider it contemptible to believe this or that and to live accordingly, without first having given themselves *an account of the final and most certain reasons pro and con* [my emphasis], and without even troubling themselves about such reasons afterward: . . . But what is goodheartedness, refinement or genius to me, when the person who has these virtues tolerates slack feelings in his faith and judgments and when he does not account *the desire for certainty* as his inmost craving and deepest distress . . .[38]

Here Nietzsche sets up the arena in which truth claims are to be justified. If truth is independent of our cognitive capacities but dependent on our cognitive interests, then it is dependent on what is intelligible or conceivable to us, and thus dependent on our best reasons for holding a belief. The point here is that regardless of what information we come by in the future, the acquisition of such information cannot falsify our perspectival take on the world in a radical sense. In other words, the acquisition of further information will not globally falsify our best justified theory. This is because the acquisition of information must enter into the justificatory sphere of giving reasons if it is to make a difference to our knowledge, in which case it is recognisable by us and not radically divorced from our knowledge.

Nietzsche's argument here is somewhat similar to one proffered by Donald Davidson. Davidson argues that it is conceivable that there are beings with superior cognitive capacities to our own. Such a being would be what Davidson terms the omniscient interpreter. According to him, the omniscient interpreter can only deem our beliefs false by entering into cognitive communication with us. The possibility of such communication, however, presupposes a background of agreement on most matters. Thus, Davidson contends that 'objective error can occur only in a setting of largely true belief'.[39] The omniscient interpreter can cast our perspectival belief into massive error only from within the framework of our own standards of rational acceptability. The possibility of massive error, in other words, must be translatable into a rational format familiar to us. Metaphysical realism, in the specifically historical form that Nietzsche rejects, is one such untranslatable position. Such an untranslatable viewpoint can have, in his view, no cognitive purchase for us. It would be a view from Nowhere, an impossible attempt to 'look around our own corner'.

According to Nietzsche's argument, cognitive interests represent our best standards of rational acceptability (our best reasons for holding a theory to be true) and are to be clearly demarcated from our cognitive capacities. Our cognitive capacities refer to the manner of our acquisition of a belief as opposed to the manner of its justification. By emphasising the importance of justification and the giving of reasons, Nietzsche distinguishes between an interest that has entered the arena of justifying its epistemic credentials as opposed to any interest that we may have whatever. An interest is cognitive when it seeks to support its view with reasons for and against in a particular context. That Nietzsche distinguishes between perspectives that can be considered cognitive in this sense and any interest whatever can be discerned from *The Gay Science* where he insists on 'intellectual conscience' and the justification of belief in opposition to what he calls the religious interpretation of experience:

> they thirst after things that go *against reason,* and they do not wish to make it too hard for themselves to satisfy it. So they experience 'miracles' and 'rebirths' and hear the voices of little angels! But we, we others who thirst after reason, are determined to scrutinize our experiences as severely as a scientific experiment – hour after hour, day after day. We ourselves wish to be our experiments and guinea pigs.[40]

In addition to establishing the boundaries of human rational thought, dependence on our cognitive interests is designed to facilitate the overcoming of the appearance/reality dichotomy. This dichotomy has traditionally manifested itself in an oscillation between that which is 'found' and that which is 'made', that is, between metaphysical realism on the one hand, and an idealism that construes reality as metaphysically dependent on subjects on the other. In order to overcome this dichotomy Nietzsche must allow that there are real properties in the world, that reality is subject-independent, without licensing this possibility to cast doubt on our truths. He must hold that reality is not found merely by direct and extra-perspectival means but rather is *made known by us* without falling into the idea that this reality is constituted by us and so merely apparent. Dependence on our cognitive interests, for Nietzsche, stipulates that understanding reality as subject-independent is problematic only if that reality is radically inaccessible to our knowledge. Nietzsche argues, however, that the idea of such a radically inaccessible realm of reality is unintelligible. In so doing, he puts in place the necessary steps for an overcoming of the appearance/reality distinction.[41]

Nietzsche puts forward this argument in section 9 of *Human, All Too Human* and surrounding passages, where he presents an argument from indifferentism, which in turn is based on both an argument from genealogy and an argument from conceivability, against the idea of a metaphysical world that is radically inaccessible to our knowledge.[42] Nietzsche's reference to the possibility of a 'metaphysical world' in section 9 is a little ambiguous.[43] He argues whilst it is possible that there is a metaphysical world, this possibility can have no practical bearing on the epistemic status of our best justified beliefs. This is because, Nietzsche concludes, the only form of metaphysical world that is intelligible to us is one that, although independent of us, is in principle available to our knowledge.

The indifferentist argument claims that the idea of the thing-in-itself is epistemically impotent; it cannot make any practical difference to us because it is unable to cast our best justified beliefs into massive error.

There are two reasons why it cannot have such consequences. First, genealogical investigation reveals that the idea of a metaphysical world inaccessible to our human mode of knowing is founded on flawed reasoning. By tracing the genealogy of our belief in such a metaphysical world, Nietzsche contends that this belief originates in a false estimation of the world. He writes:

> but all that has hitherto made metaphysical assumptions *valuable, terrible, delightful* to them, all that has begotten these assumptions, is passion, error and self-deception; the worst of all methods of acquiring knowledge, not the best of all, have taught belief in them.[44]

Nietzsche argues that once we reveal the erroneous methods informing our belief in a thing-in-itself, this belief will be 'refuted'. The idea of an inaccessible reality, according to Nietzsche, can be understood as part of a host of inherited errors that wanted to explain the origin of change by appealing to an unchanging realm.[45] Here he suggests that the idea of an inaccessible thing-in-itself is in fact a human projection that makes sense only in the context of the many inherited errors that continue to inform our judgements. Second, Nietzsche contends that a metaphysical world defined as radically inaccessible to our knowledge is something completely unintelligible to us in positive terms. A metaphysical world that is radically divorced from our knowledge, he claims, can only be defined negatively. He writes: 'For one could assert nothing at all of the metaphysical world except that it was a being-other, an inaccessible, incomprehensible being-other; it would be a thing with negative qualities.'[46] Thus to the purely theoretical possibility of a radically inaccessible metaphysical world that remains after the argument from genealogy, Nietzsche contends that theoretical possibility is not very likely to cause men worry since it alone cannot carry any serious epistemic consequences for our best justified beliefs. Nietzsche argues that the idea of a thing-in-itself defined thus negatively cannot coincide with the epistemic possibility of casting our best justified beliefs into massive error. This is because the idea of a radically inaccessible thing-in-itself is parasitic on our experience of the empirical world and can be understood only in opposition to this experience. The mere idea of a thing-in-itself cannot therefore bear any weighty epistemic consequences for our knowledge of the empirical world.[47]

Consequently, Nietzsche combines an indifferentist argument with one from genealogy and conceivability, suggesting the idea of a metaphysical world that is radically inaccessible to our knowledge cannot make any practical difference to us because the idea of a thing-in-itself is 'empty of significance' and cannot be articulated in a familiar rational format.[48] On the basis of the above arguments Nietzsche concludes that the idea of an inaccessible metaphysical world is epistemically void for us. It carries no practical consequences for the epistemic worthiness of our best justified beliefs. However, Nietzsche claims we are far from arriving at our best justified beliefs. He argues that we have inherited many intellectual 'errors' from which we are yet to extricate ourselves.[49] This is what he means when he writes that we exist in the realm of 'idea'.[50] He writes: 'That which we now call the world is the outcome of a host of errors and fantasies, which have gradually arisen and grown entwined with one another in the course of the overall evolution of the organic being.'[51] Nevertheless, he suggests that we can escape the realm of ideas or inherited errors through 'physical and historical explanations' that 'lift us up out of the entire proceeding'.[52] Consequently, Nietzsche argues both that the notion of a radically inaccessible thing-in-itself is unintelligible and that our 'ideas' are capable of refinement through careful 'scientific' analysis.[53] Once the epistemic threat posed by the idea of a thing-in-itself is overcome and the distortions posed by inherited errors are in principle surmountable, Nietzsche paves the way for a complete overcoming of the distinction between appearances and inaccessible reality. That is, reality is now defined as that which is in principle available to our knowledge without being reducible to our 'ideas'. Consequently, Nietzsche allows that reality is subject-independent, but in principle accessible to our knowledge.

According to Nietzsche, every perspective that is justified according to our best standards is a perspective in the world. The fact that the world transcends, in the particular sense of not being reducible to our interests, does not entail that the world is inaccessible and unknowable in principle. What Nietzsche's perspectival theory of knowledge does rule out, however, is the possibility of a supra-perspectival and therefore God's Eye view of the world. Rejecting the latter's commitment to a recognition-transcendent view of truth, what John Haldane terms the ultra-realist insistence on 'the unconditional transcendence of reality over our natural means of coming to know about the world',[54] Nietzsche puts forward an internal realism, holding that reality is internal to our perspectival practices of justification. According to Nietzsche, a perspective, the condition under which seeing becomes seeing *something*, is the determinate manner in which the world is known.[55]

Nietzsche, then, rejects the idea that objectivity entails a God's Eye View from Nowhere in favour of a perspectival viewpoint that overcomes the metaphysical realist decoupling of truth and justification.

This is achieved by rejecting the notion of truth-in-itself in favour of Nietzsche's conception of truth *for us* whereby our actual and best practices of justification determine truth.[56] Metaphysical realism, as Nietzsche understands it, defines objectivity as that which is radically divorced from our human perspectives. That is, even our best justified beliefs might be massively in error. Nietzsche's account of objectivity, in contrast, entails the consideration of multiple points of view with regard to a matter, writing, as we have seen, that '*the more* affects we allow to speak about a matter . . . that much more complete will our "concept" of this matter, our "objectivity" be'.[57] Here Nietzsche suggests that if objectivity is defined by our perspectival take on the world, then truth cannot globally transcend our best justified human beliefs. This reading takes considerable steps in rebutting the idea that Nietzsche's perspectivism is a negative thesis that claims that our knowledge is 'merely' perspectival.[58] The negative view sees perspectives as playing a limiting role as in Kant where the categories, understood as transcendental conditions of the possibility of experience, limit our knowledge to that of appearances. Owing to the constitutive role of the categories, Kant's appearances, according to Nietzsche, are mere perspectival objects of knowledge divorced from how things are in themselves.[59] The negative reading allows for the possibility of a decoupling of justification and truth by conceding that our best perspectival practices of justification may be massively in error. In contrast, Nietzsche puts forward the positive internal realist thesis that our perspectives are rooted within the world and not divorced from it. This thesis culminates in Nietzsche's empiricism, the focus of our next section. When combined with his perspectivism, Nietzsche's empiricism puts in place the final step in his overcoming of the traditional metaphysical realist downgrading of empirical reality as an object of knowledge.

NIETZSCHE'S EMPIRICISM

Nietzsche's empiricism is particularly significant for his attempt to overcome metaphysical dualism. The latter view is rooted, he claims, in a philosophy of resentment that rejects the empirical world of our lived experience by positing another inaccessible world as the standard of the true and the real. Nietzsche argues that overcoming resentment requires an affirmation of the empirical world as a valid arena for philosophical inquiry, stating that all evidence for our most conscientious and trustworthy truths come from the senses.[60] That this appeal to empirical criteria is intended as an affirmative response to the anti-empirical dualistic philosophy of resentment can be seen from Nietzsche's claim that 'In Christianity neither morality nor religion come into contact with reality at any point'.[61] Nietzsche's perspectivism succeeds in overcoming this anti-empirical tendency by establishing that the empirical world plays a role in our epistemic claims without acting as an extra-perspectival epistemological foundation for those claims. That is, according to Nietzsche's internal realism, the empirical world of our lived experience is the arena within which our truth claims are worked out, and not a standard extrinsic to our actual practices of justification.

Abandoning the quest for pure conceptual or *a priori* access to the 'true' world unhindered by appeal to sense-experience Nietzsche argues that sense-knowledge represents the parameters of human conceivability and intelligibility. He writes in *Thus Spoke Zarathustra*:

> God is a supposition: but I want your supposing to be bounded by conceivability.
>
> Could you *conceive* a god? – But may the will to truth mean this to you: that everything shall be transformed into the humanly-conceivable, the humanly evident, the humanly palpable! You should follow your own senses to the end![62]

Although highlighting the role of sense-experience Nietzsche denies that sense-experience can act as a non-propositional and, therefore, supra-perspectival foundation for the justification of our epistemic claims. This can be witnessed principally in Nietzsche's rejection of Positivism's appeal to the epistemic transparency of sense-experience. Writing that 'facts are precisely what there is not, only interpretations',[63] he contends, contrary to the Positivist, that sense-experience cannot legitimately be taken as a self-evident basis for our knowledge. Nietzsche argues that our sensations are always already permeated with value judgements, by which I take him to mean that what we are acquainted with are sensory beliefs or perspectives rather than 'uninterpreted' sense-data.[64] He states:

> There could be no judgments at all if a kind of equalization were not practised *within sensations* [my emphasis]: memory is possible only within a continual emphasizing of what is already familiar, experienced. – Before judgment occurs, the process of assimilation must already have taken place; thus here, too, there is an intellectual activity that does not enter consciousness, as pain does as consequence of a wound. Probably an inner event corresponds to each organic function; hence assimilation, rejection, growth, etc.[65]

According to Nietzsche, if sensations are to have a justificatory role, then they must always already be interpreted. He writes: 'Believing is the primal beginning even in every sense-impression: a kind of affirmation the first intellectual activity.'[66] What we are fundamentally acquainted with, he maintains, are not pristine, non-conceptual sensory contents but rather sensory contents that are already conceptually informed. Consequently, for Nietzsche, the component of empirical importance is not the individual sense-impression, but rather the interpretive structure within which we are acquainted with sense-impressions as already interpreted. Sense-experience must always be perspectivally oriented in order for it to play an epistemic role in the justification of our beliefs. It seems, then, that Nietzsche was aware of the epistemic impotence of foundational empiricism. Uninterpreted sense-data, Nietzsche argues, cannot act as an extra-perspectival foundation of our judgements. As Michael Williams points out, the knowledge involved in grasping sensory data independently of its interpretation by the mind is non-propositional or ineffable, and therefore incapable of constraining our judgements.[67]

For Nietzsche, then, we are dealing with the world not as 'given' but as 'taken'. According to Nietzsche, our perspectives are internal to empirical reality rather than divorced from it. This internal realism reins in the metaphysical excesses of the Kantian thing-in-itself and, in so doing, establishes a reconnection between the issues of justification and truth.

However, this interpretation encounters a difficulty. For statements abound in Nietzsche's writings, claiming that what we ordinarily take to be true is in fact a falsehood. Although we addressed this issue briefly in Chapter 1, explaining Nietzsche's description of our truths as errors in the context of his argument for the mind-independence of the world, a more substantial engagement with the issue is required here not only because of the sheer complexity of interpreting those sections of Nietzsche's writings where he mentions the falsification thesis, but also because of the difficulty that these passages pose for Nietzsche's argument that our knowledge is perspectival but objective. If Nietzsche is committed to the falsification thesis, then he undermines his internal realism. There have been some attempts to argue that Nietzsche rejects the falsification thesis in his latest writings and that this alleviates the interpretive challenge posed by his use of the language of error to describe our epistemic claims. Such an argument is put forward by Maudemarie Clark and it is principally founded on her view that Nietzsche abandons the falsification thesis in his last six books, that is, from *On the Genealogy of Morality* onwards. By abandoning the position that our beliefs may be radically, in the sense of globally, false Clark maintains that Nietzsche abandons the Schopenhauerian claim of his earlier writings that our empirical beliefs are mere illusions.[68] However, there is evidence to suggest that Nietzsche, contrary to Clark's claim, never abandoned the language of falsification. I shall draw on an argument put forward by Lanier Anderson in presenting this evidence.[69]

First, in *On the Genealogy of Morality*, which Clark maintains signals Nietzsche's rejection of the falsification thesis, Nietzsche continues to employ the language of falsification. In section 24 of the third treatise he identifies interpretation with falsification. This, coupled with his claim in section 12 of the same treatise that interpretation is an essential component of knowledge, suggests that for Nietzsche our human claims to knowledge involve error. Second, despite Clark's claims to the contrary there is little to suggest that Nietzsche radically altered his view in his last six books. Clark maintains that the passage in *Twilight of the Idols* entitled 'How the "Real World" at last Became a Myth' provides evidence that Nietzsche, at this stage of his career, has abandoned the falsification thesis and the view that our knowledge is apparent rather than real. In support of this claim Clark maintains that Nietzsche distinguishes between steps 5 and 6 of the aforementioned passage:

5. The 'real world' – an idea no longer of any use, not even a duty any longer – an idea grown useless, superfluous, *consequently* a refuted idea: let us abolish it!
   (Broad daylight; breakfast; return of cheerfulness and *bons sens*; Plato blushes for shame; all free spirits run riot.)
6. We have abolished the real world: what world is left? the apparent one, perhaps? — But no! *with the real world we have also abolished the apparent world!*
   (Mid-day; moment of the shortest shadow; end of the longest error; zenith of mankind; INCIPIT ZARATHUSTRA.)[70]

According to Clark, stage 5 represents Nietzsche's view up to and including book 5 of *The Gay Science*, that is, in her estimation, a simultaneous commitment to both phenomenalism and subjective idealism, whilst stage 6 is said to represent Nietzsche's realist view from *On the Genealogy of Morality* onwards. Step 6 represents, Clark contends, a rejection of the falsification thesis because there, she argues, Nietzsche has abandoned the view that our empirical knowledge is merely apparent. However, steps 5 and 6, contrary to Clark's claim that they are separate positions, may in fact be construed as two aspects of just one position. Nietzsche's use of two steps to make one point is consistent within the overall structure of his outline of the history of philosophy in *Twilight of the Idols*. For the initial two steps represent two aspects of just one metaphysical position, that is, the metaphysics of Platonism/Christianity. Consequently, the significant aspect of Nietzsche's outline of the history of philosophy, and which also appears in *The Gay Science*, 354 (which belongs, in Clark's view, to Nietzsche's earlier period and so is subject to the falsification thesis), is the rejection of the 'true' world in stage 5. With this rejection the justification for denigrating the empirical world as apparent should be removed. Furthermore, the removal of the appearance/reality distinction should, in turn, entail a rejection of the language of falsification. However, Nietzsche's conclusion that *'with the real world we have also abolished the apparent world'* does not result in his abandonment of the falsification thesis. In *The Gay Science*, 354 Nietzsche claims that the opposition between the thing-in-itself and appearances is an illegitimate one whilst also writing that 'all becoming conscious involves a great and thorough corruption, falsification, reduction to superficialities, and generalization'.[71] Therefore Nietzsche continues to employ the term 'appearance' despite his claim that 'No shadow of a right remains to speak here of *appearance*'.[72] Considering this, Anderson's argument correctly concludes, contrary to Clark, that we have no internal evidence to suggest that Nietzsche abandoned the falsification thesis or that he altered his view between book 5 of *The Gay Science* and *On the Genealogy of Morality*.[73]

It might appear, on the basis of this alone, that the internal realist interpretation of Nietzsche's philosophical project reaches an impasse. Nietzsche's claim to have dissolved the appearance/reality dichotomy seems only to castigate our knowledge as 'merely' apparent. The view that our knowledge is 'merely' apparent suggests that it is radically divorced from the 'true' nature of reality, thus reopening the question of scepticism. The critic who wishes to embrace this reading and suggest that Nietzsche is inconsistent in his rejection of scepticism has the evidence presented above that Nietzsche never abandoned the language of falsification to fuel their claim.

However, any earnest attempt to present Nietzsche as a sceptic merely serves to present him as grossly contradictory and therefore of diminished philosophical interest. I therefore suggest that we should adopt the principle of interpretive charity when approaching Nietzsche's writings. Acceptance of this principle demands that we try to make the most philosophical sense of Nietzsche's claims and thus that we avoid, wherever possible, committing him to inconsistencies. This is not only possible with regard to Nietzsche's writings but is demanded by those very writings themselves, particularly by those sections where he both criticises the appearance/reality distinction and deems our perspectival theories to be false in the same passage or where he continues to speak of the 'apparent' world even after declaring it to be an illegitimate philosophical practice. These sections suggest that Nietzsche was aware of this inconsistency, implying that the inconsistency is apparent and not real and that Nietzsche considers the two seemingly inconsistent positions expressed in such passages to be compatible. Our concern is to ascertain how these inconsistencies can be resolved in such a way as to take proper account of Nietzsche's internal realist stance.

Such a resolution can be reached by questioning the meaning of Nietzsche's continued use of the language of falsification in light of the fact that he presents many of his claims to be true. For example, in *Beyond Good and Evil*, 229 he begins by promising to reveal 'palpable truths' that have remained unuttered for centuries, whilst simultaneously positing a 'fundamental will of the spirit' that is attracted to appearances.[74] Although the logic of Nietzsche's perspectivism does not support scepticism he still suggests that many of our ordinary ways of viewing the world are in error. However, they are in error not because they are globally false but because they are simplifications or coarse perceptions of reality.[75] Materialistic atomism, he claims, is a coarse understanding of reality that is unworthy of being credited with serious meaning besides a convenient 'everyday' use, as an 'abbreviated' expression of the nature of things.[76] Atomism, taking the senses at face value, construes the fundamental constituents of reality as Humean distinct existences, and so is unable to explain the nature of causal connection.[77] Rejecting the idea that atomistic and non-dispositional substances can affect each other, Nietzsche construes causality as the activity of force in nature to be a more comprehensive understanding of things.[78] A comprehensive perspective for Nietzsche is one that has explanatory power across a variety of perspectives and that seeks to penetrate the evidence of the senses rather than merely describing it. We shall discuss this issue in greater detail in Chapter 4.[79] For now it is sufficient to note that simplified theories such as materialistic atomism are not completely divorced from reality, in Nietzsche's view, although he considers them to be less comprehensive perspectives on reality. That Nietzsche distinguishes between less and more comprehensive perspectives can be seen from his claim in the following passage that his appeal to 'appearances' is not intended to draw a strict opposition between appearance and reality as it is in itself. Rather, Nietzsche distinguishes between lesser and more comprehensive perspectives within the world as it shows up for us, what he calls 'lighter' and 'darker' shades of appearance:

> Really, why should we be forced to assume that there is an essential differ-ence between 'true' and 'false' in the first place? Isn't it enough to assume that there are degrees of apparency and, so to speak, lighter and darker shadows and hues of appearance . . .?[80]

Nietzsche's continued use of the term 'appearance', even after he has abandoned the distinction between the 'true' world and the 'apparent' world in both step 6 of his outline of the history of philosophy and *The Gay Science*, 354, can thus be made intelligible.[81] The distinction between lesser and greater comprehensive perspectives saves Nietzsche from an appearance/reality distinction according to which our appearances may be globally in error. Nietzsche's appeal to appearance stipulates that our knowledge is perspectival and empirical but not that reality is radically divorced from us. Hence, the dualism of apparent world and the world as it is in itself is dissolved. The internal realist view from somewhere is now complete. Nietzsche concludes that 'The antithesis of the apparent world and the true world is reduced to the antithesis "world" and "nothing"'.[82] Nietzsche's internal realism allows for an interested conception of human knowing that is in principle capable of adequately capturing the character of the world. This is because his internal realism holds that our human perspectives are rooted in the empirical world, rendering empirical reality internal to our perspectival practices of arriving at objective knowledge.

Our next chapter focuses on Nietzsche's 'early' epistemic commitments, ascertaining the extent to which internal realism is already emerging in his early writings. We shall see that Nietzsche's emerging internal realism carries with it far-reaching consequences by forming the basis for the will to power metaphysics of his later thought.

NOTES

1. The most notable discussion of this issue in the context of Nietzsche studies has been put forward by Maudemarie Clark, *Nietzsche on Truth and Philosophy* (Cambridge: Cambridge University Press, 1990). However, others, such as David Owen, *Nietzsche, Politics and Modernity* (London: SAGE Publications, 1995) and Lanier Anderson, 'Truth and Objectivity in Perspectivism', *Synthese*, Vol. 115, No. 1, 1998, pp. 1–32, have contributed to the debate. I argue that Nietzsche's particular understanding of metaphysical realism is entwined with what Michael Williams calls 'epistemic realism'. (Michael Williams, *Unnatural Doubts: Epistemological Realism and the Basis of Scepticism* [Oxford: Blackwell, 1991].)

2. Friedrich Nietzsche, *On the Genealogy of Morality*, translated by Maudemarie Clark and Alan J. Swensen (Indianapolis, IN: Hackett, 1998 [1887]), III, 12. Henceforth cited as *GM*. See also Friedrich Nietzsche, *The Will to Power*, edited by R. J. Hollingdale, translated by Walter Kaufmann (New York: Vintage Books, 1968 [1901]), 426. Henceforth cited as *WP*.

3. Nietzsche, *GM*, III, 10. See also Friedrich Nietzsche, *Ecce Homo*, translated by R. J. Hollingdale (London: Penguin, 1992 [1908]), 'Daybreak', 2. Henceforth cited as *EH*.

4. Nietzsche, *WP*, 585.

5. For a discussion of the issues of cognitivism and non-cognitivism in Nietzsche, see John T. Wilcox, *Truth and Value in Nietzsche* (Ann Arbor, MI: The University of Michigan Press, 1974).

6. Friedrich Nietzsche, *Twilight of the Idols*, included in *Twilight of the Idols/The Anti-Christ*, translated by R. J. Hollingdale (London: Penguin, 1990 [1889]), '"Reason" in Philosophy', 4. Henceforth cited as *TI*. See also Nietzsche, *WP*, 409.

7. Nietzsche, *TI*, '"Reason" in Philosophy', 3.

8. Nietzsche, *WP*, 12A.

9. Friedrich Nietzsche, *Human, All Too Human*, translated R. J. Hollingdale (Cambridge: Cambridge University Press, [1878–86], Volume I, 'Of First and Last Things', 1). Henceforth cited as *HAH*.

10. Friedrich Nietzsche, *The Gay Science*, translated by Walter Kaufmann (New York: Vintage Books, 1974 [1882/1887]), 2. Henceforth cited as *GS*.

11. Nietzsche, *HAH*, Volume I, 'Of First and Last Things', 9.

12. Nietzsche, *GM*, III, 27.

13. Nietzsche, *WP*, 5.

14. Nietzsche, *TI*, 'How the "Real World" at last Became a Myth'.

15. I have borrowed this term from Michael Williams, 'Realism and Scepticism', in *Reality, Representation and Projection* (Oxford: Oxford University Press, 1993), pp. 193–215.

16. Nietzsche, *WP*, 458.

17. Nietzsche, *GS*, 57; See also Nietzsche, *GM*, III, 12.

18. Friedrich Nietzsche, *Beyond Good and Evil*, translated by Marion Faber (Oxford: Oxford University Press, 1998 [1886]), 21. Henceforth cited as *BGE*; Nietzsche, *TI*, '"Reason" in Philosophy', 5; Nietzsche, *GS*, 10.

19. Nietzsche, *GM*, III, 12; Nietzsche, *TI*, 'Morality as Anti-Nature', 5 and 7.

20. Nietzsche, *HAH*, Volume I, 'Of First and Last Things', 2.

21. Ibid., 2.

22. Nietzsche, *BGE*, 23.

23. Nietzsche, *WP*, 408.

24. Roux argued that we need to appeal to the inner struggle between the constituent parts of an organism in order to explain their functional harmony. This inner struggle involving the 'overcompensation' or extreme development of the individual parts in their struggle for existence and the capacity of the organism for self-regulation is intended as an explanation of the 'finer inner purposefulness of animal organisms'. (Roux, cited by Wolfgang Müller-Lauter, *Nietzsche: His Philosophy of Contradictions and the Contradictions of His Philosophy*, translated by David J. Parent [Urbana and Chicago, IL: University of Illinois Press, 1999 (1971)], p. 168). Roux rejects the Darwinian conception of the struggle for existence as the basis of evolution, arguing that organisms operate according to a law of assimilation whereby they are driven involuntarily to increase their intake of nutrition rather than by an instinct for self-preservation. Rolph's law of insatiability claims that the variety and multiplicity of nature can be explained, not as the result of a Darwinian instinct for self-preservation but rather as a desire for growth and assimilation. See also Gregory Moore, *Nietzsche, Biology and Metaphor* (Cambridge: Cambridge University Press, 2002), pp. 37–8 for a further discussion of this issue.

25. Nietzsche, *GS*, 333.

26. Nietzsche, *WP*, 481.

27. Steven D. Hales and Rex Welshon argue that to think of a perspective as a belief is 'to slip from a statement is held true (or believed true) in a perspective' to 'a statement is true in a perspective' (Steven D. Hales and Rex Welshon,

Nietzsche's Perspectivism [Urbana and Chicago, IL: University of Illinois Press, 2000], p. 20). They take this to mean that a perspective, if identified with a belief, could not possibly be false. They argue that Nietzsche did not hold the latter view because he 'holds that there can be untrue beliefs within a perspective, and this would not be possible if a perspective were defined as a set of beliefs' (ibid., pp. 19–20). Thus Hales and Welshon argue that the chief difficulty with the identification of perspectives and beliefs is that 'it would make people infallible' (ibid., p. 20). Furthermore, they maintain that this identification precludes the possibility of discovery. They ask, 'If belief is sufficient for truth, then how could anyone *discover* something to be true?' (ibid., p. 20).

Hales and Welshon thus suggest that the identification of perspectives with beliefs renders our epistemic claims unrevisable and fixed. However, a perspective might be understood as a set of beliefs where some beliefs occupy a default position within the set. Within this context periphery beliefs can be abandoned without abandoning the perspective. When this happens we say that the perspective has been revised. Furthermore, Hales' and Welshon's claim that the identification of a perspective with a set of beliefs reduces truth to mere consistency (ibid., p. 19) stands only if one presupposes that our perspectives are cut off from the world rather than immersed in it.

28. See Michael Williams, *Problems of Knowledge* (Oxford: Oxford University Press, 2001), p. 164. Nietzsche's appeal to a physiology of drives and instincts, for example, is central to his rejection of previous philosophical ideas about humankind's purely rational essence, but his appeal to physiology is justified in the context of the current state of the biological sciences in the latter half of the nineteenth century.

29. Nietzsche, *WP*, 293.

30. Nietzsche, *GS*, 374.

31. Nietzsche, *WP*, 522.

32. Ibid., 387.

33. Nietzsche, *GM*, III, 12.

34. Clark, *Nietzsche on Truth and Philosophy*, p. 48. See also p. 98. Note that in his outline of the history of philosophy from *TI* cited earlier, Nietzsche describes the idea of the 'real' world as 'useless' at stage 5.

35. Clark, *Nietzsche on Truth and Philosophy*, p. 48.

36. Peter Poellner raises some objections to Clark's argument. Arguing that Clark fails to differentiate adequately between cognitive capacities and interests ultimately reducing the latter to the former, he maintains that her definition of metaphysical realism shrinks to the view that 'there might be real items which cannot be known by any conceivable knowers, whatever their cognitive capacities'. Poellner contends that rejection of this proposition places no constraint on what can be considered to be the case because nobody has ever subscribed to this proposition. (Peter Poellner, 'Perspectival Truth', in John Richardson and Brian Leiter (eds), *Nietzsche* [Oxford: Oxford University Press, 2001], p. 96n).

I am not so much concerned with Clark as with the general light that the distinction between cognitive interests and cognitive capacities sheds on Nietzsche's argument. Poellner's objection to Clark can only be understood as an objection to my argument (and hence to my appropriation of Clark) if we do not clearly distinguish between cognitive interests and capacities. I take this to be a distinction between the justification and the acquisition of knowledge. By placing the emphasis on justification, Nietzsche disallows appeals to privileged forms of cognitive insight. However, he allows that we may acquire more information. Such information, however, can only be accepted as such and allowed to make a discernible difference to our knowledge if it enters the sphere of justification.

The acquisition of knowledge is not, then, a privileged insight that transcends our possible recognition. Rather, it must be recognised by us in order to be justified. Construed in this way cognitive interests cannot be so readily reduced to cognitive capacities in the manner that Poellner's argument suggests.

37. Clark suggests as much when she writes that 'abilities are superior to our own if they would allow greater correspondence to things as they are in themselves independently of all possible knowers and conceptualization' (Clark, *Nietzsche on Truth and Philosophy*, p. 50). I take Clark's reference to possible knowers to be a reference to possible 'human' knowers. However, this is obviously the source of Poellner's concerns with Clark's argument (see note 36).

38. Nietzsche, GS, 2.

39. Donald Davidson, 'The Method of Truth in Metaphysics', in *Inquiries into Truth and Interpretation* (Oxford: Oxford University Press, 1984), p. 200.

40. Nietzsche, GS, 319.

41. According to Nietzsche, one cannot debunk his argument from perspectivism against metaphysical realism on the basis that the perspectival thesis is itself a perspective. Nietzsche holds that his claim about the perspectival character of our knowledge is a 'better' perspective than that put forward by the various forms of metaphysical realism because Nietzsche's claim has been justified by both genealogical argumentation and by showing that the idea of a view from nowhere is incoherent and inconsistent.

42. Nietzsche, *HAH*, Volume I, 'Of First and Last Things', 9. Peter Poellner attributes 'metaphysical indifferentism' to Nietzsche in 'Perspectival Truth', p. 111. However, I attribute indifferentism to Nietzsche in a different sense from Poellner. I see Nietzsche's indifferentist argument as combined with an argument from genealogy and conceivability. Poellner thinks that indifferentism and the argument from conceivability are two separate and incompatible arguments.

43. Nietzsche oscillates between describing the 'metaphysical world' in scientific terms and in terms of epistemic inaccessibility. He describes the metaphysical world as 'inaccessible' and 'incomprehensible' whilst also describing its knowability as a 'scientific problem', comparing it to 'knowledge of the chemical analysis of water'. Despite the confusion, however, it is clear that Nietzsche thinks the idea of a radically inaccessible thing-in-itself can be 'refuted' by applying 'scientific' rigour to our inquiries (Nietzsche, *HAH*, Volume I, 'Of First and Last Things', 21).

44. Ibid., 9.

45. Ibid., 16.

46. Ibid., 9.

47. Since Nietzsche gives us good reasons for rejecting the idea of a thing-in-itself as an intelligible possibility, I understand his reference to the theoretical possibility of a metaphysical world as an appeal to epistemic modesty (ibid., 9, 10). Nietzsche acknowledges we do not have complete knowledge and that our knowledge is in need of further development. This does not, however, entail the intelligibility of the idea of a radically inaccessible reality, but rather entails a commitment to the possibility of progress in our knowledge. Moreover, when Nietzsche writes that metaphysical knowledge 'would be the most useless of all knowledge: more useless even than knowledge of the chemical composition of water must be to the sailor in danger of shipwreck' (ibid., 9) I take him to be claiming not that an inaccessible metaphysical world is an intelligible possibility, but rather as issuing a warning that we need to be cognisant of the value of truth in order to avoid asceticism in our pursuit of knowledge. See Nietzsche, GM, III, 24 for a similar argument.

48. Nietzsche, *HAH*, Volume I, 'Of First and Last Things', 16.

49. Ibid., 16.
50. Ibid., 10.
51. Ibid., 16.
52. Ibid., 16–17.
53. Ibid., 16.
54. John Haldane, 'Mind–World Identity Theory and the Anti-Realist Challenge', in John Haldane and Crispin Wright (eds), *Reality, Representation and Projection*, (Oxford: Oxford University Press, 1993), p. 34.
55. Nietzsche, *GM*, III, 12.
56. For a similar argument, see Brian Leiter, 'Perspectivism in Nietzsche's *Genealogy of Morals*', in Richard Schacht (ed.), *Nietzsche, Genealogy, Morality* (London: University of California Press, 1994), p. 349.
57. Nietzsche, *GM*, III, 12.
58. See, for example, Bernd Magnus, 'The Deification of the Commonplace' in Robert C. Solomon and Kathleen M. Higgins (eds), *Reading Nietzsche* (Oxford: Oxford University Press, 1988), pp. 152ff. See also Arthur Danto, *Nietzsche as Philosopher* (New York: Columbia University Press, 1980 [1965]), pp. 76ff.
59. Bernard Reginster makes a similar point in his discussion of Nietzsche's rejection of objective descriptivism. See Bernard Reginster, *The Affirmation of Life: Nietzsche on Overcoming Nihilism* (Cambridge, MA: Harvard University Press, 2006), pp. 84–5.
60. Nietzsche, *BGE*, 134.
61. Friedrich Nietzsche, *The Anti-Christ*, included in *Twilight of the Idols/The Anti-Christ*, translated by R. J. Hollingdale (London: Penguin, 1990 [1895]), 15.
62. Friedrich Nietzsche, *Thus Spoke Zarathustra*, translated by R. J. Hollingdale (London: Penguin, 1969 [1883–92]), Part Two, 'On the Blissful Islands'.
63. Nietzsche, *WP*, 481.
64. Ibid., 505.
65. Ibid., 532.
66. Ibid., 506.
67. Michael Williams, *Groundless Belief: An Essay on the Possibility of Epistemology* (Princeton, NJ: Princeton University Press, 1999), pp. 28–9.
68. See Clark, *Nietzsche on Truth and Philosophy*, chapter 4.
69. Lanier Anderson, 'Overcoming Charity: the Case of Maudemarie Clark's *Nietzsche on Truth and Philosophy*', *Nietzsche-Studien*, Vol. 25, 1996, pp. 307–41, especially pp. 317ff. See also Michael Steven Green, *Nietzsche and the Transcendental Tradition* (Urbana and Chicago, IL: University of Illinois Press, 2002), pp. 28–34. For further discussions of Clark, see Peter Poellner, *Nietzsche and Metaphysics* (Oxford: Clarendon Press, 1995), pp. 22–4; Hales and Welshon, *Nietzsche's Perspectivism*, pp. 28–31.
70. Nietzsche, *TI*, 'How the "Real World" at last Became a Myth'.
71. Nietzsche, *GS*, 354.
72. Nietzsche, *WP*, 567.
73. That Nietzsche did not intend any distinction to be made between *BGE* and *GM*, and indeed that he considered them as continuous, can be seen from the fact that on the title-page of the first edition of *GM* Nietzsche included a note indicating that *GM* was written as a 'supplement and clarification' of *BGE* (see Anderson, 'Overcoming Charity', p. 322).
74. Nietzsche, *BGE*, 229. See also *BGE*, 202, 230.
75. Ibid., 230. In *BGE*, 23 Nietzsche distinguishes between psychological interpretations that are informed by either 'prejudices' or 'insights'. In *GS*, 333 he examines what he calls 'the fight of these onesided views'.
76. Nietzsche, *BGE*, 12.

77. Note that Nietzsche is not against sense-evidence as we have seen from our discussion of his empiricism. However, he thinks that materialistic atomism takes the senses at face value and so can offer us only descriptions rather than explanations of the empirical world (Nietzsche, *BGE*, 14).
78. For Nietzsche's account of causality as 'a continuum and a flux', see *GS*, 112.
79. Nietzsche describes perspectives as simplifications of reality in *BGE*, 230. However, a cognitive perspective is one that attempts to 'appropriate' others and so become comprehensive. As we shall see in our discussion of his will to power thesis in Chapter 4, Nietzsche's appeal to multi-perspectivism does not entail viewing one thing from many different perspectives in a merely additive sense, but rather entails understanding a range of phenomena from the point of view of a unifying comprehensive perspective.
80. Nietzsche, *BGE*, 34.
81. To remind the reader: in *GS*, 354, Nietzsche claims that perspectivism entails 'a great and thorough corruption, falsification, reduction to superficialities, and generalization' whilst also stating that 'It is even less the opposition of "thing-in-itself" and appearance [that concern me]; for we do not "know" nearly enough to be entitled to any such distinction'.
82. Nietzsche, *WP*, 567. Furthermore, in *Ecce Homo* Nietzsche writes: 'The "real world" and the "apparent world" – in plain terms: the *fabricated* world and reality' (Nietzsche, *EH*, Foreword, 2).

Chapter 3

Nietzsche's Emerging Internal Realism

This chapter examines Nietzsche's early writings, arguing that his later views regarding the perspectival yet objective character of human knowledge are present in an embryonic form in his early thought.[1] Nietzsche struggles to articulate, through a critical engagement with Kant and Schopenhauer, a possible reconciliation of self and world, central to which is his rejection of both Kant's constitutive conception of knowledge and his transformation of the idea of the thing-in-itself into a sphere of reality which, although irreducible to human minds, is nonetheless knowable by us in principle. What is notable about Nietzsche's early writings is that although he rejects the idea of the thing-in-itself, which in its Kantian guise is unknowable to beings with our cognitive constitution and in its Schopenhauerian guise only accessible independently of the forms of our knowledge, he does not reject metaphysics.[2] Although most commentators to date have interpreted Nietzsche's early metaphysics as a reference to the thing-in-itself which he would later abandon, I shall argue that his early metaphysical struggles are, to a large extent, continuous with his later attempts to reconcile human knowledge with the nature of reality.

These conclusions, however, can only be reached after a considerable degree of interpretive engagement with the texts. In the early writings Nietzsche investigates a number of possible responses to the issue of the relationship between self and world and it is often difficult to decipher precisely which response, if any, he intended to endorse. Moreover, it is often difficult to distinguish between the different responses themselves as he does not always indicate with any degree of transparency that he has altered his view or that he is occupying a new perspective. Therefore, any engagement with the early writings requires that the reader take on themselves the responsibility of attributing to Nietzsche a particular view which, although certainly implicit in the writings, has not been explicitly differentiated from the other views. In attempting to so differentiate, the interpretive methodology adopted in this chapter involves a degree of simplification. This simplification is instructive in detecting Nietzsche's emerging internal realist solution to the problem of the opposition of self and world, which despite interpretive complications is supported by the general logic of Nietzsche's early thought.

The principal interpretive challenge confronting the reader of these writings is the problem of squaring Nietzsche's use of Kantian and Schopenhauerian language with his criticisms of these thinkers. Nietzsche's criticisms of both Kant and Schopenhauer suggest that he desires to distinguish his own philosophy from what he considers to be their respective failures to overcome the opposition of self and world. However, his immersion in the conceptual and linguistic framework adopted by these two thinkers makes it difficult for the reader to decipher where Nietzsche has moved beyond the thought of Kant and Schopenhauer. To the extent that Nietzsche remains embedded in the thought of these thinkers he is unable to extricate himself completely from the appearance/reality distinction whereby our human knowledge is said to be divorced from the nature of reality, motivating the view that Nietzsche reduces the status of our human knowledge to an illusion.

I shall contend that whilst this interpretation of Nietzsche's project is largely correct with regard to 'On Truth and Lies in a Nonmoral Sense' (TL), it is not an accurate representation of his argument in either The Birth of Tragedy (BT) or the unpublished notes belonging to the early period other than TL spanning the years 1867–78. The arguments presented in BT and the unpublished notes are complex, which when sufficiently disentangled indicate the emergence of an alternative position that attempts to overcome the distinction between appearances and reality and with it the view that our human truths are illusions. The emergence of an alternative view in BT to that offered in TL and its similarity to Nietzsche's later arguments regarding the status of our human truths justifies a thematic non-chronological treatment of these early texts. That is, although TL bears the date 1873, one year after the publication of BT, the arguments in BT resemble his later stance more closely than those offered in TL. Our concern here is to address the embryonic emergence of Nietzsche's later views in the early writings rather than to engage in a chronological examination of his philosophical development.

Beginning with TL, then, as a paradigm of the philosophical difficulties that he was grappling with in his early career, we see that Nietzsche's uncritical acceptance of Kant results in sceptical idealism, entailing the view that knowable reality, constituted by and reducible to the human mind, is divorced from how things are in themselves. However, contrary to the predominant view that Nietzsche also reduces our human truths to illusions in *BT* as a result of his commitment to Schopenhauerian dogmatism, the idea that we can have extra-perspectival privileged insight into the nature of reality as an otherwise unknowable thing-in-itself, I argue that he begins his project of overcoming the opposition of self and world. Appealing to his understanding of the relationship between Apollo and Dionysus in *BT* and his conception of both the instinctive intellect and the primordial intellect in the early notes, we see that the logic of Nietzsche's early thinking does not advocate the idea of an extra-cognitive insight into the thing-in-itself nor does he advocate the idea that knowable reality is reducible to the forms of our knowledge. I conclude that Nietzsche ultimately engages critically with Kant and Schopenhauer, denying that our human truths are divorced from the world.

'ON TRUTH AND LIES IN A NONMORAL SENSE'

Many commentators view Nietzsche's early unpublished essay, *TL*, as representative, not only of his early views on truth, knowledge and language but also of his more mature position on these issues. They thus take Nietzsche's argument in *TL* that our truths are illusions as representative of both his early and late thought.[3] Whilst *TL* certainly calls into question the cognitive status of our human truths, this conclusion is representative of neither Nietzsche's mature writings nor his other early writings. Rather, *TL* sets the background against which we can measure to what extent Nietzsche frees himself from his uncritical engagement with Kant and Schopenhauer in other writings of the early period.

This uncritical engagement is manifest in *TL* in Nietzsche's undermining of the cognitive status of our human truths. He does this in two ways: the first entails the strong claim that we can know that our human knowledge is inadequate; the second is a weaker claim that maintains that the question of whether our knowledge is adequate to reality is not one that we can intelligibly answer. Despite the obvious differences between these two views, they have one thing in common: they both conclude that our specifically human truths are, at least, potentially illusory.

The first strong view maintains that our human truths are illusions and lies because they fail to correspond to reality as it is in itself. Nietzsche writes:

> We believe that we know something about the things themselves when we speak of trees, colors, snow, and flowers; and yet we possess nothing

but metaphors for things – metaphors which correspond in no way to the original entities.[4]

Furthermore, Nietzsche states:

all the material within and with which the man of truth, the scientist, and the philosopher later work and build, if not derived from never-never land, is at least not derived from the essence of things.[5]

Here Nietzsche reveals his commitment to the distinction between appearance and reality. Our human truths are confined to the sphere of appearances because they are unable to capture how things are in themselves. Nietzsche's strong claim that we can know that our human truths are inadequate to reality presupposes the existence of things-in-themselves that are divorced from our knowledge in addition to the idea that we can access these things-in-themselves by bypassing the specifically human conditions of our knowledge. This privileged form of insight acts as a standard according to which we can ascertain that our human truths are illusory.

Maudemarie Clark contends that Nietzsche provides the seeds for an alternative argument in *TL*, undermining his initial claim that human truths are illusory by doing away with the idea of transcendent truths in the guise of the thing-in-itself. As a result, she maintains, Nietzsche dismantles the basis of his initial claim that all our truths are in fact falsehoods. She argues that Nietzsche arrives at this alternative position by rejecting the very idea of correspondence to the thing-in-itself, what he calls '"an adequate expression of the object in the subject"', as a 'contradictory impossibility'.[6] She maintains that if Nietzsche rejects the idea of correspondence to the thing-in-itself as a contradictory impossibility, then he also rejects the basis for devaluing the cognitive status of our human truths. However, Clark's argument holds only if Nietzsche rejects the very idea of a thing-in-itself. But rather than doing that in *TL*, Nietzsche in fact reiterates his initial position by denying that our human truths adequately capture this reality. He writes that 'between two absolutely different spheres, as between subject and object, there is no causality, no correctness, and no expression'.[7] What Nietzsche rejects is not the thing-in-itself but the possibility of our knowing it. Contrary to Clark, then, the metaphysical possibility of a thing-in-itself and the attendant epistemological view that we cannot adequately represent the world remains. Nietzsche's claim that the idea of correspondence to the thing-in-itself is incoherent represents not an alternative position to his initial strong claim that our human truths are inadequate but rather a modified version of his initial view.

Nietzsche's strong claim that our truths are inadequate to reality, however, presupposes prior direct knowledge of the thing-in-itself independent of the human conditions of our knowledge. The realisation that he is stepping beyond the permitted parameters of our knowing leads him to adopt a second and weaker agnostic position, which maintains that we cannot know whether our truths capture reality. He writes:

> we should not presume to claim that this contrast does not correspond to the essence of things: that would of course be a dogmatic assertion and, as such, would be just as indemonstrable as its opposite.[8]

The weaker agnostic claim leaves the doubt that our human knowledge can capture how things are in themselves, although one might expect that it also entails the possibility that our knowledge is in fact adequate this transpires to be the lesser possibility. Nietzsche's agnosticism in *TL* leans towards the negative possibility that our knowledge is inadequate rather than the positive one that it captures the essence of things, because he is ultimately committed in this text to the view that the human mind plays a constitutive role in our knowledge such that the mind imposes forms that emanate from itself on reality. This reduces knowable reality to the forms of our knowledge and prevents any correspondence between human knowledge and things as they are in themselves, which by definition are beyond these forms.

In response to both the strong claim that we can know that our human truths are illusions because they do not correspond to things-in-themselves and the weaker agnostic claim that our human truths may or may not capture things-in-themselves Nietzsche proceeds to adopt what Peter Poellner terms 'metaphysical indifferentism'.[9] This is the view that there either is or may be a way things are that transcends our capacity for knowing them, but that such knowledge is useless for beings with our practical rather than purely theoretical cognitive interests. In adopting this position Nietzsche puts forward the view that it is only worth striving for knowledge that is practically useful. He states that knowledge 'apart from its consequences' is of no interest to us and therefore is 'not in the least worth striving for'.[10] He claims that our empirical reality may in fact be a dream, but for as long as that dream is uniform and coherent there is no *practical* criterion to distinguish it from reality as it is in itself.[11] As we saw in Chapter 2, Nietzsche also adopts a form of metaphysical indifferentism in section 9 of *Human, All Too Human*. As in *TL* Nietzsche maintains there that the theoretical possibility of a thing-in-itself does not carry any practical consequences for us and should be of no concern to us. However, despite its similarities with

TL the theoretical possibility entertained in *Human, All Too Human* is considerably weaker. In *Human, All Too Human*, Nietzsche argues that once we engage in genealogical and historical inquiry whereby we trace the origin and development of a belief, we will understand that the belief in the thing-in-itself is a human invention and not a justified claim about the nature of things. If the idea of the thing-in-itself as a realm of reality that lies beyond all possible human knowledge is really a hoax, then the sceptical challenge of the thing-in-itself is, in Nietzsche's view, considerably diminished. However, according to Nietzsche in *TL*, we either know that our human truths are inadequate to reality or we simply cannot say whether our empirical truths represent ultimate reality.[12] Both the strong and the weak claims leave the sceptical challenge of the thing-in-itself intact by allowing that it represents a coherent threat to the status of our epistemic claims.

Thus although both Nietzsche's strong claim that we know that our human knowledge is inadequate to reality and his weaker agnostic standpoint that this question is one that we cannot intelligibly answer seem at odds they are both in fact informed and unified by Nietzsche's commitment to sceptical idealism in this text. Implicit in this idealism is the view that if reality is not constituted by and reducible to the forms of our knowledge, then it is at least potentially radically divorced from the possibility of our knowing it. The question of whether we can ascertain that it is so divorced depends on whether we allow some privileged insight independent of our specifically human manner of knowing the world. Whether or not Nietzsche allows privileged insight, he remains committed to the idealism for which he elsewhere criticises Kant. He argues that all our human truths are restricted to the sphere of appearances constituted by us, writing: 'All that we actually know about these laws of nature is what we ourselves bring to them – time and space, and therefore relationships of succession and number'.[13] Consequently, he maintains that all our knowledge is confined to the realm of appearance, which is constituted by the *a priori* and inherited forms of our cognition.[14] Nietzsche agrees with Schopenhauer that objects of our experience are constituted by our transforming subjective sensation into objective perception through the injection of *a priori* forms of space and time.[15] However, in this text Nietzsche is not clear on where he stands with regard to the issue of causality. Schopenhauer argues that through the *a priori* law of causality the Understanding construes subjective sensations as the effect of an external cause;[16] Nietzsche writes, however, that the 'inference from the nerve stimulus to a cause outside of us is already the result of a false and unjustified application of the principle of sufficient reason'.[17] Here Nietzsche argues that the empirical objects of our experience are mind-dependent representations constituted by us and that we are not justified in claiming knowledge of anything beyond these. However, to the extent that Nietzsche does refer to an extra-mental sphere he refers to it as both an extra-mental common-sense object such as 'trees, colors, snow, and flowers' on the one hand, and a thing-in-itself on the other.[18] By denying us cognitive access to either, however, Nietzsche ultimately conflates the former with the latter. Although in other early writings Nietzsche transforms the thing-in-itself into something that is in principle accessible to us and which for that reason ceases to be a thing-in-itself in an objectionable sense, in TL he adopts what he understands to be the Kantian view that if there is an external cause of our sensations, it is an unknowable thing-in-itself that is beyond the justifiable remit of the principle of sufficient reason and our knowledge. Nietzsche reaches the conclusion that our human truths are illusory in TL as a result of his uncritical acceptance of the Kantian–Schopenhauerian appeal to both the constitutive and hence mind-dependent character of the object of our knowledge on the one hand, and the mind-independent thing-in-itself on the other. Consequently, both Nietzsche's strong claim that we can know that our truths are illusory and the weaker contention that our truths may be illusory are informed by his Kantian-inspired sceptical idealism. Moreover, his view that in practice the purely theoretical problem of the thing-in-itself is unworthy of our consideration renders him guilty of the further charge that he levels at Kant. We saw in Chapter 2 that Nietzsche charges Kant with having divorced theory from practice and, as a result, with having set up two standards of justification and truth.[19] We can see that here Nietzsche is also guilty of separating theory and practice and thus of inducing an opposition between self and world. Although Nietzsche continues to be preoccupied with the issue of self and world in other writings of this early period, these writings, conversely, attempt to unify self and world by abandoning the sceptical idealism that informs his arguments in TL.

The general view held by Nietzsche scholars, however, is that in the other writings of the early period Nietzsche persists in his denial that our human truths correspond to things-in-themselves by appealing to dogmatic metaphysics. Maudemarie Clark, for example, writes: 'Regarding truth, BT and TL differ only in relation to BT's claim that Dionysian experience alone gives us access to things-in-themselves.'[20] According to this view, although Nietzsche abandoned the possibility in TL, in BT he writes that we can access the nature of things-in-themselves by bypassing the specifically human forms of our knowledge. The problem with this is that it sees Nietzsche as working uncritically within a Kantian–Schopenhauerian framework that commits him to the distinction between appearances and things-in-themselves despite his later denial that this was what he was doing in *BT*.[21] However, further examination of the relationship between the Apolline and the Dionysiac shows, contrary to the general interpretation, that in addition to rejecting the possibility of unmediated direct knowledge Nietzsche also denies the distinction between appearance and reality in favour of the view that our knowledge adequately captures the world. By supplementing his arguments in *BT* with his appeal to both the idea of a non-human primordial intellect and a human instinctive intellect in the early notes, Nietzsche seeks to extricate himself from the framework of appearance and reality by critically engaging with Kant and Schopenhauer with regard to both the constitutive nature of the human intellect and things-in-themselves.

THE BIRTH OF TRAGEDY

Nietzsche describes *BT* as an 'impossible book'. In retrospect he claims that he ought to have developed a language of his own instead of 'labouring . . . to express strange and new evaluations in Schopenhauerian and Kantian formulations, things which fundamentally ran counter to both the spirit and taste of Kant and Schopenhauer'.[22] In *BT*, then, there is a fundamental tension between what it actually says and what Nietzsche, in retrospect, claims it was struggling to say. Thus, on the one hand, we find an orthodox adoption of Schopenhauer accompanied by some extensive citations from Schopenhauer's writings, and on the other, we have Nietzsche's own declaration that he was attempting to formulate a decidedly anti-Schopenhauerian and anti-Kantian thesis.[23] According to the predominant interpretation of Nietzsche commentators, the relationship that Nietzsche sets up between the Apolline and the Dionysiac in *BT* demonstrates the Schopenhauerian influence on his argument, which ultimately commits him to dogmatic metaphysics in this book.[24] According to this view, Nietzsche is not only committed to a Kantian distinction between mind-dependent appearances and mind-independent things-in-themselves, but by understanding the Apolline and the Dionysiac in terms of an opposition where the Dionysiac is prioritised over the Apolline, he also thinks that we can access the nature of things-in-themselves independently of the forms of the Understanding, revealing that our specifically human truths are illusory. The suggestion that Nietzsche is committed to dogmatic metaphysics and the illusory status of human truth in *BT* rests, then, on how Nietzsche understands the relationship between the Apolline and the Dionysiac.

Although Nietzsche articulates the relationship between the Apolline and the Dionysiac on multiple levels, which include the psychological and the aesthetic, it is at the metaphysical and epistemological levels that we enter into controversy regarding the role that each of the gods plays and their relationship to each other.[25] Metaphysically speaking, there are two possible readings of the relationship between the Apolline and the Dionysiac.[26] The first, which is appealed to in support of the predominant interpretation of *BT*, considers the two gods to be in eternal conflict and in so doing it exacerbates the problem of self and world by maintaining that mind-dependent appearances are opposed to mind-independent reality. This view is suggested by Nietzsche's claim that the empirical world of our experience constituted by the Apolline forms of individuation may be compared to a dream. By appealing to Schopenhauer, Nietzsche contends that empirical reality is semblance and that all people and things are phantoms or dream images.[27] This commits him to a dualism whereby our anthropocentric manner of knowing the world and how reality appears to us (Apolline) may be radically different from how the world is in itself (Dionysiac). Moreover, we can know this, so the interpretation goes, owing to the fact that we have direct insight into the nature of things in themselves by bypassing the Apolline forms of our cognition.[28]

The predominant interpretation is supported by the fact that, on the surface at least, Nietzsche presents the Apolline and the Dionysiac in terms of an opposition in *BT*. He traces the etymological origin of Apollo as the god of light, the 'luminous one' (*der Scheinende*), which serves to emphasise its apparent nature.[29] He employs Schopenhauer's metaphor of the veil of Maya to describe the Apolline as the cognitive forms of individuation. The Apolline is thus said to be responsible for our cognitive acquaintance with the individuated forms of the empirical world. Nietzsche also suggests that Apolline appearances (*Erscheinungen*) are in fact illusions (*Scheine*) because they do not faithfully correspond to the Dionysiac. The Dionysiac, operating on two levels, is presented as both the metaphysical primal 'oneness' that lies behind the Apolline world of empirical illusion and a form of direct intuitive insight into this reality. In presenting the two impulses in this way, Nietzsche sees them as representing appearance and reality respectively.[30] Thus, he identifies Dionysus with nature and truth and Apollo with culture and illusion:

> The contrast between this genuine truth of nature and the cultural lie which pretends to be the only reality is like the contrast between the eternal core of things, the thing-in-itself, and the entire world of phenomena; and just as tragedy, with its metaphysical solace, points to the eternal life of that

core of being despite the constant destruction of the phenomenal world, the symbolism of the chorus of satyrs is in itself a metaphorical expression of that original relationship between thing-in-itself and phenomenon (*Erscheinungswelt*).[31]

Here Nietzsche articulates the relationship between the Apolline and the Dionysiac in terms of an appearance/reality dualism that can be overcome through direct intuitive insight that abandons the Apolline forms of phenomenal individuation.

However, this interpretation can only be upheld if we take a particular literal and simplified reading of *BT*. Such a reading does not fully consider Nietzsche's own claims that he is struggling to articulate a non-Schopenhauerian and non-Kantian thesis, and his explicit declaration that he is attempting to overcome the opposition between reality and appearances.[32] Allowing these comments to direct our reading we find that Nietzsche is engaging in something far more complex than a simple opposition between appearances and things-in-themselves in the form of the two Greek gods. That Nietzsche has something quite different in mind can be discovered by a closer examination of the interdependent rather than oppositional relationship that he sets up between the Apolline and the Dionysiac. Nietzsche argues that rather than representing an opposition the Dionysiac and the Apolline mutually limit and define one another. He states that the Apolline is intimately related to the Dionysiac:

> The Apolline Greek, too, felt the effect aroused by the *Dionysiac* to be 'Titanic' and 'barbaric'; at the same time he could not conceal from himself the fact that he too was related inwardly to those overthrown Titans and heroes.[33]

Central to Nietzsche's understanding of the interdependency of the two gods is both his development of an anti-dogmatic stance by rejecting the possibility of direct or privileged access to reality independently of the specifically human forms of our knowledge and his transformation of the notion of the thing-in-itself from something divorced from the empirical sphere of our experience into something that is knowable by us in principle.

Although it is difficult to ascertain the logic behind Nietzsche's description of the relationship between the Apolline and the Dionysiac as one of 'reciprocal necessity' from an examination of *BT* alone, consideration of some comments that he makes in 'On Schopenhauer' (1868) brings his reasoning into sharper focus. In this early unpublished essay Nietzsche criticises Schopenhauer's efforts to reconcile self and world as a form of dogmatic metaphysics.[34] Schopenhauer accepts the dualistic framework of the Kantian distinction between the thing-in-itself and appearance, but attempts to overcome the unknowability of Kant's thing-in-itself by adopting the view that the thing-in-itself is accessible to us as the Will independently of the forms of our Understanding. However, Nietzsche contends that Schopenhauer retreats to an impossible extra-cognitive standpoint.[35] He argues that Schopenhauer can begin to describe the thing-in-itself as Will only by employing the forms of human Understanding.[36] In so doing, Nietzsche draws our attention to his own view regarding the impossibility of immediate knowledge and his contention that we cannot bypass the conditions of our knowledge in the way that Schopenhauer suggests. The reciprocal relationship between the Dionysiac and the Apolline in *BT* is arguably designed to make just this point. By presenting the two gods as reciprocal partners Nietzsche draws our attention to his view that knowledge of reality must be mediated and conditioned by the forms of our knowing. He thus suggests that the Dionysiac process, whereby subject and object become one, must be articulated in the language of Apollo.[37]

However, this interpretation encounters a difficulty. There are some passages in *BT* where Nietzsche seems almost to retract his view that Dionysiac truth must be articulated in the language of Apollo by appealing to the notion of extra-conceptual or non-Apolline access to things as they are in themselves. For example, he writes:

> whereas lyric poetry depends utterly on the spirit of music, music itself, in its absolute sovereignty, has no *need* at all of images and concepts but merely *tolerates* them as an accompaniment.[38]

Here we are confronted by one of the difficulties and tensions inherent in *BT*. Nietzsche maintains that unmediated pure Dionysiac knowledge is unintelligible whilst also suggesting that Dionysiac music as a form of insight into the nature of reality is independent of the Apolline forms of our knowledge. In spite of this, his description of Dionysiac knowledge as non-conceptual does not necessarily mean that he appeals to privileged insight independently of Apolline form. Rather, what Nietzsche arguably has in mind here is Schopenhauer's criticism of the notion of explicit judgement.[39] Explicit judgement entails the conscious and explicit appeal to a concept as a rule of action, which is extrinsic to the action itself. Schopenhauer claims that although pure concepts are necessary for the communication of thought they are not necessary for, and can indeed hinder, action. Perceptual rather than purely conceptual knowledge, Schopenhauer argues, is conducive to action. He states: 'in the case of billiards-playing, fencing, tuning an instrument, or singing, knowledge of perception must directly guide activity; passage through reflection makes it uncertain, since it divides the attention, and confuses the executant.' Thus he claims: 'it is of no use for me to be able to state in the abstract in degrees and minutes the angle at which I have to apply my razor, if I do not know it intuitively, in other words, if I do not know how to hold the razor.'[40] Perceptual knowledge as opposed to explicit judgement, according to Schopenhauer, is informed by the forms of the Understanding rather than the purely conceptual forms of the faculty of Reason. Perceiving the world in spatio-temporal and causal terms, our intuitive apprehensions or perceptions, he maintains, are informed by the *a priori* and constitutive forms of human Understanding. We shall see later that Nietzsche's view of perception differs from Schopenhauer's in an important respect. That is, Nietzsche ultimately rejects Schopenhauer's idealist view that the forms of our knowledge are imposed on reality by the human mind rather than belonging to reality itself. Nevertheless, the comparison with Schopenhauer is instructive here in that it shows that Nietzsche's description of the Dionysiac as non-conceptual in *BT* can be understood to be a rejection of the idea of explicit judgement and not an appeal to a form of knowing that transcends the Apolline forms of our cognition. Nietzsche's point is that the Apolline forms of our cognition are always already implied in our perceptual knowledge. According to Nietzsche, our perceptual knowledge is intellectual and contains within it an inferential character. His appeal to music, therefore, far from retreating to dogmatism, in fact further develops his argument against the possibility of dogmatic metaphysics and supports my interpretation that in *BT* the Dionysiac must be articulated in terms of the Apolline. This interpretation is borne out by the fact that Nietzsche ultimately contends that Apolline forms are not divorced from Dionysiac music but rather achieve their greatest significance through music. He argues that Apolline images and concepts 'acquire a heightened significance' when combined with Dionysiac music, which he describes as 'the kind of music which truly corresponds to them'.[41] When Nietzsche claims that music is extra-conceptual, what he has in mind by the term 'conceptual' are pure concepts that are divorced from the content of our knowledge.[42]

His claim that music is extra-conceptual can best be explained, then, as a rhetorical introduction to his criticism of the dogmatism of Socrates. Socrates, according to Nietzsche, separates Reason and instinct.[43] Whereas Schopenhauer emphasises direct unmediated insight into the nature of the thing-in-itself through experience of our bodily willing selves independently of the forms of our Understanding,[44] Socrates places the emphasis on pure conceptual knowledge. The Socratic theoretical man, as Nietzsche interprets him, believes that Reason can penetrate the nature of reality as it is in itself and thus formulate one true, unrevisable description of this reality. Nietzsche states of the theoretical man that 'his desire finds its highest goal in a process of unveiling which he achieves by his own efforts and which is always successful'.[45] Here Nietzsche attributes to the theoretical man the view that reality as it is in itself is accessible via pure concepts. In contrast to such 'optimism' Nietzsche claims that the nature of reality is impenetrable. By this he means that reality is not accessible by pure concepts alone and he maintains the Socratic theoretical man will be confronted with the impenetrability of Being by pure concepts and thus that science/theory will eventually be confronted with its own limits. He suggests that when logic and scientific theory reach their limits they give way to art. He states that the metaphysical pretension of the theoretical man 'leads it to its limits time after time, at which point it must transform itself into *art, which is actually, given this mechanism, what it has been aiming at all along*'.[46] Art differs from the logicism of the scientific theoretical man in that it attempts to bring together the rational and the instinctive.[47] By synthesising the Apolline and the Dionysiac Nietzsche attempts to reconcile self and world without escaping to either an extra-cognitive (Schopenhauer) or extra-sensuous (Socrates) position. Consequently, the relationship that Nietzsche sets up between the Apolline and the Dionysiac in *BT* disallows dogmatic metaphysics.

That Nietzsche also abandons the appearance/reality distinction is, however, less clear. The rejection of dogmatic metaphysics does not on its own guarantee the non-illusory status of our human truths. But this conclusion follows only if Nietzsche actually abandons the intelligibility of things-in-themselves. That he is beginning to question the meaningfulness of the idea is clear from 'On Schopenhauer'. In this text Nietzsche responds critically to Schopenhauer's distinction between appearances and things-in-themselves, arguing that the thing-in-itself is not capable of a positive definition. Nietzsche maintains that we can only define the thing-in-itself negatively, conceiving it in opposition to the predicates that we ascribe to the empirical world. The thing-in-itself is thus 'something lying wholly outside the sphere of cognition, a list of *negative* properties . . .'.[48] In response to what he sees as Schopenhauer's demand for a positive definition, however, Nietzsche maintains that a positive definition can be had only by ascribing the very same predicates that we ascribe to experience to the thing-in-itself. To do so, however, is to fail to distinguish between the empirical world and the thing-in-itself at all. Nietzsche states:

> Schopenhauer requires that something which can never be an object should nevertheless be thought of objectively. But on this route we can reach only an apparent objectivity, given that a totally obscure, inconceivable X is being decked out, as if in brightly coloured clothes, with predicates drawn from a world alien to it, the world of appearance. Subsequently we are required to regard the surrounding clothes – the predicates – as the thing in itself: that is the meaning of the sentence 'if it is nevertheless to be thought of objectively, it must borrow name and concept from an object.' Thus 'because it must be so', the concept 'thing in itself' is secretly moved aside and another pressed into our hands in its stead.[49]

The concept of the thing-in-itself, according to Nietzsche, merely engages in a dubious metaphysics of opposites 'despite the fact that between thing in itself and appearance not even the concept of opposition has any meaning'.[50] He contends that Schopenhauer's best defence of his view that the distinction between things-in-themselves and appearances is meaningful is to claim that, despite Nietzsche's critique, the distinction 'can nevertheless be thought'.[51] However, Nietzsche argues that this defence is a weak one and reduces the status of the thing-in-itself to a 'guess' that cannot be adequately supported. He writes:

> There can be a thing in itself yet only in the sense that in the region of transcendence everything is *possible* that ever was hatched in a philosopher's brain. This possible thing in itself can be the will: a possibility which, arising as it does out of the connection of two possibilities, is only the negative power of the first possibility, in other words a strong move towards the other pole, that of impossibility.[52]

What we ultimately learn from Schopenhauer, according to Nietzsche, is that the most that can be said about the thing-in-itself is that it is a 'totally obscure inconceivable X' which can be positively described only in terms of the spatio-temporal and causal predicates that we apply to the empirical world of our experience.[53] Moreover, in response to what he sees as Schopenhauer's failure to explain the origin of the individuated human intellect in the thing-in-itself, Nietzsche writes that there are no criteria available to distinguish the thing-in-itself from the empirical world of our experience:

> Thus the Schopenhauerian thing in itself would be the *principium individuationis* and at the same time the ground of necessitation – in other words, just the ordinary world that is present to hand. Schopenhauer wanted to

find the X in an equation; his calculation yields the result that it = X, which means that he has not found it.[54]

That similar reasoning informs Nietzsche's view of the reciprocal relationship between the Dionysiac and the Apolline in *BT* can be discerned by comparing his argument in *BT* with a later one in *The Gay Science*. In *BT* Nietzsche writes of the empirical world individuated by the forms of the Apolline that 'we imagine the dreamer calling out to himself in the midst of the dream world, but without disturbing it, "It is a dream, I will dream on"'.[55] Here Nietzsche presents the empirical world of our experience as an appearance.[56] In *The Gay Science* Nietzsche reiterates his point that the empirical sphere is an apparent one but emphasises that this appeal to appearances does not imply a contrasting sphere of things-in-themselves. He writes:

> I suddenly woke up in the midst of this dream, but only to the consciousness that I am dreaming and that I must go on dreaming lest I perish – as a somnambulist must go on dreaming lest he fall. What is 'appearance' for me now? Certainly not the opposite of some essence: what could I say about any essence except to name the attributes of its appearance! Certainly not a dead mask that one could place on an unknown x or remove from it![57]

The similarities between Nietzsche's position in *BT*, 'On Schopenhauer' and *The Gay Science* and his denial in the latter text that his description of the empirical sphere as apparent implies a distinction between appearances and things-in-themselves indicates that the distinction between the Apolline and the Dionysiac is not intended to be such a distinction either. In a draft for a preface to *BT* Nietzsche claims that he aims to put forward a one-world view that overcomes the tension between appearance and reality.[58] He maintains his aim is to overcome the appearance/reality distinction and a world-view founded on the juxtaposition of opposites. Moreover, in *BT* Nietzsche contends that he is interested in the art of comfort in *this* world as opposed to another unknowable metaphysical realm.[59] One might be forgiven for thinking that Nietzsche's description of reality as an appearance in the context of his self-proclaimed dismantling of the distinction between appearance and reality entails a form of subjective idealism that reduces reality to our mental representations, holding him firmly within the general constitutive, mind-dependent framework of both Kant and Schopenhauer. In the previous chapter we saw how Nietzsche avoids this conclusion in his later writings. That he also avoids it in *BT*, however, can be discerned from an examination of the specific metaphysical background that informs his argument in this book. This metaphysical background contends that the empirical world of our experience, although accessible to the human intellect, is nevertheless irreducible to it.

However, it is precisely this aspect of Nietzsche's thought that has led to the view, despite his claims to the contrary, that *BT* perpetuates the appearance/reality distinction. It is not difficult to ascertain the reason for this. When Nietzsche writes that rather than constituting an opposition the Dionysiac functions as a 'delicate line'[60] within the Apolline he does so in the context of a complicated metaphysics that appeals to the notion of a primordial intellect, which on the surface does not appear to be very different from Schopenhauer's appeal to the thing-in-itself as Will. Nietzsche suggests that the empirical world of our experience is an image or appearance projected by the primordial intellect, or what he also calls the Dionysian world-artist. Although this metaphysics is often interpreted as signalling Nietzsche's early commitment to the thing-in-itself, in the next section I shall argue, contrary to the predominant view, that it is intended to dismantle the appearance/reality distinction by rejecting both the Kantian thesis that knowable reality is reducible to the forms of our knowledge but divorced from the thing-in-itself and the Schopenhauerian thesis that the thing-in-itself is accessible independently of the cognitive forms of human Understanding. This will initially involve an examination of Nietzsche's notion of the human instinctive intellect, which is supposed to dissolve the gap between our human knowledge and ultimate reality understood as a primordial intellect. In his early unpublished notes Nietzsche claims that the instinctive intellect is a non-constitutive intellect immersed in rather than divorced from reality. As we shall now see, the instinctive intellect is fundamental to the emergence, in an inchoate form, of Nietzsche's later internal realism in the early writings.

INSTINCTIVE INTELLECT

Nietzsche intends to overcome the opposition of self and world in the guise of the appearance/reality distinction by outlining the specifically non-constitutive character of the human instinctive intellect. In particular, instinctive intellect is designed to overcome the constitutive account of knowledge by rejecting what Nietzsche sees as Kant's and Schopenhauer's extra-empirical subject of knowing.[61] The constitutive account leads to sceptical idealism, according to Nietzsche, as a result of its view that the sphere of our empirical experience is both constituted by and reducible to the human mind. The realm of our empirical experience is thus said to be narrowly anthropocentric and divorced from how things are in themselves. Nietzsche's appeal to the instinctive intellect maintains that rather than constituting reality whereby empirical reality is reducible to the forms of the human intellect and unconnected to things in themselves, the human intellect participates in reality. This reality is not a thing-in-itself, according to Nietzsche, because it is in principle available to our knowledge. Nietzsche's notion of instinctive intellect represents an attempt to formulate a mode of knowing that is rooted in and has access to the nature of the world.

In a collection of early notes entitled 'On the Origins of Language' (1869–70) Nietzsche outlines his proposal of an unconscious and instinctive intellect. He writes: 'Instinct is one with the innermost kernel of a being. This is the real problem of philosophy, the unending expediency of organisms and the unconsciousness in their coming to be.'[62] Nietzsche's conception of the instinctive intellect attempts to naturalise it and so reject the constitutive conception of the knowing self that is said to order the world from an extra-empirical vantage point. He puts forward the view that the human intellect is part of nature in opposition to the idealist view which he attributes to both Kant and Schopenhauer that the transcendental intellect constitutes the empirical world of individuated objects. According to Nietzsche such idealism goes hand in hand with either scepticism or dogmatic metaphysics. Both Kant's and Schopenhauer's particular brand of idealism entails, in Nietzsche's view, a distinction between how things are constituted by the human mind and how they are constituted in themselves. Nietzsche articulates the type of idealism that he attributes to both Kant and Schopenhauer in the following passage:

> Even the Kantian theory of knowledge was immediately employed by man for his own self-glorification: the world has its reality only in man. It is tossed back and forth like a ball in the heads of men. In truth however this theory means only this: Though one might think that there exists both a work of art and a stupid man to contemplate it, of course the work exists as a cerebral phenomenon for this stupid man only to the extent that he is himself an artist as well and contributes the forms [to the work]. He could boldly assert, 'the work of art has no reality outside of my brain.'[63]

The view that Nietzsche attributes to Kant here is that the human mind constitutes an otherwise unformed chaos of sensations into an individuated realm of empirical objects. Nietzsche's desire to overcome this idealism entails a rejection of what he calls the 'conscious intellect' as the key to knowledge, which, he claims, mistakenly takes the human intellect to be the constitutive centre of things. To privilege the conscious intellect, according to Nietzsche, entails the idealist view that *a priori* forms are imposed on an unformed realm of sensations. In contrast, Nietzsche puts forward the view that our capacity for rational thought is inextricably bound up with our affective natures. Identifying the unconscious and instinctive human intellect with perceptual thinking he writes:

> Unconscious *inferences* set me to thinking: it is no doubt a process of passing from *image* to *image*. The image which is last attained then operates as a stimulus and motive. Unconscious thinking must take place apart from concepts: it must therefore occur in *perceptions (Anschauungen)*.[64]

Here Nietzsche describes unconscious perception as extra-conceptual. However, as suggested in our earlier examination of his description of the Dionysiac as non-conceptual, it transpires that intuition, in Nietzsche's view, is merely non-abstract. Our perception does not entail the imposition of *a priori* form on extra-conceptual content. Rather, our perceptions are always already intellectually informed. Furthermore, in the early notes Nietzsche describes *Anschauung* as *Anordnung*.[65] Here he suggests that our perceptual experience is always an orderly one. In so doing, he puts forward the view that, contrary to initial appearances, there is no great distinction to be made between perception and intellect as perception, he claims, is a form of unconscious thinking.[66] In his later writings Nietzsche continues to maintain that, properly understood, there is very little difference between unconscious and conscious thought because one is really a form of the other. He states:

> Having long kept a strict eye on the philosophers, and having looked between their lines, I say to myself: the largest part of conscious thinking has to be considered an instinctual activity, even in the case of philosophical thinking; we need a new understanding here, . . . 'consciousness' is scarcely *opposite* to the instincts in any decisive sense – most of a philosopher's conscious thinking is secretly guided and channelled into particular tracks by his instincts.[67]

According to Nietzsche our cognitive constitution is embedded in our affective nature; our capacity for rational thought is distinctly embodied. We do not impose the forms of our knowing on the world. Rather, the instinctive intellect is immersed in the world.

By attempting to liberate himself from both Kant and Schopenhauer, Nietzsche strives to overcome the view that human minds constitute the realm of our empirical experience. However, as already indicated, Nietzsche's argument is formulated against a metaphysical background. This background can be discerned from some of the early notes where he posits a metaphysical *Ur-Eine* or Will, which projects itself as an appearance. He maintains that space, time and causality belong to these appearances. However, unlike Kant and Schopenhauer, Nietzsche holds that these forms are not transcendental forms imposed by a human subject but rather they emanate from the self-objectifying Will itself. He states:

> I hesitate to trace space, time and causality from the pitiful human consciousness; they belong to the will. They are the condition for all symbolics of appearance: man himself is such a symbol, as is the state, the earth. This symbolism is not unconditionally there for man alone.[68]

Here Nietzsche contends, contrary to both Kant and Schopenhauer, that the properties we predicate of the realm of experience are projections of the willing Ur-intellect. Space, time and causality are not *a priori* forms imposed on reality by the human intellect. This is because both the naturalised human subject or instinctive intellect and the spatio-temporal empirical world are appearances projected by a primordial intellect. According to Nietzsche, our empirical experience is an image viewed by a primordial intellect whilst simultaneously being one with that intellect. Nietzsche writes: 'We are in one sense pure *Anschauung* (that means projected images of a completely enraptured being, which has the highest repose in this viewing), on the other hand we are the one being itself.'[69] Nietzsche maintains that our conscious intellect cannot access the nature of the Ur-intellect 'directly'.[70] The conscious intellect gives us access to appearances of appearances. That is, the conscious intellect gives us representations of the empirical world, which is, in turn, a projection of the Ur-intellect. However, he contends that the Ur-intellect is not cut off from us. For we can access the character of the Ur-intellect through the instinctive intellect:

> The *individiatio* is in any case not the work of conscious knowing, rather the work of the Ur-intellect. The Kantian-Schopenhauerian Idealists did not recognize this. Our intellect *never* carries us further than to conscious knowledge: insofar as we are, however, also intellectual instinct, we can venture to say something about the Ur-intellect. No arrow reaches beyond this.[71]

Nietzsche writes: 'The conscious intellect a weak thing, really only the tool of the will. But the intellect itself and the will are one.'[72] Moreover, he contends, 'All growth in our knowledge arises out of the making conscious of the unconscious.'[73] That is, by bringing what we know unconsciously or instinctively to the level of conscious knowing Nietzsche suggests that we can succeed in overcoming the opposition of self and world. He writes: 'Suppose there is an inseparable connection between the intellect which produces concepts and representations and the perceptual world!'[74]

According to Nietzsche, as unconscious or instinctive intellect we are an appearance of the Ur-intellect. That the unconscious intellect is a projection or appearance is suggested by Nietzsche's claim that 'individuation is *not* the birth of conscious mind'.[75] The instinctive intellect, therefore, belongs to the empirical world of individuated phenomena. However, as an appearance of the Ur-intellect it also participates in the Ur-intellect. Thus Nietzsche writes: 'Every appearance is also the *Ur-Eine* itself.'[76] Nietzsche's point here, though rather obscure, seems to be that as a projection of the primordial intellect and the manner in which that intellect views itself, our experiences as an instinctive intellect, although unconscious, are also the experiences of the primordial intellect.[77] On the basis of his appeal to the instinctive intellect Nietzsche formulates a decidedly anti-sceptical and therefore, in his view, anti-Kantian thesis. He states:

> The *forms* of the intellect have gradually arisen out of the matter. It is plausible in itself that these forms are strictly adequate to the truth. For where is an apparatus which could invent something new supposed to have come from?[78]

This anti-sceptical stance can be further discerned from his reference to Trendelenburg. He writes, contrary to Kant, 'it still remains entirely *possible* that the world is as it appears to us to be.'[79]

This metaphysics also informs Nietzsche's argument in *BT*. His views regarding the reciprocal relationship between the Apolline and the Dionysiac are formulated against the metaphysical background of a primordial intellect and its supposed harmony with the human instinctive intellect. In *BT* he contends that the empirical world is a projection of what he calls the Dionysiac world-artist. This explains why he describes the empirical world of our experience as apparent in this book. He states:

> The more I become aware of those all-powerful artistic drives in nature, and of a fervent longing in them for semblance, for their redemption and release in semblance, the more I feel myself driven to the metaphysical assumption that that which truly exists, the eternally suffering and contradictory, primordial unity, simultaneously needs, for its constant release and redemption, the ecstatic vision, intensely pleasurable semblance.[80]

Although it is difficult to ascertain clearly the precise nature of the primordial intellect, Nietzsche intends it to support his thesis that there is no epistemic gap between our human knowledge and the nature of the world. Moreover, he is also concerned to establish that human knowledge of reality is possible if understood along the lines of a non-constitutive instinctive intellect. One might ask, however, what Nietzsche means by reality. Is he referring to the primordial intellect or to empirical reality? For Nietzsche, at least on the most charitable reading of his early writings, the answer must not come in the form of a disjunction. He does not consider the primordial intellect and empirical reality to be two different things. Rather, his appeal to the primordial intellect is intended to capture the inner nature of appearances. This is suggested by both his description of the primordial intellect as the 'innermost kernel' of things and his claim that appearances and the primordial intellect share a unity.[81] Consequently, Nietzsche's appeal to the primordial intellect is intended to safeguard rather than undermine the sphere of appearance. Nietzsche's distinction between the primordial intellect and empirical reality is not intended to be one between appearance and reality. Rather, to use one of his later descriptions, they stand for lighter and darker shades of appearance.[82]

However, despite his protestations to the contrary, one might still ask whether Nietzsche has relapsed into dogmatism here. Although on the face of it his appeal to the primordial world-artist is uncomfortably reminiscent of the Schopenhauerian dogmatic metaphysics that he claims to reject, he denies that they are the same thing. In the early notes, Nietzsche articulates his intention to remain firmly within the anthropocentric boundaries of our knowledge:

[Let us] not [forget] that this whole process is only our necessary form of appearance and to that extent utterly lacking in any metaphysical reality; [and] that, however, with all our proofs we cannot get past these barriers, and at most we are able to recognize them as such. If above I dared to speak of Genius and appearance as if I had access to a knowledge surpassing those limits and as if I were able to look out from the *one*, great eye of the world [*Weltauge*], let me state after the fact that I don't believe I have stepped outside of the anthropomorphic circle with that figurative language . . .[83]

On the issue of dogmatism, then, Nietzsche is cautious. He does not claim unmediated or privileged insight into the nature of things but presents the primordial intellect as an anthropocentric explanatory posit intended to make intelligible his view that reality operates according to intrinsic principles of order rather than principles supplied by the human mind. Describing his appeal to a primordial world-artist as a 'metaphysical assumption' in *BT* Nietzsche's recourse to the primordial intellect as an explanatory posit is a regulative modification of Kant's anthropocentrism.[84] Rather than reducing reality to the forms of our knowledge we explain the operations of reality analogously to our specifically human experience. He writes:

> The progress of philosophy: It was first thought that men were the authors of all things. Gradually one *explained* [my emphasis] things to himself by analogy with particular human qualities.[85]

Despite the ambiguity surrounding Nietzsche's appeal to the primordial intellect, it nonetheless clearly indicates that his engagement with Kant and Schopenhauer in the early writings is predominantly critical. At this stage of his philosophical development Nietzsche is concerned to establish, contrary to Kant and Schopenhauer, that the human mind does not constitute the empirical world of our experience and that the empirical world is mind-independent in this specific sense.[86] Moreover, conscious knowledge, if properly understood and brought into closer contact with the non-constitutive human instinctive intellect, is no longer divorced from things-in-themselves. Rather, the traditional thing-in-itself is transformed in Nietzsche's writings and becomes a regulative explanatory posit to explain how the non-constitutive human mind can have knowledge of reality without engaging in dogmatic metaphysics.[87] According to this explanatory posit, the primordial intellect is not radically divorced from our experience of reality since its spatio-temporal experiences and ours as unconscious intellect are identical.

Nevertheless, arguing that reality is ordered from within and should not be understood as reducible to human minds, Nietzsche's epistemological commitments lead him to metaphysics. Despite our charitable interpretation of this metaphysics as entailing an appeal to the inner nature of things that share a unity with appearances, the notion of a primordial intellect ultimately remains obscure. In order to overcome what he considers to be Kant's reductive and narrow anthropocentrism Nietzsche finds himself appealing to a non-human and arguably superfluously purposive intellect to account for both the character of things and the objectivity of our knowledge. In his later writings Nietzsche concedes that his appeal to a primordial intellect cannot achieve what he wants. Despite his early efforts to unite the primordial intellect with the realm of appearances and our knowledge of them, he reflects on his earlier appeal to a primordial intellect, realising that it renders the empirical world a 'dream and fiction of a God'. His 'convalescent' self understands that he must not 'bury the head in the sand of heavenly things' but rather he must speak of the meaning of 'the earth'.[88] Although he does not give up on the need for regulative metaphysical explanations in his later writings, he becomes aware that such explanations can be more successfully understood to obtain at the level of empirical reality. The metaphysical issue of the intrinsic nature of reality, articulated in the early notes as the problem of reconciling multiplicity with unity,[89] continues to preoccupy him throughout his philosophical career and is articulated in his later writings in terms of uniting, at the level of empirical reality, the relational character of things with their intrinsic natures. Nietzsche formulates this argument in his thesis of the will to power by further engaging with Kant on the issue of the thing-in-itself and constitutive knowledge. As we shall see in the next chapter, Nietzsche's later metaphysics, in a similar fashion to that of his early writings, emerges from his epistemology.

NOTES

1. I take Nietzsche's early work to comprise all his writings up to 1878. This includes both published and unpublished writings up to, but not including, *Human, All Too Human*. Although I shall argue for the continuity of Nietzsche's thought throughout the early and late periods, I think that it is possible for practical reasons to distinguish between an early and late Nietzsche. As the analysis in this chapter shows, Nietzsche wavers between alternative philosophical positions in the early writings. This is to be distinguished from his somewhat more confident adoption of internal realism from *Human, All Too Human*, where he formulates explicit reasons why the belief in the thing-in-itself is unreliable (see Chapter 2). However, I shall argue that Nietzsche sows the seeds of his later internal realist position in the early writings.
2. For an alternative interpretation of Schopenhauer see, for example, Bryan Magee, *The Philosophy of Schopenhauer* (Oxford: Oxford University Press, 1997), chapter 21.
3. See Sarah Kofman, 'Metaphor, Symbol, Metamorphosis', in David B. Allison, *The New Nietzsche* (London: MIT Press, 1994), p. 207. See also Arthur Danto, *Nietzsche as Philosopher* (New York: Columbia University Press, 1980 [1965]), chapter 2. According to these commentators, Nietzsche concludes that our truths are illusions on the basis of an argument regarding the metaphorical character of language. Maudemarie Clark, in contrast, claims that he arrives at it on the basis of his commitment to representationalism and the thing-in-itself. (Maudemarie Clark, *Nietzsche on Truth and Philosophy* [Cambridge: Cambridge University Press, 1990], chapter 3).
4. Friedrich Nietzsche, 'On Truth and Lies in a Nonmoral Sense' (1873), in *Philosophy and Truth: Selections from Nietzsche's Notebooks of the Early 1870's*, edited and translated by Daniel Breazeale (London: Humanities Press, 1991), pp. 82–3. As in the main text I refer to this book in the abbreviated form *TL* in the notes.
5. Ibid., p. 83.
6. Ibid., p. 86. See Clark, *Nietzsche on Truth and Philosophy*, p. 92.
7. Nietzsche, *TL*, p. 86.
8. Ibid., pp. 83–4. Grimm argues that Nietzsche adopts this agnostic position throughout his career. See Rüdiger Hermann Grimm, *Nietzsche's Theory of Knowledge* (Berlin: Walter de Gruyter, 1977).
9. Peter Poellner, 'Perspectival Truth', in John Richardson and Brian Leiter (eds), *Nietzsche* (Oxford: Oxford University Press, 2001), p. 111.
10. Nietzsche, *TL*, p. 82.
11. Ibid., p. 87.
12. As Hill has pointed out, Nietzsche's genealogical method first appears in *TL*.

However, in *TL* it is confined to what Hill terms a social constructivist account of the drive for truth, explaining where the drive for truth comes from. See R. Kevin Hill, *Nietzsche's Critiques: The Kantian Foundations of His Thought* (Oxford: Clarendon Press, 2003), p. 114 n37. However, in *Human, All Too Human*, Nietzsche's genealogical method applies to our belief about what truth is, that it comprises correspondence to things-in-themselves. Friedrich Nietzsche, *Human, All Too Human*, translated by R. J. Hollingdale (Cambridge: Cambridge University Press, 1996 [1878–86]), Volume I, 'Of First and Last Things', 11. Henceforth cited as *HAH*.

13. Nietzsche, *TL*, p. 87.
14. Ibid., p. 84. Nietzsche argues that we have inherited our cognitive apparatus due to its utility for survival.
15. Arthur Schopenhauer, *The World as Will and Representation*, Volume I, translated by E. F. J. Payne (New York: Dover, 1966 [1819]), p. 7. Henceforth cited as *WWR*, I.
16. Ibid., p. 19.
17. Nietzsche, *TL*, p. 81.
18. Nietzsche refers to these common-sense objects as 'things themselves' as opposed to things-in-themselves (Nietzsche, *TL*, p. 83).
19. Friedrich Nietzsche, *The Will to Power*, edited by R. J. Hollingdale, translated by Walter Kaufmann (New York: Vintage Books, 1968 [1901]), 458. Henceforth cited as *WP*.
20. Clark, *Nietzsche on Truth and Philosophy*, p. 90. Hill also thinks that *BT* and *TL* form a unitary view. He argues that both texts restrict our knowledge to phenomena that have been constructed by us. However, he contends that *BT* presents reflective judgements about things-in-themselves (Hill, *Nietzsche's Critiques*, p. 103).
21. Nietzsche, *WP*, 853. However, Arthur Danto sees Nietzsche's Apolline/Dionysiac distinction in *BT* as constituting a distinction between appearance and reality (Danto, *Nietzsche as Philosopher*, pp. 97–8).
22. Friedrich Nietzsche, *The Birth of Tragedy and Other Writings*, translated by Ronald Speirs (Cambridge: Cambridge University Press, 1999 [1872]), 'An Attempt at Self-Criticism', p. 10 section 6. As is my practice in the main text, I refer to this book in the abbreviated form, *BT*, in the Notes. Interestingly, in a letter to Overbeck, in July 1885, Nietzsche claims that his mature philosophy is already obscurely expressed in *BT*. (Friedrich Nietzsche, *Sämtliche Briefe. Kritische Studienausgabe*, edited by Giorgio Colli and Mazzino Montinari, 8 volumes, [Munich: dtv; Berlin and New York: de Gruyter, 1986], 7, p. 67).
23. Hill also argues that Nietzsche's position in *BT* is Kantian rather than Schopenhauerian. However, Hill contends that Nietzsche retains both Kant's mind-imposition thesis and the thing-in-itself. According to my interpretation, Nietzsche rejects the constitutive view of knowledge and transforms the thing-in-itself beyond its Kantian meaning. See Hill, *Nietzsche's Critiques*, chapter 3.
24. See, for example, Alexander Nehamas, *Nietzsche: Life as Literature* (Cambridge, MA: Harvard University Press, 1985), pp. 42–3. Richard Schacht also contends that Nietzsche's arguments in *BT* are heavily influenced by Schopenhauer. Richard Schacht, *Nietzsche* (London: Routledge, 1992 [1983]), chapter VIII. See also Walter Kaufmann, *Nietzsche: Philosopher, Psychologist, AntiChrist* (Princeton, NJ: Princeton University Press, 1974 [1950]).
25. According to Silk and Stern we can understand the relationship between the Apolline and the Dionysiac on three levels: the psychological, the aesthetic and the metaphysical (M. S. Silk and J. P. Stern, *Nietzsche on Tragedy* [Cambridge: Cambridge University Press, 1981], p. 288). Nietzsche's three-tiered interest in

Apollo and Dionysus are intimately intertwined. On the psychological level, the Apolline and the Dionysiac represent a plurality of drives through which we relate to the world. Silk and Stern describe the Apolline and the Dionysiac on the level of psychology as 'creative human impulses, *Triebe*, under which are subsumed modes of perceiving, experiencing, expressing and responding to reality' (ibid., p. 288). As a psychological impulse the Apolline experiences the world as ordered and stable whilst the Dionysiac experiences the dissolution of this order and thus experiences the world as being in flux. The aesthetic understanding of the two gods is founded on the psychological analysis. As aesthetic criteria, the Apolline and the Dionysiac are said to represent 'cultural tendencies' which express the psychological impulses. Thus sculpture is characterised as Apolline and music as Dionysiac; sculpture represents Apolline order whilst music expresses Dionysiac flux. The contrast here is between 'dream' and 'intoxication', respectively. As metaphysical ideas the two gods refer, on the surface, to appearances and reality.

I have also indicated that the Apolline and Dionysiac can be understood epistemologically because they are psychological drives. As such the Apolline and the Dionysiac are also forms of knowing reality. In *Beyond Good and Evil* Nietzsche writes that his physico-psychology of drives is the key to the 'basic issues' (Friedrich Nietzsche, *Beyond Good and Evil*, translated by Marion Faber [Oxford: Oxford University Press, 1998 (1886)], 23. Henceforth cited as *BGE*). Additionally, by understanding the Apolline and Dionysiac as drives, Nietzsche aims to overcome the idea of disinterested knowledge. In *On the Genealogy of Morality*, he refers to objective knowledge as an interplay between 'affective interpretations' (Friedrich Nietzsche, *On the Genealogy of Morality*, translated by Maudemarie Clark and Alan J. Swensen (Indianapolis, IN: Hackett, 1998), III, 12). Henceforth cited as *GM*).

26. It may be objected that Nietzsche is more interested in the existential issue of life-affirmation than with questions of knowledge and reality. However, the existential and the epistemological–metaphysical are not separate from one another according to Nietzsche. See the Introduction for a discussion of this issue.

27. Nietzsche, *BT*, pp. 14–15, section 1. Although Schopenhauer had intended his idealism to close the gap, in Berkeleian fashion, between representations and objects, his comparison of the empirical world to a dream or illusion arguably reopens this gap (Schopenhauer, *WWR*, I, pp. 34–5).

28. Nietzsche's use of Schopenhauerian language here suggests that, epistemologically speaking, the Apolline and the Dionysiac refer to two ways of knowing that correspond to the Understanding's forms of individuation and intuitive insight that is independent of these forms respectively (see Nietzsche, *BT*, p. 77, section 16). See also Clark, *Nietzsche on Truth and Philosophy*, p. 90.

29. Nietzsche, *BT*, p. 16, section 1.

30. Ibid., p. 19, section 2.

31. Ibid., pp. 41–2, section 8.

32. Ibid., 'An Attempt at Self-Criticism', p. 12, section 7. Here Nietzsche emphasises the notion of '*this world*'.

33. Nietzsche, *BT*, p. 27, section 4. Nietzsche describes the relationship between the Apolline and the Dionysiac as a 'mysterious marriage' (Nietzsche, *BT*, p. 28, section 4) and a 'mysterious unity' (ibid., p. 28, section 5).

34. In 'Schopenhauer as Educator' Nietzsche praises Schopenhauer's aim to reconcile knowledge and Being or to overcome the opposition of self and world (Friedrich Nietzsche, 'Schopenhauer as Educator', 3 [1874], in *Untimely Meditations*, translated by R. J. Hollingdale [Cambridge: Cambridge University

Press, 1994 (1873–76)]). However, he thinks that Schopenhauer's appeal to 'immediate certainties' fail to achieve this aim (Nietzsche, *BGE*, 16).

35. It may be argued that Schopenhauer, contrary to Nietzsche's view, does allow that we have cognition of the true nature of things-in-themselves in aesthetic experience, which does not bypass the cognitive subject because aesthetic experience involves, for him, the Idea and the pure subject of knowing (Schopenhauer, *WWR*, I, p. 209). However, Schopenhauer's account of aesthetic experience involves, as Patrick Gardiner explains, the view that 'the forms of consciousness in which the sense of oneself as a persisting separate individual vanishes and where the ordinary distinction between percipient and perceived seems to lose hold' (Patrick Gardiner, *Schopenhauer* [Harmondsworth: Penguin, 1963], p. 202). To the extent, then, that Schopenhauer thinks that an intuition of the nature of things as they are in themselves involves overcoming the forms of empirical knowledge, it seems correct to say that he bypasses the cognitive subject. The subject of aesthetic experience evoked by Schopenhauer is of the 'spectatorial' kind which Nietzsche does not, in my view, support (see note 39).

36. In a supplementary chapter in *WWR* Schopenhauer modifies his claim regarding the subject-independent nature of our intuition of the Will. Here he argues that our knowledge of the Will, although independent of the forms of space and causality, is not independent of time. He argues that we can know the Will 'only in its successive individual *acts*, not as a whole, in and by itself' (Arthur Schopenhauer, *The World as Will and Representation*, Volume II, translated by E. F. J. Payne [New York: Dover, 1966 (1844)], p. 197. Henceforth cited as *WWR*, II).

37. Nietzsche, *BT*, p. 30, section 5.

38. Ibid., p. 36, section 6. Nietzsche attempts to explicate the nature of the unity of the Apolline and the Dionysiac by turning to an examination of lyric poetry. Music, Nietzsche maintains, 'produces a copy of the primordial unity' (Nietzsche, *BT*, p. 30, section 5), which he describes as a repetition of the world and a second copy of it. However, music must be 'represented'. Under the influence of the Apolline, music becomes visible in a symbolic dream image:

> The image-less and concept-less reflection of the original pain in music, with its release and redemption in semblance, now generates a second reflection, a single symbolic likeness (*Gleichnis*) or *exemplum*. The artist has already given up his subjectivity in the Dionysiac process; the image which now shows him his unity with the heart of the world is a dream scene which gives sensuous expression to the primordial contradiction and pain, along with its primal lust for and pleasure in semblance. (Ibid., p. 30, section 5)

Although passages such as this one are sometimes interpreted in the Nietzsche literature as putting forward the view that aesthetic experience involves the overcoming of our subjective attachments in favour of a spectator approach to the question of knowledge, this chapter suggests an alternative understanding. When Nietzsche claims in this passage that the artist overcomes his subjectivity I take him to mean that it is possible to attain objective knowledge of reality. That Nietzsche does not mean to suggest that such objective knowledge involves overcoming the 'subjective' forms of cognition can be seen from his further claim that such 'Dionysiac' knowledge is not independent of 'semblance' or the Apolline forms of our cognition. Nietzsche, therefore, puts forward a different view from Schopenhauer's.

39. See Nietzsche's praise of Schopenhauer's 'immortal doctrine[s] of the intellectuality of intuition' in *The Gay Science*, translated by Walter Kaufmann (New York: Vintage Books, 1974 [1882/1887]), 99. Henceforth cited as *GS*. For

Schopenhauer's view that perception is intellectual, see Schopenhauer, *WWR*, I, p. 443.

40. Schopenhauer, *WWR*, I, p. 56.
41. Nietzsche, *BT*, p. 79, section 16.
42. Whereas Schopenhauer contends that the forms of our Understanding are non-conceptual, Nietzsche arguably disagrees. He advocates that concepts are necessary for the recognition of objects when he writes that the purely intuitive man has no concept of world. The purely intuitive man, according to Nietzsche, 'does not understand how to learn from experience and keeps falling over and over again into the same ditch' (Nietzsche, *TL*, p. 91).

   Nietzsche's identification of Apolline imagery with concept use (Nietzsche, *BT*, p. 79, section 16) and his views on the interdependency of the Apolline and the Dionysiac suggest, contrary to Schopenhauer, that the ability to classify and recognise objects, an ability evident in Schopenhauer's illustration of playing billiards, for example, entails an implicit rather than an explicit use of concepts. Furthermore, in *TL* Nietzsche hints that the opposition between self and world might be overcome by what he terms the 'liberated intellect'. Although he states of this liberated intellect that it 'will now be guided by intuitions rather than by concepts', he also maintains that this liberated intellect will speak in 'unheard-of combinations of concepts' (Nietzsche, *TL*, p. 90). On occasion Schopenhauer agrees with Nietzsche, writing, contrary to Kant, that 'Philosophy, therefore, is for him a science *of* concepts, but for me a science *in* concepts . . .' (Schopenhauer, *WWR*, I, p. 453). See Christopher Janaway, *Self and World in Schopenhauer's Philosophy* (Oxford: Clarendon Press, 1989), p. 164 and Julian Young, *Schopenhauer* (London: Routledge, 1994), pp. 44ff. for a further discussion of these issues.
43. See Friedrich Nietzsche, *Ecce Homo*, translated by R. J. Hollingdale (London: Penguin, 1992 [1908]), 'The Birth of Tragedy', 1 for Nietzsche's criticism of Socrates' separation of reason and instinct. Henceforth cited as *EH*.
44. Schopenhauer, *WWR*, II, p. 195.
45. Nietzsche, *BT*, pp. 72–3, section 15. In contrast to Socratic rationalism, as he sees it, Nietzsche espouses the virtues of ongoing and regulative research. He speaks of 'why Lessing, the most honest of theoretical men, dared to state openly that *searching* [my emphasis] for the truth meant more to him than truth itself . . .' (ibid., p. 73, section 15).
46. Ibid., p. 73, section 15.
47. In *BT* Nietzsche suggests that an artistic Socrates is not a contradictory idea (Nietzsche, *BT*, p. 71, section 14). In *HAH*, referring to a 'double-brain', Nietzsche contends that art and science work in tandem to the extent that art makes imaginative conjectures that must be constrained by scientific thinking (Nietzsche, *HAH*, Volume I, 'Tokens of Higher and Lower Culture', 251).
48. Friedrich Nietzsche, 'Zu Schopenhauer' [1868], *Werke und Briefe. Historisch-Kritische Gesamtausgabe* (München: C. H. Beck'sche Verlagsbuchhandlung, 1933–42), 3, pp. 352–61. I have consulted 'On Schopenhauer', included as an Appendix to Christopher Janaway, *Willing and Nothingness: Schopenhauer as Nietzsche's Educator* (Oxford: Clarendon Press, 1998), p. 262. Henceforth cited as *OS*.
49. Nietzsche, *OS*, p. 262.
50. Ibid., p. 260.
51. Ibid., p. 261.
52. Ibid., p. 261.
53. Ibid., p. 262.
54. Ibid., p. 264.

55. Nietzsche, *BT*, p. 25, section 4.
56. Superficially this claim seems to be very similar to Nietzsche's indifferentism in *TL*, where he describes the apparent world as 'an eternally repeated dream' (Nietzsche, *TL*, p. 87). However, as we shall see in our examination of the metaphysical background to *BT* in the next section, Nietzsche abandons the constitutive account of knowledge that informs *TL*. This means that in *BT* Nietzsche is not a sceptical idealist and, as a result, his description of our knowledge as apparent does not necessarily imply the idea of an opposing sphere of things-in-themselves as it does in *TL*.
57. Nietzsche, *GS*, 54. James I. Porter also notices the similarity in his *The Invention of Dionysus: An Essay on The Birth of Tragedy* (Stanford, CA: Stanford University Press, 2000), pp. 30–5.
58. Nietzsche, *WP*, 853.
59. Nietzsche, *BT*, 'An Attempt at Self-Criticism', p. 12, section 7.
60. Ibid., p. 16, section 1.
61. What Nietzsche criticises here is Schopenhauer's appeal to the Kantian transcendental intellect, although Nietzsche maintains that Schopenhauer is confused about the nature of the intellect (Nietzsche, *OS*, pp. 263–4). According to Nietzsche, Schopenhauer is unable to explain his view that the knowing intellect is transcendental and yet identical to the brain. By appealing to the non-constitutive character of the instinctive intellect Nietzsche argues that Schopenhauer's attempted naturalisation of Kant, identifying the knowing intellect with the brain, should carry non-idealistic consequences. Nietzsche concludes, contrary to Schopenhauer, and presumably Friedrich Lange, that the world can conceivably be reducible to the human mind only if the human intellect is a Kantian transcendental intellect. If the human intellect is identified with the brain, then the mind is a part of the natural world and the world cannot be reducible to it. (Nietzsche argues similarly in *BGE*, 15.) For an account of Lange's naturalisation of Kant, see George J. Stack, *Lange and Nietzsche* (New York: Walter de Gruyter, 1983); Claudia Crawford, *Nietzsche's Theory of Language* (New York: Walter de Gruyter, 1988), chapter 6.
62. Friedrich Nietzsche, 'Vom Ursprung der Sprache' [1869/70], *Gesammelte Werke*. Musarionausgabe (München: Musarion Verlag, 1920–29), 5, p. 468. I have consulted Claudia Crawford's translation, 'On the Origins of Language', included as an Appendix to her *Nietzsche's Theory of Language*, p. 223.
63. Friedrich Nietzsche, 'The Philosopher: Reflections on the Struggle between Art and Knowledge', paragraph 106, in Breazeale (ed.), *Philosophy and Truth*. There is a similarity between Nietzsche's description of transcendental idealism here and his description of empirical idealism in *BGE*, 15. Nietzsche does not clearly distinguish between transcendental and empirical idealism, following Schopenhauer's interpretation of Kant's transcendental idealism as a form of subjective idealism (Schopenhauer, *WWR*, I, pp. 434–5).
64. Nietzsche, 'The Philosopher: Reflections on the Struggle between Art and Knowledge', paragraph 116.
65. Nietzsche, *Werke und Briefe. Historisch-Kritische Gesamtausgabe*, 2, pp. 255–6. I have consulted Crawford's translation, 'Untitled Notes', included as an Appendix to *Nietzsche's Theory of Language*, p. 292.
66. Claudia Crawford articulates Nietzsche's argument in his early writings when she writes that under the influence of Hartmann rather than Schopenhauer:

> Nietzsche comes to visualize a completely unconscious process of thinking which has a certain logic or inferential quality of its own and which functions as a basis for conscious discursive activity. It is a process which consists of

an 'interblending of the discursive and intuitive methods' of the unconscious and conscious aspects of mental activity. (Crawford, *Nietzsche's Theory of Language*, p. 49)

Nietzsche differs from Schopenhauer because he thinks that perception involves thinking.

67. Nietzsche, *BGE*, 3.
68. Friedrich Nietzsche, *Sämtliche Werke. Kritische Studienausgabe*, edited by Giorgio Colli and Mazzino Montinari (Berlin and München: Walter de Gruyter and dtv, 1980), 7, pp. 114–15, 5 [81]. Henceforth cited as *KSA*. Claudia Crawford groups a selection of these notes from 1870–71 under the title 'Anschauung Notes' as an Appendix to her *The Beginnings of Nietzsche's Theory of Language*. The present reference is to p. 270 of that Appendix. Henceforth cited as *AN*.
69. Nietzsche, *AN*, p. 277. *KSA*, 7, p. 214, 7 [201].
70. Ibid., p. 278. *KSA*, 7, p. 215, 7 [201].
71. Ibid., p. 268. *KSA*, 7, p. 111, 5 [79].
72. Ibid., p. 271. *KSA*, 7, p. 128, 5 [123].
73. Ibid., p. 270. *KSA*, 7, p. 116, 5 [89].
74. Ibid., p. 271. *KSA*, 7, p. 120, 5 [99].
75. Ibid., p. 268. *KSA*, 7, p. 111, 5 [79].
76. Ibid., p. 272. *KSA*, 7, p. 200, 7 [157].
77. Ibid., p. 273. *KSA*, 7, pp. 203–4, 7 [168]. Nietzsche's appeal to the primordial intellect is rather unclear. When he writes of the 'irreality of space and time' (ibid., p. 273. *KSA*, 7, p. 204, 7 [168]) he suggests that the Will, although non-spatio-temporal, projects and views itself in spatio-temporal terms. Yet he also refers to the 'presupposition of the reality of individuation' (Nietzsche, *AN*, p. 268. *KSA*, 7, p. 112, 5 [79]) in contrast to which our conscious representations are deemed to be appearances of appearances (that is, appearances of the appearances projected by the Ur-intellect). Here Nietzsche suggests that the instinctive intellect is rooted firmly within the individuated sphere of space and time. On the surface it is unclear where the unity of the Ur-intellect/Will and the instinctive intellect lies, especially in light of Nietzsche's denial that he is a dogmatist. Their unity must lie, then, in the unity of their respective experiences.
78. Nietzsche, 'The Philosopher: Reflections on the Struggle between Art and Knowledge', paragraph 106.
79. Ibid., paragraph 84.
80. Nietzsche, *BT*, pp. 25–6, section 4.
81. Nietzsche, 'On the Origins of Language', p. 223, *Gesammelte Werke*, 5, p. 468.
82. Nietzsche, *BGE*, 34.
83. James I. Porter, whose translation I use here, draws our attention to the passage in *The Invention of Dionysus*, p. 124. See Nietzsche *KSA*, 14, p. 541.
84. Nietzsche, *BT*, pp. 24–6, section 4.
85. Nietzsche, 'The Philosopher: Reflections on the Struggle between Art and Science', paragraph 103. Kevin Hill recognises Nietzsche's appeal to regulative explanations in the early writings. However, in contrast to Hill's contention that these judgements are cognitively impotent and amount to little more than wishful thinking on Nietzsche's part (Hill, *Nietzsche's Critiques*, p. 115), Nietzsche argues in a later note that such maxims can yield knowledge (Nietzsche, *WP*, 333), even though he retrospectively considers his appeal to the primordial intellect as extravagant. See Friedrich Nietzsche, *Thus Spoke Zarathustra*, translated

by R. J. Hollingdale (London: Penguin, 1969 [1883–92]), Part One, 'Of the Afterworldsmen'. Henceforth cited as Z.

86. Hill contends that the primordial intellect understood as a perceiver is similar to Kant's notion of the thing-in-itself as an intuitive understanding (Hill, *Nietzsche's Critiques*, p. 104). The difference here for Nietzsche, however, is that he suggests that the thing-in-itself is knowable. As such, it ceases to be a thing-in-itself in the objectionable sense.

87. According to Nietzsche, the human mind can have knowledge of reality because it is not divorced from reality. Nietzsche's reference to an unconscious intellect sets up this alternative picture wherein the subject is an evolving part of a larger evolving whole:

> Now man has evolved slowly, and knowledge is still evolving: his picture of the world thus becomes ever more true and complete. Naturally it is only a clearer and clearer *mirroring*. But the mirror itself is nothing entirely foreign and apart from the nature of things. On the contrary it too slowly arose as [part of] the nature of things. We observe an effort to make the mirror more and more adequate. The natural process is carried on by science. Thus the things mirror themselves ever more clearly, gradually liberating themselves from what is all too anthropomorphic. (Nietzsche, 'The Philosopher: Reflections on the Struggle between Art and Knowledge', paragraph 102)

88. Nietzsche, Z, Part One, 'Of the Afterworldsmen'.
89. For his discussion of multiplicity and unity, see Nietzsche, AN, p. 270. KSA, 7, p. 114, 5 [80].

Part II
Metaphysics

Chapter 4

Justifying the Will to Power

So far we have seen that Nietzsche's perspectivism dispenses with Kant's oscillation between realism, entailing a God's Eye View, and idealism, where reality is thought to be reducible to the forms of our knowledge. The following three chapters show how Nietzsche's will to power thesis plays an important role in overcoming this oscillation. The present chapter does this by examining the arguments informing Nietzsche's proposal of the will to power, demonstrating that it operates as a metaphysics that not only derives from his perspectival account of knowledge but, as a result of its doing so, challenges traditional substantialist accounts of the nature of self and world. Denying that reality is a non-relational thing-in-itself knowable only by extra-perspectival means on the one hand, or that it is reducible to human minds on the other, Nietzsche puts forward the thesis that forces motivated by the desire for power are the ultimate constituents of reality and that both self and world are composed of these forces.[1] However, in light of the Nietzsche literature to date the suggestion that Nietzsche proposes the will to power as a metaphysical thesis is controversial. Responses to the doctrine among Nietzsche commentators have been mixed and can be divided into two groups. Members of the first group, appealing to Nietzsche's perspectivism and playing down the significance of the will to power thesis, argue that Nietzsche is not a metaphysical thinker. Proponents of the second view, however, emphasising his comments on the will to power, argue that Nietzsche's philosophy is predominantly metaphysical.[2] Although advocates of this second position take Nietzsche's metaphysics of the will to power seriously they do little to dispel the fears of the first group because they do not address the issue of with what justification Nietzsche puts forward the will to power thesis. In particular, they do not address the issue of how a metaphysical thesis such as that of the will to power can be deemed compatible with Nietzsche's perspectivism. Metaphysics as we use the term here denotes not a non-empirical domain such as Kant's thing-in-itself but rather the idea of one reality subject to a single overall explanation.[3] The will to power is metaphysical, according to Nietzsche, because it captures the true nature of reality. As the suggestion that the will to power is intended to fulfil this criterion is contentious our discussion must begin with an account of Nietzsche's justification of the doctrine, demonstrating how he arrives at the thesis from within the parameters of his perspectival view of knowledge. The task, however, is made difficult by the degree of opposition to any attempted justification of the thesis.

Two dominant lines of argument designed to weaken the significance of the will to power thesis within Nietzsche's philosophy as a whole have surfaced in the secondary literature. The first is the textual argument, which claims by appealing to various passages in Nietzsche's published writings that he does not articulate the will to power as a true metaphysical theory. As a result, this argument proposes there is no need for us to seek out Nietzsche's justification of the doctrine. The second is the philosophical argument, which claims that the will to power thesis is incompatible with Nietzsche's perspectivist epistemology. This consideration derives from the view that if the will to power is intended to be a true metaphysical thesis, then it represents an extra-perspectival claim to knowledge. Implicit here is the idea that Nietzsche's perspectivism does not facilitate an engagement with metaphysics. As a result of these two arguments few commentators have attempted to interpret the doctrine of the will to power as working in tandem with his perspectivism.[4]

In what follows I suggest these arguments are flawed, and moreover, that Nietzsche's will to power thesis represents, contrary to these two views, an important component in his philosophical enterprise. The chapter is divided into two sections. The first, addressing the above objections and ascertaining the epistemic commitments that inform Nietzsche's proposal of the will to power thesis, argues that it is both textually and philosophically defensible. Its philosophical defence resides in Nietzsche's prioritisation of epistemology over metaphysics, whereby he remains faithful to his perspectival view of knowledge in his proposal of the will to power, arguing that the latter derives from and is compatible with the former. According to Nietzsche, the will to power is a comprehensive perspective that has explanatory scope across multiple perspectives.[5] The second section illustrates how the metaphysics of the will to power emerges against the background of Nietzsche's perspectivism, avoiding a metaphysics of opposites by incorporating the 'objective' point of view of the physical sciences and the 'subjective' point of view of the anthropological sciences under one comprehensive explanatory perspective.[6] Central to this is Nietzsche's appropriation of the concept of force, which he argues constitutes an important step towards overcoming the oscillation between realism and idealism.

TWO OBJECTIONS TO THE WILL TO POWER

The textual objection to Nietzsche's will to power thesis centres on the question of whether Nietzsche intends his articulation of the doctrine to be true or no more than a hypothesis. With regard to this, Maudemarie Clark, the principal proponent of the textual argument, claims that the metaphysical version of the will to power as it appears in the published writings is not presented as a true doctrine but merely a value judgement, a 'construction of the world from the viewpoint of his moral values' rather than something that Nietzsche has 'reason to believe'.[7] Clark appeals to *Beyond Good and Evil*, 36 (*BGE*) and the surrounding passages to support her claim. In this book Nietzsche puts forward the hypothesis 'that nothing real is "given" to us apart from our world of desires and passions, assuming that we cannot ascend or descend to any "reality" other than the reality of our instincts'. This develops into the conjecture that there is only one form of causality operative in the world and that is the action of Wills:

> The question is ultimately whether we really recognize that the will can *effect* things, whether we believe in the causality of the will: if we do (and to believe in *this* is basically to believe in causality itself) we *must* experiment to test hypothetically whether the causality of the will is the only causality. A 'will' can have an effect only upon another 'will', of course, and not upon 'matter' (not upon 'nerves', for example): one must dare to hypothesize, in short, that wherever 'effects' are identified, a will is having an effect on another will – and that all mechanical events, in so far as an energy is active in them, are really the energy of the will, the effect of the will.[8]

Clark argues that if we interpret this section in the context of the passages that surround it, then we see that rather than committing himself to the truth of the will to power Nietzsche actually undermines the metaphysical version of the doctrine. She contends that acceptance of the thesis as it appears in *BGE*, 36 would involve attributing to Nietzsche *a priori* knowledge of the Will as an indubitable knowledge in a similar fashion to the supposed certainty and indubitable character of Descartes' 'thoughts'. According to Clark this would merely serve (contrary to Nietzsche's aims) to devalue the world of empirical experience. Thus she argues that the claims made in *BGE*, 36 are in conflict 'with Nietzsche's denial in *BG* 16 that there are "immediate certainties," including "I think" or "I will"'.[9] It is also incompatible, according to Clark, with Nietzsche's criticism in *BGE*, 19 of philosophers like Schopenhauer, who 'speak of the will as if it were the best-known thing in the world'. Clark's argument relies on her claim that, despite the suggestions made in *BGE*, 36, Nietzsche rejects both the foundationalism of extra-perspectival knowledge and the causality of the Will. She maintains that their rejection takes place in the passages surrounding *BGE*, 36 and in other passages where Nietzsche discusses the concept of causality. Here, she contends, Nietzsche undermines the will to power as a true metaphysical doctrine, rendering his presentation of the thesis a mere hypothesis rather than an initial conjecture supported by reasons.[10] However, in these passages Nietzsche, contrary to Clark's claim, merely rejects extra-perspectival knowledge and not the causal efficacy of the Will. I will cite two relevant passages for the convenience of the reader. The first is from *The Gay Science*:

> *Aftereffects of the most ancient religiosity.* – Every thoughtless person supposes that will alone is effective; *that willing is something simple, a brute datum, underivable, and intelligible by itself* [my emphasis]. He is convinced that when he does something – strike something, for example, – it is he that strikes, and that he did strike because he *willed* it. He does not see any problem here; the feeling of *will* seems sufficient to him not only for the assumption of cause and effect but also for the faith that he *understands* their relationship. He knows nothing of the mechanism of what happened and of the hundredfold fine work that needs to be done to bring about the strike, or of the incapacity of the will in itself to do even the tiniest part of this work. The will is for him a magically effective force; the faith in the will as the cause of effects is the faith in magically effective forces.[11]

The second passage is from *BGE*:

> Philosophers tend to speak about the will as if everyone in the world knew all about it; Schopenhauer even suggested that the will was the only thing we actually do know, know through and through, know without additions or subtractions. But I continue to think that even in this case Schopenhauer was only doing what philosophers simply tend to do: appropriating and exaggerating a *common prejudice*. As I see it, the act of willing is above all something *complicated*, something that has unity only as a word – and this common prejudice of using only one word has overridden the philosophers' caution (which was never all that great anyway).[12]

Nietzsche's aim in these passages is not to deny that we have a contentful idea of causal power or that our experience of willing entails some acquaintance with causal efficacy.[13] Nietzsche is not rejecting the causality of the Will but rather rejecting what he considers to be the incomplete analysis of the Will. In particular, Nietzsche criticises the view that the Will is something simple and intuitively known, establishing as his target Schopenhauer's view that we have unmediated intuitive knowledge of the Will. Schopenhauer argues that the Will is immediately known as 'the inner nature of the world':

> the concept of *will* is of all possible concepts the only one that has its origin *not* in the phenomenon, *not* in the mere representation of perception, but which comes from within, and proceeds from the most immediate consciousness of everyone. In this consciousness each one knows and at the same time is himself his own individuality according to its nature immediately, without any form, even the form of subject and object, for here knower and known coincide.[14]

The Will, for Schopenhauer, is the knowable thing-in-itself that is made manifest in various phenomenal instantiations that are, in his view, 'quite different' from the nature of the Will.[15] Access to the Will within Schopenhauer's philosophy, according to Nietzsche, relies on the possibility of extra-perspectival knowledge. Writing that Schopenhauer 'has eliminated the character of the will by subtracting from it its content, its "whither"', rendering the Will 'a mere empty word', Nietzsche argues, in contrast, that the Will is defined and justified contextually.[16] Although contextualism appeals to default beliefs that frame the comprehensible parameters of an inquiry, these beliefs do not provide an intrinsically credible atomistic base for our knowledge. Rather, default beliefs are themselves supported holistically in terms of their relations to other beliefs within the particular context that gives them meaning. Outside of this context they are not basic in any sense at all.[17] Consequently, to say that the will to power is justified contextually is to say that it is given content only in a particular context and that it is defined by its context. As such, it is not something immediately known independently of the form in which it appears. According to Nietzsche, power does not constitute one thing, but varies according to context just as what constitutes playing an instrument well depends on the instrument. I might say, for example, that I play the guitar well if I know the relevant chords and string configurations. In contrast, playing the flute well requires both breathing technique and knowledge of keys rather than strings. Similarly, I might say that in some contexts an individual is powerful who can actively influence the opinion of others through argumentative persuasion whilst in another context physical strength might best characterise power.[18]

By emphasising the contextual character of the will to power Nietzsche rejects the extra-perspectival implications of Schopenhauer's appeal to the Will. Despite his rejection of extra-perspectival knowledge, however, Nietzsche upholds his thesis regarding the causality of the Will. Both Nietzsche's rejection of the extra-perspectival conception of the Will as something immediately known and acceptance of the causality of the Will can be seen from *BGE*, 19. Here he is at pains to demonstrate that the Will is not a simple unity but rather a complicated phenomenon that is a unity 'only as a word'.[19] Nietzsche upholds the causal efficacy of the Will as a complex process involving both the affect of commanding and the affect of obeying. The causal efficacy of the Will entails, Nietzsche argues, a hierarchical relationship between commanding and obeying wills. In so explaining the phenomenon of willing, Nietzsche actually restates the thesis outlined in *BGE*, 36 that causality entails the activity of wills.

Whilst Clark concedes that Nietzsche allows we have some idea of causal efficacy, she denies he models it on the interpretation of causality we derive from the experience of willing, claiming Nietzsche nowhere accepts the causality of the Will on which his argument in *BGE*, 36 relies.[20] Although Clark is correct to stress Nietzsche's rejection of the transparent immediacy of introspection as a basis for knowledge, her claim that Nietzsche rejects the causality of the Will is nonetheless shortsighted.[21] The causality of the Will to which Nietzsche subscribes in *BGE*, 36 is not the same as that which he criticises, for example, in *Twilight of the Idols*. In the latter book Nietzsche denies that we can take the notion of willing, understood as entailing unity, freedom and introspective transparency, as our guide for understanding either ourselves or the world. The causality of the Will to which Nietzsche appeals in *BGE*, 36 entails none of these things. Rather, in *BGE* the causality of the Will entails hierarchical and complex relations between the individual wills that make up the self as they organise themselves to pursue collectively an agenda that is essential to their natures.[22] Here causality of the Will entails an acceptance of necessity, non-transparency and multiplicity rather than the freedom, simplicity and unity that he rejects in *Twilight of the Idols*. Moreover, contrary to Clark, the causality of the Will that Nietzsche accepts in *BGE*, 36 is not of the primitive type that he criticises in *The Gay Science* and that construes causality in terms of 'a personal willing being'.[23] Nor is it an instance of the 'primeval mythology' endorsed by Schopenhauer. According to Nietzsche, Schopenhauer 'never even attempted an analysis of the will because, like everybody else, he had *faith* in the simplicity and immediacy of all willing'. Nietzsche maintains, in contrast, that willing requires a more refined explanation, writing that 'willing is actually a mechanism that is so well practiced that it all but escapes the observing eye'.[24] Although Nietzsche does not attribute the Will to nature in this passage, it nonetheless indicates that he rejects not the causality of the Will *per se*, but only a simplified account of what willing properly entails. Consequently, Clark's claim that Nietzsche undermines the metaphysical doctrine of the will to power in the published writings other than *BGE* is mistaken. Nietzsche thinks, contrary to Clark's view, that he can uphold the causal efficacy of the Will as the initial premise in his development of the will to power thesis in *BGE*, 36 whilst still rejecting the extra-perspectival implications of Schopenhauer's appeal to the Will. As a result we cannot as readily dismiss the doctrine of the will to power, as Clark suggests, as merely an expression of Nietzsche's own values.

However, Nietzsche must also demonstrate that he is justified in putting forward a true metaphysical thesis from within the parameters of his perspectival theory of knowledge. This entails showing that our perspectival truths are not confined to particular contexts but that we can legitimately adopt an overarching comprehensive perspective that adequately captures the nature of reality. Nietzsche must hold, therefore, that there is one world to which our epistemic claims are more or less adequate and that the will to power thesis is a comprehensive perspective that captures the nature of this reality. However, the *philosophical argument* against its justification claims that if Nietzsche intends the will to power to be a true doctrine about the nature of reality, then he is appealing to extra-contextual and therefore extra-perspectival knowledge. The objection holds that we can appeal to the realist idea of one world to which our epistemic claims are more or less adequate only if we allow for the possibility of knowledge outside all contexts. Such extra-contextual knowledge entails privileged insight into the nature of reality. Since Nietzsche's perspectivism is designed to disallow extra-contextual and direct insight, the argument goes, it is incompatible with the will to power thesis. Implicit in this objection is the idea that only an extra-perspectival view facilitates the making of objective or adequate metaphysical claims about the nature of reality. The objection maintains that if Nietzsche seriously wants to put forward the will to power as a metaphysical thesis, then he must prioritise the metaphysics of the will to power over his perspectival epistemology because we simply cannot get from the latter to the former.[25]

That Nietzsche does not prioritise in this way can be discerned from his introduction of the will to power in *BGE*, 36 as an experiment in philosophical method. The experiment centres on the question of whether we can posit the will to power as a fundamental explanatory principle. Making a plea for the principle of explanatory economy he writes:

> Assuming, finally, that we could *explain* [my emphasis] our entire instinctual life as the development and differentiation of *one* basic form of the will (namely the will to power, as *my* tenet would have it); assuming that one could derive all organic functions from this will to power and also find in it the solution to the problem of procreation and alimentation (it is all one problem), then we would have won the right to designate *all* effective energy unequivocally as: the *will to power*.[26]

BGE, 36 thus articulates both an epistemological and a metaphysical thesis. That is, this passage is concerned to articulate both a theory of knowledge and a metaphysical doctrine of forces. However, Nietzsche gives priority to the epistemic thesis, writing in a different text that the 'most valuable insights are arrived at last; but the most valuable insights are *methods*'.[27] We can appreciate what is entailed by Nietzsche's appeal to the importance of method and explanatory economy by considering his notion of philology as the 'art of reading well', which also expresses his concern with method. The art of reading well, according to Nietzsche, contains 'the prerequisite for a cultural tradition, for a uniform science'.[28] He indicates that what he elsewhere calls a 'regulatory total picture of things', such as the one set out in the will to power thesis, can be deemed justified if it has explanatory power across both the physical and the anthropological sciences such that we incorporate both the 'outside' view of the former and the 'inside' view of the latter.[29] In *Human, All Too Human* he writes: 'Historical philosophy . . . can no longer be separated from natural science, the youngest of all philosophical methods . . .'.[30] Nietzsche's appeal to the uniformity of our knowledge and explanatory economy is thus to the possibility of comprehensive perspectives on things. (A comprehensive perspective is one that has explanatory scope across multiple perspectives.) Consequently, Nietzsche's intention to curb any pretensions to extra-perspectival conceptions of justification and truth whilst still making legitimate metaphysical claims about the nature of reality can be discerned from his view that the will to power thesis is true within human perspectives rather than outside all human perspectives.[31] In this way, Nietzsche avoids appealing to extra-perspectival self-justifying beliefs which in turn justify the rest of our beliefs, arguing that it is only in their 'connection' [*Zusammenhange*] and 'relation' [*Beziehung*] that our judgements can be deemed epistemically secure.[32] He writes: 'the conclusions of science acquire a complete rigorousness and certainty in their coherence with one another [*in ihrem Zusammenhange mit einander*].'[33]

Nietzsche's justification of the will to power thesis emerges against his view that our truths must be warranted contextually. Although the will to power is not confined to one particular context, it is not extra-perspectival. This is because, for Nietzsche, the will to power is intra-contextually warranted. In other words, Nietzsche's will to power is contextual because it must be warranted in each particular context. It is intra-contextual because it is justified within a multiplicity of human perspectives. Accordingly, any metaphysical conclusions that Nietzsche reaches using this method of inquiry will be perspectivally justified. However, before we examine how Nietzsche illustrates this argument through his appropriation of the concept of force there are two possible objections to his contextualist thesis that must be addressed. The first objection argues that Nietzsche's claim to capture the nature of reality is not compatible with a justification 'from within'.[34] The second objection makes the same claim by denying the possibility of a one-world reading of Nietzsche. It does so by arguing that since truth is a contextual matter and so relative to a perspective or conceptual scheme, there are multiple possible worlds rather than one world to which our epistemic claims are adequate. According to this view, Nietzsche's perspectivist justification of the will to power, as an explanation that applies to multiple contexts, is not viable.[35]

The initial objection to Nietzsche's perspectivism claims that our perspectival knowledge fails to capture the world and thus a thesis that is justified intra-contextually cuts off justification from the world. The charge is that Nietzsche's perspectivism leads to sceptical idealism that can only be overturned by adopting a dogmatically realist position that appeals to direct extra-perspectival insight into reality. Neither of these positions serves Nietzsche's argument that his perspectivist epistemology is compatible with his will to power metaphysics. In response, Nietzsche can overcome the objection if it can be shown that the theory-independent notion of world that informs the oscillation between dogmatic realism and sceptical idealism is vacuous. The dogmatic realist makes theory-independent claims about how the world is in itself. As a result, the dogmatic realist makes extra-perspectival claims to knowledge. Nietzsche thinks he has shown that any appeal to knowledge that is supposed to be true outside all perspectives is unintelligible. Not only this, he maintains that such claims are epistemically impotent. Nietzsche argues that to attempt to get at the world from no point of view at all is simply to lose any contentful notion of world. Describing it as 'a thing with negative qualities' he contends there is nothing we could state about such a world 'except that it was a being-other, an inaccessible, incomprehensible being-other'.[36]

Nevertheless, the objection maintains that if one rejects the possibility of extra-perspectival knowledge, then one has no alternative but to embrace sceptical idealism whereby justification is cut off from the world. That this objection is incoherent, however, can be discerned from the fact that sceptical idealism also relies on the notion of a theory-independent world that Nietzsche rejects. The charge that our perspectival knowledge is cut off from the world entails a contentless view of the world as something divorced from all points of view. The sceptical idealist charge is thus committed to the intelligibility of an unknowable thing-in-itself, a notion Nietzsche has argued should be abandoned. Once it is abandoned the sceptical idealist objection falls away too. Freed from the shackles of this notion, Nietzsche can maintain that our perspectives always have the world in view to varying degrees. Writing that 'there would be no life at all if not on the basis of perspectivist assessments and appearances', Nietzsche denies that our knowledge is cut off from the world. He maintains that once we dissolve the distinction between 'appearances' on the one hand, and a theory-independent 'true' world on the other, it is 'enough to assume that there are degrees of apparency and, so to speak, lighter and darker shadows and hues of appearance'.[37] Rather than cutting us off from the world, to have a perspective is, for Nietzsche, already to capture the world. Michael Williams, although not commenting on Nietzsche, captures the general thrust of the objection and Nietzsche's response when he writes:

> One can become haunted by the picture of one's belief system incorporating all sorts of internal relations of justification while, as a whole, floating above the world with no point of contact. But this worry is incoherent, because the concept of 'the world' which is operative here is completely vacuous. As soon as we start thinking of that with which belief has to make contact as congeries of elementary particles, patterns of retinal irradiation, or relational arrays of sensuous colour-patches, we are operating within some particular theory of the way the world is, and the question of how belief relates to the world no longer seems puzzling. The question can exert its paralysing effect only as long as (and indeed because) the notion of 'the world' is allowed to remain as the notion of something completely unspecifiable.[38]

By adopting a theory-dependent conception of world Nietzsche can avoid the oscillation between dogmatic realism and sceptical idealism. He argues that a theory-internal view of justification and truth, far from being divorced from reality, always captures the nature of reality to a greater or lesser extent.

The second objection, however, argues that a theory-dependent conception of world leads to relativism. Christoph Cox, for example, maintains that, for Nietzsche, the concept world only has meaning under some description or other and that all perspectives are 'incongruent' in the strong sense of being 'incompatible' with one another.[39] As a result, according to Cox, Nietzsche holds that we most correctly speak of world in the plural rather than in the singular:

> This view proceeds from the naturalistic premise that we never encounter 'the world as it is in itself' but always 'the world as it appears under a particular description.' Because there is no comparing 'a description of the world' with 'the world as it is under no description at all,' this latter notion turns out, at best, to be superfluous. All we ever can do is compare descriptions with other descriptions. And because there is no One True World, there is no description that could show itself to be the One True Description by 'corresponding to' that World. Thus there will always be many descriptions and no single, independent world that they all describe. Each *description*, then, is actually a *prescription* that constructs a world, leaving us with no World but many worlds.[40]

According to Cox's Nietzsche 'there is no uniquely correct "way the world is" but rather as many "ways the world is" as there are warranted theories'.[41] As a result of his identification of 'interpretation' with 'the world' Cox maintains that the world, for Nietzsche, is metaphysically reducible to the multiplicity of interpretations. If Cox is correct in attributing to Nietzsche the view that we can only speak of the world in the plural rather than the singular, then we cannot appeal to the will to power as a thesis that captures the one true nature of reality.

However, Cox's objection can be overcome by appealing to two particular passages from Nietzsche's writings that suggest that he is concerned to maintain the very metaphysical independence that Cox denies. The first passage is from *BGE*, where Nietzsche insists on the metaphysical independence of the world from interpretations of it. Considering the physicist's notion of conformity to law as an example of bad interpretive practice, Nietzsche suggests that interpretations can be epistemically rated in terms of their adequacy to reality. Of the physicist's interpretation Nietzsche argues:

> it is not a factual matter, not a 'text', but rather no more than a naïve humanitarian concoction, a contortion of meaning that allows you to succeed in accommodating the democratic instincts of the modern soul! . . .

> But, as I say, this is interpretation, not text; and someone could come along with the opposite intention and interpretative skill who, looking at the *very same nature and referring to the very same phenomena*, [my emphasis] would read out of it the ruthlessly tyrannical and unrelenting assertion of power claims.[42]

Nietzsche's practice of referring to his own doctrine of the will to power as an interpretation whilst still presenting it as a true metaphysical thesis suggests that it is not a theory's status as an interpretation that Nietzsche is questioning here, but rather its epistemic merit as an adequate interpretation of reality. Although he welcomes the possibility that its credentials may also be subject to challenge, Nietzsche nonetheless thinks that the will to power can be awarded greater epistemic status than previous interpretations of reality due to what he considers to be the methodologically more scrupulous birth of his own doctrine. This is because, in Nietzsche's view, the will to power thesis is justified intra-contextually rather than dogmatically. His desire to retain the metaphysical independence of the world from its interpretations can be further witnessed in his account of philology as the art of reading well in *The Anti-Christ*:

> Philology is to be understood here in a very wide sense as the art of reading well – of being able to read off a text *without* falsifying it by interpretation, *without* losing caution, patience, subtlety in the desire for understanding. Philology as *ephexis* [indecisiveness] in interpretation.[43]

Here Nietzsche appeals to the philological virtues of truth and honesty, comparing reality to a text, which he urges us to read well. Similarly, in *Human, All Too Human* Nietzsche argues, by applying philological standards of interpreting books to the interpretation of nature, that nature is irreducible to and consequently metaphysically independent of its many erroneous interpretations:

> It requires a great deal of understanding to apply to nature the same kind of rigorous art of elucidation that philologists have now fashioned for all books: with the intention of comprehending *what the text intends to say* [my emphasis] but without sensing, indeed presupposing a *second* meaning. But as even with regard to books the bad art of elucidation has by no means been entirely overcome and one still continually encounters in the best educated circles remnants of allegorical and mystical interpretations: so it is in respect to nature – where, indeed, it is even far worse.[44]

Cox's argument that our perspectives are fundamentally incompatible can also be overcome by re-examining the passage to which Cox appeals in support of this claim. In this passage Nietzsche argues that our many perspectives are 'incongruent'.[45] Cox interprets this as a strong claim arguing for the incompatibility of perspectives. However, it is possible to interpret Nietzsche as making an alternative point, which claims the multiplicity of perspectives are non-reducible to each other. The non-reducibility of perspectives, moreover, does not entail their essential incompatibility, it merely stipulates that truth is a contextual issue. The will to power thesis as an objective truth, true within perspectives, does not violate this clause because as an intra-contextual truth it respects the priority of context. Emerging as a comprehensive perspective, the will to power is justified in the context of both the anthropological and the physical sciences. The will to power as an intra-contextual truth does not stand over and above the various sciences moulding their data to the thesis. Rather, the metaphysical thesis of the will to power emerges from within a reflection on these data and how they hang together as a methodological unity. Consequently, Nietzsche's appeal to comprehensive perspectives that are intra-contextually justified is demanded by his doctrine of economy of principles. This demand requires that although there are many perspectives or contexts in which our truths are justified, these perspectives are of one world and can be unified by an overall perspective that has comprehensive explanatory scope. Nietzsche indicates that the will to power satisfies what is required of a comprehensive perspective when he writes that 'all effective energy' in the physical world can be described as will to power. In addition to having explanatory power in the physical sciences, Nietzsche claims in BGE that the explanatory scope of the thesis extends to psychology where it succeeds in offering an alternative to the mechanical account of the self.[46] Nietzsche's appeal to a single principle captures his aim to unite under one comprehensive explanation both the perspectives of the anthropological and the physical sciences. He thinks this can be achieved through recourse to a qualitative conception of the world that captures our 'subjective' experience of reality but which also offers a better explanation of the physical world than that offered by rival theories, particularly that of mechanical science. Nietzsche contends that the will to power satisfies these requirements by both appropriating and supplementing the concept of force as it is expounded in Boscovich's physics. Boscovich's concept of force, according to Nietzsche, points the way to overcoming the quantitative view of mechanical science whilst incorporating the qualitative view of anthropological science, without relinquishing objectivity and collapsing into the subjectivism of mind-dependent idealism. The concept of force allows us, Nietzsche claims, to provide 'a *sufficient* explanation for the so-called mechanistic (or "material") world' without reducing that world to a '"representation" (in the Berkeleian or Schopenhauerian sense)'.[47] To see how Nietzsche arrives at the actual content of the will to power and how it constitutes for him a comprehensive explanatory perspective we must now turn to a more detailed examination of his appropriation of the concept of force.

NIETZSCHE'S APPROPRIATION OF THE CONCEPT OF FORCE

Nietzsche's appropriation of the concept of force paves the way for his development of a uniform science or comprehensive perspective on things. He demonstrates the need for the concept of force by outlining the philosophical problematic of materialist atomism and empirical idealism. These two philosophical modes of thought, Nietzsche argues, emphasise either the physical or the anthropological sciences. As such, they represent the danger and limitations of one-sided perspectives. By presenting such a perspective as an extra-perspectival standard of knowledge, both materialist atomism and empirical idealism, according to Nietzsche, offer only oppositional modes of explanation. He contends that although the concept of force as it is available to us in physics does not complete the project, it does take an important step in the direction of making possible a comprehensive perspective that has explanatory power across both the physical and the anthropological sciences. This step overcomes oscillation between dogmatic realism and idealism by putting forward a thesis in favour of the possibility of a metaphysics that is relational but objective. In so doing, Nietzsche argues that the concept of force captures the qualitative perspective of empirical idealism without relinquishing the need for the 'objective' viewpoint of materialism. However, Nietzsche contends that recognition of the ultimate deficiencies of the concept of force in addition to its positive implications provides us with the key to establishing the will to power as a unifying comprehensive perspective. The test of its comprehensive status will be its ability to offer better explanations in both the physical and the anthropological sciences than its competitors. Putting forward the will to power as a better explanation than materialist atomism in addition to offering a non-atomistic account of the self, Nietzsche argues that the will to power passes the test.

In *BGE*, 12 and the passages surrounding it Nietzsche makes it clear that he introduces the concept of force in order to overcome what he terms 'sensualism' in philosophy.[48] This takes two forms and Nietzsche's disagreement with both centres on the issue of the primary/secondary quality distinction. According to Nietzsche, an overemphasis on either primary or secondary qualities renders void any attempt to proffer a comprehensive explanation of the nature of things by stressing either the physical or anthropological sciences to the detriment of the other.

The first form of sensualism is manifest, according to Nietzsche, in materialistic atomism, which promotes belief in 'substance', 'matter' and particle-atoms.[49] This is the Lockean view that the world in itself is to be understood as a quantitative realm of primary qualities, depriving secondary qualities of any extra-mental existence. Nietzsche brands this model sensualism despite the fact that it distinguishes between the common-sense view which, for example, regards objects as intrinsically colourful, and the scientific view that considers colour to be the result of 'powers' in the object to produce the sensation of colour in observers. This is because materialism, as Nietzsche understands it, attempts to 'explain' our qualitative experience of the world by appealing to the quantitative view of atomistic physics. The quantitative perspective of atomistic physics is, according to Nietzsche, incorrectly taken as the standard of 'objectivity'. The realm of primary qualities is thus said to represent the way things are in themselves. Nietzsche states that 'The reduction of all qualities to quantities is nonsense'.[50] Apart from its materialist claims, then, materialistic atomism, according to Nietzsche, puts forward one true description of the world. The difficulty here, for him, is that this one true description is adopted as an extra-perspectival thesis. It is founded on the idea, contrary to Nietzsche's own, that metaphysics precedes epistemology. This is the belief that justification proceeds 'from outside'. That is, how things are, independently of our perspectival take on the world, is said to act as the ultimate court of appeal in the justification of our epistemic claims. Responding to such a view Nietzsche juxtaposes the terms 'inventing' and 'finding'.[51] In opposition to materialistic atomism, Nietzsche maintains that 'inventing' precedes 'finding'. In so doing, he suggests that justification should proceed from 'within' rather than from 'without' and thus should be an intra-perspectival affair. Consequently, in *BGE*, 20 he rejects Locke's account of the origin of our ideas as superficial.

The second form of sensualism that Nietzsche rejects is empirical idealism, because its project of reducing the world to the mental is, in his view, untenable. In the following passage Nietzsche argues that empirical idealism, the view that reality is reducible to our representations, succumbs to insurmountable difficulties. Idealism must either assume that there is an immaterial mental substance in which the empirical world, including the brain and sense organs, inheres as ideas, or else it must collapse into a *reductio ad absurdum*, holding that the brain, as part of the natural world, is also its cause:

> In order to practise physiology with a good conscience, you have to believe that the sense organs are *not* phenomena in the philosophical idealist sense, for then they could not be causes! This is sensualism as a regulative hypothesis at least, if not as an heuristic principle.
>
> What's that? And other people are actually saying that the external world is created by our sense organs? But then our body, as part of this external world, would be the creation of our sense organs! But then our very sense organs would be – the creation of our sense organs! It seems to me that this is a complete *reductio ad absurdum*: assuming that the concept *causa sui* is something completely absurd. It follows that the outer world is *not* the creation of our sense organs –?[52]

Thus, according to Nietzsche, if idealism is to avoid collapsing into absurdity, it must take the form Berkeley attributes to it. Through the voice of Philonous and in response to Hylas' materialist suggestion that the perception of ideas can be explained in terms of 'various impressions or traces . . . made in the brain', Berkeley writes:

> The brain . . . you speak of, being a sensible thing, exists only in the mind. Now, I would like to know whether you think it reasonable to suppose, that one idea or thing existing in the mind, occasions all other ideas. And if you think so, then how do you account for the origin of that primary idea or brain itself?[53]

According to Berkeley, the materialist holds that primary qualities exist in external objects and cause sensations in observers via neurophysiological processes. These sensations are subject-dependent and do not accurately represent a likeness of the external object, as can be discerned by the relativity of these sensations whereby, for example, water may feel hot to one hand and cold to another. Sensations, according to the materialist, are mind-dependent, whilst the objects that cause them are mind-independent. However, Berkeley argues that the relativity of perception argument also applies to primary qualities such that the supposedly mind-independent properties of extension and so on are in fact mind-dependent data. He argues that the relativity of perception, in addition to the fact that we cannot conceive material bodies that are, for example, extended but colourless, indicates that objects are not mind-independent but rather a collection of mental ideas. Therefore, Berkeley maintains that our neurophysiology cannot play a causal role in the production of ideas as our neurophysiological structures like all external objects are constituted by bundles of ideas.[54] Although Berkeley's idealism does not succumb to a *reductio ad absurdum*, it is nonetheless problematic for Nietzsche. The difficulty here, Nietzsche argues, is that Berkeley's empirical idealism goes to extreme lengths, reducing the natural world to mental ideas, in order to secure 'common sense'. These efforts are misguided, according to Nietzsche, because taking how we ordinarily perceive the world at face value, Berkeley reduces reality to a subjective immaterialist standard, thus failing to 'practise physiology with a good conscience'.[55]

According to Nietzsche, the one-sidedness of both materialism and idealism, operating within the confines of the primary/secondary quality distinction, is articulated in their shared view that there is an opposition to be drawn between those properties objects have intrinsically and 'in themselves' and those that are projected by us. The empirical subjective idealist maintains there are only minds and sense-data and that 'red', for example, is an intrinsic property whilst 'persistence' is a mere 'projection'. Berkeley's reduction of primary qualities to the status of secondary qualities, although intended to overcome the distinction between appearance and reality, results in a bundle theory of objects that perpetuates the distinction between intrinsic and projected properties. According to his bundle theory, objects are reducible to collections of ideas or mental representations. The idea of a persisting object is, according to this view, a projection. Berkeley maintains that the continued existence of objects, when unperceived by a finite mind, is a divine volition or decree.[56] However, the materialist maintains, in contrast to the empirical idealist, that external objects have persistence as an intrinsic property, and that 'red' is something that we project. By emphasising one or other of the polarities in these related distinctions, both forms of sensualism – empirical idealism and materialism – promote opposing forms of extra-perspectival knowledge, both making the claim that there is one correct, unrevisable description of the world or one ultimate science. Both materialism and empirical idealism, in Nietzsche's view, are one-sided arguments that give priority to either physical science (the quantitative 'objective' view) or to anthropological science (the qualitative 'subjective' view). Both views, according to Nietzsche, are guilty of taking what is a one-sided perspective and treating it as an extra-perspectival standard of justification. In so doing, both operate within the framework that prioritises metaphysics over epistemology. They do this by conflating their limited perspective regarding the ultimate nature of things with how things are in themselves, whether the thing-in-itself is mental (as in empirical idealism) or extra-mental (as in materialism). Nietzsche's doctrine of the will to power avoids this fate because it attempts to 'unify' the various sciences rather than reduce all explanation to any one of them. Rather than adopt a limited perspective and conflate it with an extra-perspectival standard, Nietzsche attempts to adopt a more comprehensive perspectival approach. This involves consideration of the perspectives of both the anthropological and the physical sciences. The will to power, which is properly speaking intra-contextual rather than reductionist, is designed to find a middle ground between the polarities of materialism and idealism. Nietzsche argues that the overcoming of these two poles is best achieved through recourse to Boscovichean physics which, in his view, succeeds in partially paving the way for a more suitable explanation of the furniture of the world than that proffered by either materialistic atomism or empirical idealism. In *BGE* Nietzsche introduces Boscovich's theory of forces claiming that

> the Pole Boscovich . . . along with the Pole Copernicus achieved the greatest victory yet in opposing the appearance of things. For while Copernicus convinced us to believe contrary to all our senses that the earth does *not* stand still, Boscovich taught us to renounce the last thing that 'still stood' about the earth, the belief in 'substance,' in 'matter,' in the bit of earth, the particle, the atom: no one on earth has ever won greater triumph over the senses.[57]

Boscovich's dynamic conception of matter emerges in response to and as an attempt to resolve problems inherent in materialist atomism. However, although Nietzsche introduces Boscovich's physics in this passage as a rejection of materialist atomism, he also intends it to overcome empirical idealism. This is because Boscovich's claim that matter can be explained in terms of centres of force undercuts the distinction between primary and secondary qualities that informs the debate between materialist atomism and empirical idealism. It does this in response to a difficulty inherent in the atomist's account of interaction.

According to the materialist atomism of the Corpuscularian theory, every physical interaction must be analysable into transfers of motion between interacting corpuscles. Atoms, according to this view, are irreducible and as such are said to characterise what is most fundamental. A problem arises, however, when we consider what happens when these fundamental atoms transfer motion by contact. This is because the mechanist's notion of causality through impact entails that bodies undergo a discontinuous change in velocity. Harré and Madden articulate this problematic in the following way:

> Being atomic they must be rigid, since the theory requires that compressibility is always explained as the possibility of the occupation of a smaller volume by a set of rigid corpuscles originally spread through a certain larger volume. But in the interaction by contact of truly rigid bodies their centres of gravity must instantaneously acquire new velocities by a finite increment, thus changing their speed discontinuously.[58]

Such an instantaneous change of velocity violates the empirically supported law of continuity 'which denies the passage from one magnitude to another without passing through intermediate stages'.[59] However, Boscovich maintained that this difficulty could be overcome by understanding bodies not in terms of extended atoms but in terms of points of force. Introducing the notion of a repulsive force that acts at small distances between bodies and which transforms into an attractive force at greater distances, he argues that there is a continuous change in velocity according to the distance between two bodies. As the degree of repulsive force increases indeterminately as the distance between them decreases the two bodies never come into contact. Boscovich's view that particles relate to one another dynamically through the forces of attraction and repulsion eliminates from physics the mechanical view of causality through impact. Bodies relate to one another, not through contact, but according to action at a distance. Furthermore, taking points of force to be the ultimate constituents of matter Boscovich rejects both the materialist emphasis on primary qualities and the empirical idealist reliance on secondary qualities. He does so by replacing both the notions of a quality-less substratum (Lockean materialism) and substance-less qualities (Berkeleian idealism) with a dynamic conception of matter, which does away with the distinction between substances and attributes.[60] In their stead Boscovich draws our attention to tertiary qualities, which are relational, dispositional and objective properties.

Locke had distinguished between primary, secondary and tertiary qualities. Primary qualities are said to be 'intrinsic' properties of a thing; they are non-relational, non-dispositional and non-subjective. Primary qualities, then, according to this view, constitute the way things are in themselves. Both secondary and tertiary qualities, however, are powers in the object to produce certain types of effect. To the extent they are understood as powers, secondary and tertiary qualities are both relational and dispositional properties. However, whereas secondary qualities are deemed to be subjective and perceiver-dependent because they produce effects on human perceivers, tertiary qualities are said to be objective because they produce effects on things other than human sensibility. For example, both 'yellow' and 'soluble' are relational properties. However, 'yellow' implies a certain relation to a human perceiver whilst 'soluble' implies a certain relation to aqua regia.[61] Despite Locke's claim that relational properties or powers are less fundamental than primary qualities, Nietzsche argues that tertiary properties are of principal importance because they allow for relations between things in the world without construing such relations as mind-dependent.[62] By emphasising the role of tertiary qualities, he thinks Boscovich overcomes both the Lockean emphasis on non-relational intrinsic properties as the standard of objectivity (physical science), and the idealist reduction of reality to subjective relational secondary properties (anthropological science).[63] Boscovich's theory of forces thus provides an essential component to the context in which Nietzsche develops his dynamist theory.

Despite his praise for Boscovich, however, Nietzsche parts company with him on the issue of the ultimate status of force. Nietzsche charges that the physicist is more concerned with balancing mathematical equations than with capturing the nature and thus causal efficacy of force.[64] As a result, the physicist, according to Nietzsche, is guilty of reducing the status of force to that of an unfamiliar and inexplicable occult quality. He contends that although science aims to explain things in terms recognisable by us it in fact achieves the opposite to this end, rendering the world opaque and unfamiliar.[65] Nietzsche thinks that if we are to capture the nature of force rather than reduce it to something mysterious, we need to attribute to it an inner character. We can do this, according to Nietzsche, by ascribing an 'inner will' to force analogously to our own experience of willing.

> The victorious concept 'force', by means of which our physicists have created God and the world, still needs to be completed: an inner will must be ascribed to it, which I designate as 'will to power', i.e., as an insatiable desire to manifest power; or as the employment and exercise of power, as a creative drive.[66]

Although we shall address the complexity of Nietzsche's argument that force must be attributed with an inner nature in the next two chapters, suffice it for present purposes to say that his ascription of an inner will to force provides the necessary key for him to offer a comprehensive perspective on things that has explanatory power across both the physical and the anthropological sciences. If Nietzsche can show that the ascription of an inner will to force has explanatory power in the anthropological sciences as well as in the physical sciences, then he will, according to his own criteria, have established the 'objectivity' or justifiability of the will to power thesis.

Having already shown how the will to power has explanatory scope in the physical sciences by providing the missing ingredient of causal efficacy to the physicist account of force, Nietzsche indicates that the will to power has explanatory scope in the anthropological sciences by developing a non-atomistic conception of the self. Thus the general task set in the following passage is to extend the rejection of atomism in physics to the atomistic conception of the soul:

> However, we must go even further and declare war, a merciless war unto the death against the 'atomistic need' that continues to live a dangerous afterlife in places where no one suspects it (as does the more famous 'metaphysical need'). The first step must be to kill off that other and more ominous atomism that Christianity taught best and longest: *the atomism of the soul*.[67]

According to Nietzsche, the self is not a self-identical substance in the traditional sense but rather an organisation of competing drives motivated by the desire for power. He conceives the self as a social structure of drives, each of which has its own agenda that it wishes to pursue and implement. He argues that the success of the drives in achieving their specific agenda depends on its relations with the other drives that compose the self. In order to attain their individual goals, each drive must enter into negotiations and agreements with the others. In *BGE* Nietzsche illustrates the complex unity that is the self by appealing to the phenomenon of willing. Willing, according to Nietzsche, is a complex process involving sensation, thought and affect. The experience of willing involves, in his view, both the affect of commanding and the affect of obeying.

> A person who *wills*: this person is commanding a Something in himself that obeys, or that he thinks is obeying.
> But let us now consider the strangest thing about the will, about this multifarious thing that the common people call by one word alone. In any given case we both command *and* obey, and when we obey we know the feelings of coercion, pressure, oppression, resistance, and agitation that begin immediately after the act of will.[68]

Understanding the self as a hierarchical organisation of drives, Nietzsche argues, is a better account of the self than its competitors because it explains, in a way that mechanism cannot, why we experience our wills as free.[69] The feeling of free will ensues, he contends, from the conflation of the affect of commanding with the affect of obeying. The identification of both feelings leads us to identify the power that carries out the task with the power that orders its implementation. Nietzsche states:

> 'Freedom of the will' – that is the word for that complex pleasurable condition experienced by the person willing who commands and simultaneously identifies himself with the one who executes the command – as such he can share in enjoying the triumph over resistance, while secretly judging that it was actually his will that overcame that resistance.[70]

According to Nietzsche, this psychological model of the will to power bears a significant resemblance to his will to power physics.[71] The similarity resides in Nietzsche's hypothesis that both the world and the self can best be explained as a struggle between power-seeking forces and drives. According to Nietzsche, each quantum of force in the physical world desires to manifest its nature and overcome resistances by other forces that are similarly motivated. Likewise, in Nietzsche's social account of the self, individual drives strive to implement their respective ends, overcoming resistances from competing drives to do the same. As a result of this similarity, Nietzsche takes it that he has successfully demonstrated the status of his will to power thesis as a comprehensive perspective that explanatorily unifies the anthropological and the physical sciences and that offers better explanations than its competitors in both domains. Nietzsche thinks that his metaphysics, which derives from but is not constituted by his commitment to a perspectival epistemology, is justified within its parameters. As the most comprehensive perspective on things, the will to power, Nietzsche suggests, works in tandem with his perspectivism.

Having now established the manner of its justification we must move on to examine the full metaphysical repercussions of Nietzsche's will to power thesis. In the next chapter we shall see how Nietzsche's supplementation of force with an inner will emerges from his taking up a project initiated by the early Kant but abandoned by him in his later separation of appearances from how things are in themselves. The project is that of demonstrating both the possibility and necessity of a metaphysics that holds that the fundamental constituents of reality are intrinsic and relational.

NOTES

1. Friedrich Nietzsche, *The Will to Power*, edited by R. J. Hollingdale, translated by Walter Kaufmann (New York: Vintage Books, 1968 [1901]), 1067. Henceforth cited as *WP*.
2. Some commentators argue that Nietzsche's perspectivism does not entitle him to make metaphysical claims such as those made in the will to power thesis. Such commentators include Maudemarie Clark, *Nietzsche on Truth and Philosophy* (Cambridge: Cambridge University Press, 1990) and Arthur Danto, *Nietzsche as Philosopher* (New York: Macmillan, 1965). Equally, there is a camp within Nietzsche studies that strives to emphasise the importance of his metaphysics. The most notable of such commentators is Martin Heidegger, *Nietzsche*, translated by David Farrell Krell (San Francisco: HarperCollins, 1991 [1961]). Another writer who takes Nietzsche's will to power seriously but denies that it is a traditional metaphysics designed to capture the 'essence' of reality in favour of the view that it is a pluralist and empirical ontology of force is Gilles

Deleuze, *Nietzsche and Philosophy*, translated by Hugh Tomlinson (London: Athlone Press, 1992 [1962]). See also the 'New Nietzsche' strand of Nietzsche scholarship, David B. Allison (ed.), *The New Nietzsche: Contemporary Styles of Interpretation* (London: MIT Press, 1994).

3. Although we shall not consider it here, we shall see in subsequent chapters that Nietzsche thinks force operates in the empirical world that is available to our knowledge and not in a non-empirical domain such as the Kantian thing-in-itself.

4. Walter Kaufmann argues that the will to power is compatible with Nietzsche's perspectivism by reducing the status of the will to power to that of an empirical theory in psychology, which he maintains is compatible with perspectivism in a similar manner to other empirical theories (Walter Kaufmann, *Nietzsche: Philosopher, Psychologist, Antichrist* [Princeton, NJ: Princeton University Press, 1974], p. 206). For an exception to attempts to dilute the metaphysical import of the will to power whilst still maintaining its compatibility with perspectivism, see R. Lanier Anderson, 'Nietzsche's Will to Power as a Doctrine of the Unity of Science', *Studies in History and Philosophy of Science*, Vol. 25, No. 5, 1994, pp. 729–50. See also Hales' and Welshon's argument that Nietzsche's critique of the appearance/thing-in-itself distinction requires a perspectival ontology. Steven D. Hales and Rex Welshon, *Nietzsche's Perspectivism* (Urbana and Chicago, IL: University of Illinois Press, 2000), pp. 76ff. R. Kevin Hill, *Nietzsche: A Guide for the Perplexed* (London: Continuum, 2007), pp. 105–6 argues similarly.

5. The arguments presented here are particularly indebted to both Anderson, 'Nietzsche's Will to Power as a Doctrine of the Unity of Science' and Hales and Welshon, *Nietzsche's Perspectivism*.

6. For his rejection of the metaphysics of opposites, see Friedrich Nietzsche, *Human, All Too Human*, translated by R. J. Hollingdale (Cambridge: Cambridge University Press, 1996 [1878–86]), Volume I, 'Of First and Last Things', 1. Henceforth cited as *HAH*. See also Friedrich Nietzsche, *Beyond Good and Evil*, translated by Marion Faber (Oxford: Oxford University Press, 1998 [1886]), 2. Henceforth cited as *BGE*.

    I use the term 'science' to capture Nietzsche's view of a cognitive perspective. Cognitive perspectives for Nietzsche are ones that are epistemically responsible, adhering to strict methodological constraints. Scientific perspectives are thus to be distinguished from non-cognitive perspectives such as the religious point of view, which, according to Nietzsche, shows less concern for such constraints. See Friedrich Nietzsche, *The Gay Science*, translated by Walter Kaufmann (New York: Vintage Books, 1974 [1882/1887]), 295–7, 319. Henceforth cited as *GS*. See also Friedrich Nietzsche, *The Anti-Christ*, included in *Twilight of the Idols/The Anti-Christ*, translated by R. J. Hollingdale (London: Penguin, 1990 [1895]), 59. Henceforth cited as *AC*.

    Arguing that scientific investigation in all its forms is a human perspective and not a presuppositionless model of inquiry (Friedrich Nietzsche, *On the Genealogy of Morality*, translated by Maudemarie Clark and Alan J. Swensen (Indianapolis, IN: Hackett, 1998 [1887]), III, 24. Henceforth cited as *GM*), Nietzsche denies that the perspective of either physical science or anthropological science is superior to the other. The aim of incorporating both is to show that the traditional opposition is one-sided and can be replaced fruitfully with a comprehensive perspective that overcomes the opposition. See also Nietzsche, *GM*, III, 25, where he describes 'science' in a broad way, including under this description both the 'natural' and the 'unnatural' sciences.

7. Clark, *Nietzsche on Truth and Philosophy*, p. 227.

8. Nietzsche, *BGE*, 36.

9. Clark, *Nietzsche on Truth and Philosophy*, pp. 213–14.

10. Clark argues that the hypothetical form of its presentation in *BGE*, 36 suggests Nietzsche does not intend the will to power to be taken as a true metaphysical doctrine. However, contrary to Clark, Nietzsche's hypothetical presentation merely suggests its regulative status, which does not prohibit the possibility of its being true. (See Chapters 1 above and 5 below for arguments in favour of this view.) For further commentators who interpret Nietzsche's will to power as merely hypothetical, see George J. Stack, *Lange and Nietzsche* (New York: de Gruyter, 1983); Claudia Crawford, *Nietzsche's Theory of Language* (New York: de Gruyter, 1988). The latter two interpretations, examining the will to power in the context of Lange's influence on Nietzsche, interpret Nietzsche's hypothetical proposals as emerging from a commitment to sceptical idealism.

11. Nietzsche, *GS*, 127.

12. Nietzsche, *BGE*, 19.

13. For a similar argument, see Peter Poellner, 'Causation and Force in Nietzsche', in B. Babich (ed.), *Nietzsche, Epistemology, and Philosophy of Science: Nietzsche and the Sciences II* (Dordrecht: Kluwer Academic Publishers, 1999), p. 291.

14. Arthur Schopenhauer, *The World as Will and Representation*, Volume I, translated by E. F. J. Payne (New York: Dover, 1969 [1819]), p. 112. Henceforth cited as *WWR*, I.

15. Ibid., p. 112. For Schopenhauer's claim that we have unmediated acquaintance with the Will, see also p. 505.

16. Nietzsche, *WP*, 692.

17. For example, any inquiry into the nature of the external world must presuppose that the external world exists. This presupposition, however, is not an intrinsically credible foundationalist/extra-perspectival belief but rather is meaningful only within specific practices of inquiry requiring particular types of evidence, and so on. As Michael Williams argues, contextualism accepts a locally holistic conception of justification, rejecting both the atomism of foundationalism and the radical holism of coherentism. He thus writes of the default beliefs that frame the contexts of inquiry that

> These bedrock certainties derive their content – their meaning – from the particular practices of inquiry and justification that hold them in place. To believe in an historical past, or an external world, just is to recognize certain types of error possibility, to demand certain kinds of evidence (in appropriate circumstances), and so on. Because such certainties are *semantically embedded* in our epistemic practices – thus unintelligible apart from them – it is a mistake to see those practices as justificationally dependent on the 'presuppositions' they embed. They are not assumptions because they are not, in the relevant sense, foundational at all. (Michael Williams, *Problems of Knowledge* [Oxford: Oxford University Press, 2001], pp. 165–6)

18. Richard Schacht, *Nietzsche* (London: Routledge & Kegan Paul, 1983), p. 222 argues similarly.

19. Nietzsche, *BGE*, 19.

20. Clark, *Nietzsche on Truth and Philosophy*, p. 217.

21. For Nietzsche on introspection, see Friedrich Nietzsche, *Twilight of the Idols* included in *Twilight of the Idols/The Anti-Christ*, translated by R. J. Hollingdale (London: Penguin, 1990 [1889]), 'The Four Great Errors', 3. Henceforth cited as *TI*.

22. Nietzsche, *BGE*, 19. See also Nietzsche, *WP*, 636.

23. Nietzsche, *GS*, 127.

24. Ibid., 127.

25. See Clark, *Nietzsche on Truth and Philosophy*, p. 214. Clark argues Nietzsche

can accept the will to power as a metaphysical thesis only if he accepts the possibility of extra-perspectival knowledge. See also Danto, *Nietzsche as Philosopher*, chapter 3. Mark T. Conard, 'Nietzsche's Kantianism', *International Studies in Philosophy*, Vol. 33, No. 3, 2001, and Peter Poellner, 'Perspectival Truth', in John Richardson and Brian Leiter (eds), *Nietzsche* (Oxford: Oxford University Press, 2001) also discuss the relation between Nietzsche's perspectivism and metaphysics, arguing that the former derives from the latter. For a similar view, see John Richardson, *Nietzsche's System* (Oxford: Oxford University Press, 1996), p. 11.
26. Nietzsche, *BGE*, 36.
27. Nietzsche, *WP*, 469.
28. Nietzsche, *AC*, 59.
29. For an illustration of how Nietzsche incorporates both sciences, see *BGE*, 12. In an early essay, Nietzsche emphasises the need for a 'regulatory total picture' that sets up a 'picture of life as a whole' (Friedrich Nietzsche, 'Schopenhauer as Educator' [1874], 3, in *Untimely Meditations*, translated by R. J. Hollingdale [Cambridge: Cambridge University Press, 1994 [1873–6]]).
30. Nietzsche, *HAH*, Volume I, 'Of First and Last Things', 1.
31. See Hales and Welshon, *Nietzsche's Perspectivism*, p. 34 for a similar suggestion.
32. Nietzsche, *WP*, 530.
33. Nietzsche, *HAH*, Volume I, 'Of First and Last Things', 19.
34. See Danto, *Nietzsche as Philosopher*, pp. 76ff.
35. Christoph Cox, *Nietzsche: Naturalism and Interpretation* (London: University of California Press, 1999), p. 156.
36. Nietzsche, *HAH*, Volume I, 'Of First and Last Things', 9.
37. Nietzsche, *BGE*, 34.
38. Williams, *Groundless Belief*, p. 101.
39. Cox, *Nietzsche: Naturalism and Interpretation*, p. 156.
40. Ibid., p. 156.
41. Ibid., pp. 155–6.
42. Nietzsche, *BGE*, 22.
43. Nietzsche, *AC*, 52.
44. Nietzsche, *HAH*, Volume I, 'Of First and Last Things', 8. For a discussion of this issue, see Alan D. Schrift, *Nietzsche and the Question of Interpretation* (New York: Routledge, 1990), p. 165.
45. Nietzsche, *WP*, 568.
46. Nietzsche, *BGE*, 12. Nietzsche writes that the will to power has explanatory scope in physics, biology and psychology. The biology of the will to power, as Nietzsche sees it, holds contrary to Darwin's appeal to 'self-preservation' that an organism fundamentally strives to release force (Nietzsche, *BGE*, 13). However, since Nietzsche's naturalist account of the self construes the self as a bundle of drives and instincts, I will not treat Nietzsche's will to power thesis as biology separately from his account of the self and shall discuss only the latter, intending it also to reflect on the former. Moreover, Nietzsche's combination of the intentional character of drives with their physicality in both human and non-human organisms reflects his aim to overcome the opposition of materialism and idealism. For a discussion of these issues, see Richardson, *Nietzsche's System*, pp. 35–9 and Schacht, *Nietzsche*, pp. 234ff.
47. Nietzsche, *BGE*, 36. Nietzsche's argument is directed at both sceptical idealism and empirical subjective idealism. Sceptical idealism entails that the world as we experience it is reducible to human minds but that things-in-themselves are not so reducible. Empirical subjective idealism maintains all reality is

mind-dependent with no metaphysical remainder. Nietzsche denies that reality, either 'for us' or 'in itself', is mind-dependent, arguing that both views operate within a metaphysics of opposites, adopting the position that the 'world' is knowable only if it is mind-dependent.

48. In *BGE*, 15 Nietzsche employs the term 'sensualism' in connection with empirical idealism. That he also intends this term to be equated with materialistic atomism can be seen from his claim in *BGE*, 12 that Boscovich and Copernicus taught us to reject materialistic atomism 'contrary to all our senses'.

49. Nietzsche, *BGE*, 12.

50. Nietzsche, *WP*, 564.

51. Nietzsche, *BGE*, 12.

52. Ibid., 15.

53. George Berkeley, *Three Dialogues between Hylas and Philonous* in *Principles of Human Knowledge/Three Dialogues* (London: Penguin, 1988), Second Dialogue, p. 158. For Berkeley's account of the knowing self see his Third Dialogue, pp. 179ff.

54. Ibid., First Dialogue, pp. 121–56. I. C. Tipton argues that Berkeley is mistaken in thinking the relativity of perception argument proves objects are mind-dependent. See I. C. Tipton, *Berkeley: The Philosophy of Immaterialism* (London: Methuen, 1976), p. 255.

55. Nietzsche suggests that Berkeley's position is untenable because his mental thing-in-itself is devoid of explanatory power and so does not, despite Berkeley's claim to the contrary, 'save the phenomena'. This is because Berkeley arguably appeals to the very phenomena that require explanation as an explanation. Nietzsche argues that, in the absence of any valid appeal to God as an ultimate explanation, Berkeley can give only 'descriptions' rather than 'explanations' of how things are. This is partly what Nietzsche means when he praises Boscovich for having overcome sensualism in philosophy and for having won a 'triumph over the senses' (Nietzsche, *BGE*, 12). According to Nietzsche, we cannot rely on the senses alone to provide an explanation of our qualitative experience of the world. Rather, he suggests we must speculate and probe beyond the immediate evidence of the senses although such hypotheses are accepted only to the extent that they succeed in offering better explanations of the empirical world than competitor views.

56. Berkeley, *Three Dialogues*, Third Dialogue, p. 197.

57. Nietzsche, *BGE*, 12.

58. Rom Harré and E. H. Madden, *Causal Powers: A Theory of Natural Necessity* (Oxford: Basil Blackwell, 1975), p. 169.

59. Max Jammer, *Concepts of Force: A Study in the Foundation of Dynamics* (Cambridge, MA: Harvard University Press, 1957), p. 172.

60. Strictly speaking, Locke's account of 'real essence' is not quality-less if we consider that real essence is constituted by a thing's intrinsic or primary qualities. However, for purposes of the contrast being drawn here, Locke's real essence can be said to be quality-less to the extent it is devoid of any relational (tertiary or secondary) qualities. Real essence is quality-less, then, in so far as it is a quantitative, scientific outlook rather than a qualitative one. For a discussion of the role of force in overcoming the distinction between quality-less substances and substance-less qualities, see Harré and Madden, *Causal Powers: A Theory of Natural Necessity*, pp. 166–7.

61. John Locke, *An Essay Concerning Human Understanding*, edited by P. Nidditch (Oxford: Clarendon Press, 1975 [1689]), Book II, chapter xxiii, section 37. See Rae Langton, *Kantian Humility: Our Ignorance of Things in Themselves* (Oxford: Clarendon Press, 1998), p. 152 for a discussion of this issue.

62. This is what Nietzsche has in mind when he states of the will to power:

> I do not mean the material world as a delusion, as 'appearance' or 'representation' (in the Berkeleian or Schopenhauerian sense), but rather . . . as a kind of instinctual life in which all the organic functions . . . are synthetically linked to one another . . . (Nietzsche, *BGE*, 36)

63. See Peter Poellner, *Nietzsche and Metaphysics* (Oxford: Clarendon Press, 1995), p. 50 for a discussion of this issue.

64. Nietzsche, *WP*, 624, 629. Boscovich denies that forces are occult qualities. He writes:

> everybody knows what approach means, and what recession is; everybody knows what it means to be indifferent, & what having a propensity means; & thus the idea of a propensity to approach, or to recede, is perfectly distinctly attained. (Roger J. Boscovich, *A Theory of Natural Philosophy* [Chicago: Open Court, 1922 (1758)], p. 95)

Although he disagrees, some commentators argue that Nietzsche is also guilty of appealing to occult qualities. For example, James I. Porter argues that Nietzsche's metaphysical picture of competing centres of force is alienating (James I. Porter, *The Invention of Dionysus* [Stanford, CA: Stanford University Press, 2000], p. 27).

65. Nietzsche, *WP*, 608.

66. Nietzsche, *WP*, 619. Nietzsche's appeal to an argument from analogy here is compatible with his rejection of what he calls in *Twilight of the Idols* the 'Proof by *pleasure* as criterion of truth' (Nietzsche, *TI*, 'The Four Great Errors', 5). Nietzsche's objection to the 'proof of pleasure' is that it seeks to explain both our experience of ourselves and our experience of the world according to 'the *most common* explanations'. The usual explanations, Nietzsche contends, offer a simplified account of our experience, viewing the psychological will as simple, immediately known to us and the source of free action (ibid., 'The Four Great Errors', 3, 7). Nietzsche's argument from analogy in favour of the will to power offers an alternative, non-atomistic account of the will that is not the source of responsible free action but rather operates according to an inner necessity.

67. Nietzsche, *BGE*, 12.

68. Ibid., 19.

69. Nietzsche's account of the self as will to power also counteracts the idea that we are first and foremost acquainted with facts of consciousness. According to Nietzsche, the self is a social structure of drives whose motivations are not immediately available to consciousness (Nietzsche, *BGE*, 3; Nietzsche, *GS*, 354). We recall from Chapter 1 that Nietzsche credits Kant with having recognised that the self is not a transparent substance known immediately through introspection (Nietzsche, *BGE*, 54). Nietzsche's view of the self as will to power is intended to complete this argument by explaining why this is the case.

70. Nietzsche, *BGE*, 19. According to Nietzsche, the notion of 'free will' is a myth. See, for example, Nietzsche, *HAH*, Volume I, 'On the History of Moral Sensations', 106–7. However, he promotes the idea that freedom can be understood in an alternative way. This alternative involves affirmation of the fact that we must act in accordance with our necessary natures (Nietzsche, *GS*, 276).

71. For a further discussion of this issue, see Anderson, 'Nietzsche's Will to Power as a Doctrine of the Unity of Science', and Schacht, *Nietzsche*, pp. 234ff. For a discussion of Nietzsche's perspectivist account of the self, see Hales and Welshon, *Nietzsche's Perspectivism*, Chapter 7.

Chapter 5

The Kantian Background to Nietzsche's Metaphysics

This chapter investigates how Kant influences Nietzsche's metaphysics. By highlighting the historical context informing Nietzsche's concern with the metaphysical status of force in his will to power thesis it underscores the particular Kantian lens through which Nietzsche grapples with the metaphysical problem of the reality of causal powers.

In his articulation of the will to power thesis in *Beyond Good and Evil* Nietzsche describes the ultimate constituents of reality in causal terms, arguing that 'effective' causes have an intrinsic nature, capturing the 'world as it is seen from the inside'.[1] Whilst Nietzsche's claim in this passage that 'I do not mean the material world as a delusion . . . (in the Berkeleian or Schopenhauerian sense)' makes it clear that he intends his will to power thesis to dissociate him from Schopenhauer, what is not immediately evident is that his explicit identification of force with efficient causality entails a rejection of Schopenhauer's criticism of Kant's treatment of the concept of force.

According to Schopenhauer, the empirical world, or the world as representation, conforms to *a priori* principles of sufficient reason. Scientific causation, as one form of the principle of sufficient reason, he contends, captures the relational character of empirical phenomena but not their intrinsic natures. Distinguishing natural force from causality, he argues that forces of nature are direct objectifications of the Will in its essence ('Ideas') and not yet individuated by the principle of sufficient reason. Natural force, therefore, in Schopenhauer's view, is non-causal, non-temporal and non-spatial, although it manifests itself in those forms at the empirical level. However, Schopenhauer contends that Kant conflates force with efficient causality despite his adherence to the distinction between appearance and thing-in-itself. He writes:

> Indeed Kant himself . . . calls the forces of nature 'effective causes,' and says that 'gravity is a cause'. But it is impossible to have a clear understanding of

his thought so long as force and cause in it are not distinctly recognized as completely different; the use of abstract concepts leads very easily to their confusion, if the consideration of their origin is set aside.[2]

This confusion emerges, Schopenhauer contends, from Kant's failure to recognise the mind-dependent nature of causal laws (and hence their restriction to empirical relations constituted by us) and the mind-independent and non-empirical status of natural force. Nietzsche was acquainted with Schopenhauer's criticism of Kant's identification of causality with force as can be witnessed from his reference to Schopenhauer's 'denial of will as an "efficient cause"'.[3] However, Nietzsche sides with Kant on this issue by identifying force with efficient causality. The reasoning informing Nietzsche's position here is his view that Kant is correct to treat the issue of force at the level of empirical relations and not as a resident of the non-empirical sphere of the thing-in-itself. Consequently, Nietzsche's explicit identification of force with efficient causality in *Beyond Good and Evil* suggests, in agreement with Kant and contrary to Schopenhauer, that force does not operate beneath the relational realm of the principle of sufficient reason. Rather, Nietzsche argues that the concept of force is itself a relational property operating within the realm of empirical reality. Expressing his approval, in principle, of Kant's causal project Nietzsche praises Kant's efforts to restrict the legitimate objective applicability of this concept to the empirical world:

> Let us recall . . . *Kant's* tremendous question mark that he placed after the concept of "causality" – without, like Hume, doubting its legitimacy altogether. Rather, Kant began cautiously to delimit the realm within which this concept makes sense (and to this day we are not done with this fixing of limits).[4]

However, Nietzsche thinks that if causal powers instantiated at the level of empirical reality are to be understood as metaphysically real and therefore genuinely efficacious, they must be both relational and possessed of an intrinsic nature. According to Nietzsche, this is the very issue that drives the development of Kant's metaphysics from its 'pre-critical' beginnings as a response to the *vis viva* debate between the Cartesians and Leibnizeans to its culmination in the Copernican turn of his mature 'critical' thought. In what follows we shall see that whilst Nietzsche praises the direction of Kant's pre-critical writings in its efforts to reconcile, contrary to Descartes and Leibniz, the intrinsic nature of force with its empirical and relational character, he thinks that the ultimate solution to establishing the reality of powers entails engaging with and modifying Kant's critical arguments. This is because Kant's critical philosophy, aiming to avoid dogmatism in response to his early commitment to physico-theology, ultimately separates the relational and empirical character of force from its intrinsic nature residing in things-in-themselves. Nietzsche wants to secure the reconciliation of intrinsicality and relationality evident in Kant's early project, but from within the methodological constraints of his mature philosophical system. By engaging with Kant's constitutive/regulative distinction Nietzsche argues, contrary to the mature Kant, that forces obtaining at the level of empirical reality are metaphysically real.

NIETZSCHE'S ENGAGEMENT WITH THE PRE-CRITICAL KANT

Nietzsche's engagement with Kant on the issue of causality and force is not restricted to his later thought but spans the entire corpus of his writings from his unpublished notes dating prior to *The Birth of Tragedy*. Having argued in Chapter 3 that the philosophical aims of Nietzsche's early writings are continuous with those of his later thought, I shall draw on material from both periods in support of my interpretation of the Kantian background to Nietzsche's will to power metaphysics. Nietzsche's early unpublished notes, far from representing a passing interest in Kant, in fact shed significant light on both the context and nature of Nietzsche's proposal of the will to power thesis in *Beyond Good and Evil*. By indicating that Nietzsche's concern with Kant's treatment of causality and force incorporates both Kant's 'pre-critical' and 'critical' writings these notes help us understand Nietzsche's motivations in claiming that a robust causal account of reality such as that offered in the will to power thesis requires that effective causes be intrinsic as well as relational.

In an early unpublished piece entitled 'Philosophy in the Tragic Age of the Greeks' (1873), Nietzsche singles out for praise Kant's pre-critical project in his *Universal Natural History and Theory of the Heavens* (1755) where Kant explains the self-organising character of nature according to mechanical efficient causation.[5] According to Nietzsche, in this book we witness Kant's praiseworthy effort to overcome both his own earliest view and the predominant view in the seventeenth and eighteenth centuries that force, if it is to be metaphysically real, cannot be empirical. Highlighting both how Kant grapples with seventeenth- and eighteenth-century debates regarding the nature of force and Nietzsche's response to the development of Kant's thought, we see the beginning of Nietzsche's metaphysics of powers that are both relational and intrinsic. Moreover, we witness how he offers both an entrenched yet alternative solution to the problem of reconciling intrinsicality and relationality to that of Kant and his contemporaries.

In *Universal Natural History* Kant aims to reconcile external mechanical causes with inner intrinsic natures under one ontological description, rejecting his previous separation of the two in his earliest response to the *vis viva* debate, which was formative in the subsequent development of his metaphysical thought. The debate, initiated by Leibniz's 1686 paper 'The Memorable Errors of Descartes and Others', stemmed from a controversy between the Leibnizeans and Cartesians regarding the concept of force.[6] The controversy centred on the question whether there obtains in nature a 'living force', distinct from mechanical force, and whether this *vis viva*, should it obtain, can be quantified or measured. The debate thus concerned the metaphysical question regarding the fundamental nature of force and the mathematical question of its quantification where its quantifiability was taken to be the measure of its empirical character.

According to Descartes, empirical force is devoid of an inner intrinsic nature. He contends that force, identified with the quantity of motion, is 'dead pressure' (*vis mortua*), measurable as the product of the quantity of matter and velocity. This reduction of force to quantity of motion derives from Descartes' view that God is the only true causal agency of nature. In addition to his view that our descriptions of nature must be expressible mathematically, he argues that matter, consisting only of extension, is completely inert. Thus, there is no room in the Cartesian account for 'occult' qualities such as attraction and repulsion or sympathies and antipathies. Rather, Descartes sees himself as breaking with the occult qualities of Aristotle and medieval thought. Force for Descartes is reducible to external motion and leads to a geometrical account of motion by contact. In the following passage from the *Principles of Philosophy* he describes motion in terms of spatial transfer:

> if our aim is to assign a determinate nature to it, we may say that *motion is the transfer of one part of matter, or one body, from the vicinity of the other bodies which are in immediate contact with it, and which are regarded as being at rest, to the vicinity of other bodies.* By 'one body' or 'one piece of matter' I mean whatever is transferred at a given time, even though this may in fact consist of many parts which have different motions relative to each other. And I say 'the transfer' as opposed to the force or action which brings about the transfer, to show that motion is always in the moving body as opposed to the body which brings about the movement. The two are not normally distinguished with sufficient care; and I want to make it clear that the motion of something that moves is, like the lack of motion in a thing which is at rest, a mere mode of that thing and not itself a subsistent thing, just as shape is a mere mode of the thing which has shape.[7]

Objecting to Descartes' identification of matter with extension and his reduction of force to the motion of solid bodies by contact, Leibniz argues that extension cannot be the defining character of material substance because extension, in his view, can be reduced to more fundamental factors. He maintains that extension, a relative phenomenon of ideal relations between immaterial substances, is unable to account for the inertia of bodies or their resistance to motion.[8] Rather, Leibniz contends that force is the dynamic essence of matter, and although he concedes that its effects can be expressed mathematically as the product of the quantity of matter and the square of velocities, he denies that this measurement can capture its metaphysical reality. According to Leibniz, empirical force is a 'derivative' dynamic phenomenon caused by an underlying 'primitive' force, which he describes as the inherent tendency of monadic substances coexisting on the basis of a pre-established harmony. For Leibniz, although primitive force is metaphysically real, having an intrinsic nature, it does not obtain at the level of empirical phenomena. He writes in *Specimen Dynamicum*:

> The first thing we must recognize is that force is something fully real, even in created substances, whereas space, time and motion have something of the nature of beings of reason; they are not true or real in themselves, but only in so far as they involve the divine attributes of immensity, eternity, and activity, or the force of created substances. . . . For while force is something real and absolute, motion belongs to the class of relative phenomena; and truth is to be found not in the phenomena but in their causes.[9]

In his first published book, *Thoughts on the True Estimation of Living Forces* (1749), Kant attempts a synthesis of the Cartesian and Leibnizean estimation of force. However, what we get is not so much their reconciliation as an argument in favour of two types of causes resulting in the continued separation of mathematically quantifiable empirical force and force as a non-empirical metaphysical quality.[10] At the time of writing *Living Forces* Kant was largely ignorant of Newtonian physics, failing to recognise that motion just like rest is a state and that force is required only for the alteration of this state rather than for its maintenance.[11] Consequently, Kant argues that a physical body is subject to two types of force: external and internal force. External force is momentary and does not last for any finite length of time. Giving the example of pushing a ball across a tabletop he argues that the continuous motion of the body requires the application of a continuous and external force, subject to the principle of conservation and as such considered by Kant to be mathematically quantifiable.[12] According to Kant external force is genuinely empirical as it is expressed in the Cartesian formula of mass times velocity.

However, Kant contends a gunshot reveals a different type of motion from that of external force. In the case of a gunshot the external force disappears at the very moment that the bullet leaves the drum although it continues in motion even when the initial external force is no longer applied.[13] He appeals to an internal source of force within bodies, arguing that the motion of a bullet does not depend on an external force but rather is the effect of an inner dynamic and essentially striving force. The task of this living force, according to Kant, described in a similar fashion to Leibniz's primitive active force, as an Aristotelian entelechy and the essential nature of force, is to preserve a body in inertial motion.[14] Kant argues that a freely moving body does so according to its internal nature; it is an essential striving to maintain its state of motion. Unlike external force, however, internal force is not subject to the law of conservation and is therefore not capable of mathematical treatment.[15] By drawing a contrast between mathematics and metaphysics Kant argues that living force does not represent a physical quantity but rather a metaphysical quality.[16] Metaphysical internal force is thus divorced from mathematically quantifiable empirical force.

However, by the time Kant wrote *Universal Natural History,* a book Nietzsche praises for its attempt to reconcile the metaphysical and the empirical, he had become both versed in and a defender of Newtonian mechanics, rejecting internal force in favour of the view that there is only one form of causality. Consequently, internal force metamorphoses in *Universal Natural History* into the idea of the self-organising character of mechanical nature, reconciling under one ontological description mechanical causes acting externally and teleological 'life'. Articulating this project in terms of a concern to reconcile Newtonian physics with the notion of purpose, Kant argues the universe is self-organising and functions according to purposes that are intrinsic to the mechanical operations of nature. From within the framework of Newton's mechanical principles, he appeals to the evolution of complex systems from the simple constituents of attractive and repulsive force.[17] He writes:

> I have in fact decided with the greatest caution to forego all arbitrary specu-
> lation, I have, after I have set the world in the simplest chaos, applied no
> other forces than the forces of attraction and repulsion for the development
> of the great order of nature, two forces which both are equally certain,
> equally simple, and also equally primary and universal. Both are borrowed
> from the Newtonian philosophy of nature.[18]

Viewing his project in *Universal Natural History* as a completion and a bringing to fruition of the full implications of Newtonian mechanics, Kant contends that he adheres more strictly to Newtonian mechanical principles than had Newton's own writings. Kant argues that Newton's appeal to an 'alien hand' or divine interference in the mechanical workings of nature is inconsistent with the principles that inform his natural philosophy.[19] Writing that 'matter, though operating through the mechanism of its forces, has a certain correctness in its results and does justice with no [external] compulsion to the rules of adaptedness',[20] he contends that Newton completed the 'mathematical half' of natural philosophy and that he himself would complete the 'physical part'.[21] The mathematical half refers to Newton's articulation of the mechanical laws of motion whilst the physical half which Kant proposes comprises the specifically empirical project of investigating celestial motions and conjecturing on the basis of these investigations that nature is a self-organising whole that operates according to a necessity intrinsic and internal to itself.

Contrary to Newton's view that matter is passive, Kant contends that nature is characterised by 'essential striving'.[22] Purposes are not, then, in Kant's view, extrinsic to nature but rather are inherent in the very operations of nature according to Newtonian mechanical laws. Nature, he contends, is a beautiful and perfect self-organising whole informed by natural necessity. Moreover, this natural necessity entails the reconciliation of efficient and final causes whereby efficient causes are the mechanical vehicles for the self-organising and striving activity of nature:

> Matter, which is the original stuff of all things, is also bound to certain laws and, if freely abandoned to them, must necessarily produce beautiful connections. Matter has no freedom to deviate from the plan of perfection. As it also finds itself subject to an upmost wise purpose, it must necessarily be directed into such harmonious relations through a First Cause dominating it, *and there is a God precisely because nature can proceed even in chaos in no other way than regularly and orderly.*[23]

Here Kant denies that two types of causality operate in the mechanical world. He contends that Newton's appeal to divine interference in mechanical operations involves two types of causality: mechanical causation that operates imperfectly in the natural world and divine causation that adjusts and perfects the mechanical operations of nature from without. Kant aims to overcome this bifurcation of causality, arguing that only the mechanical perfection of the natural world as a 'well-ordered whole' is truly compatible with an 'all-sufficient highest

Reason'.[24] Moreover, unlike his appeal to internal force in *Living Forces*, the laws of mechanics in *Universal Natural History* are mathematically determinable and therefore have genuine empirical significance.

Of specific interest to Nietzsche with regard to Kant's project in *Universal Natural History* is its aim to offer only one level of explanation, that available at the level of empirical naturalistic investigation. Nietzsche writes:

> Is it not a sublime thought, to derive the magnificence of the cosmos and the marvellous arrangements of the stellar orbits wholly from a single, simple, purely mechanical movement, from a mathematical figure in motion, as it were! Instead of seeing in it the intentions and the intervening hands of a machine-god, he derived it from a type of oscillation which, once having begun, is necessary and predictable in its course and attains effects which are the equal of the wisest calculations of ratiocination; and of the utmost planning of purposiveness – but without being them.[25]

It is this task of capturing at the level of empirical reality the intrinsic nature of force that Nietzsche praises in *Universal Natural History*, suggesting that he would not support, for example, Kant's conclusions in *Living Forces*. That he would not can also be discerned from Nietzsche's expressed reluctance to separate the mathematical project of quantification and the metaphysical project of qualification.[26] However, this is by no means to suggest that Nietzsche adopts the Leibnizean solution of reducing mathematical quantities to metaphysical qualities. Although there are similarities between Leibniz's project and that of Nietzsche's desire to capture the quality of force, Nietzsche's praise for Kant's *Universal Natural History* indicates that there is a crucial difference between Leibniz's and Nietzsche's projects. According to Leibniz, the empirical sphere of mechanical relations operates according to 'derivative' force. He contends that mechanical force is ultimately grounded in 'primitive' force, which he describes as the 'substantial form' of non-empirical monads whose interaction with one another is ideal rather than real.[27] Nietzsche in his aim, like Kant in *Universal Natural History*, to combine at the level of empirical reality relational force with its intrinsic nature, rejects the idea that intrinsic natures are non-relational. Consequently, Nietzsche's refusal to separate quantities and qualities indicates that for him relational powers are physically real, intrinsic and genuinely empirical. He writes: 'all driving force is will to power . . . there is no other physical, dynamic, or psychic force except this'.[28]

However, despite his praise for the general direction and aim of Kant's pre-critical arguments, Nietzsche remains ultimately dissatisfied.

Although his comments on Kant's early writings are by no means extensive and the comments that we do possess in unpublished notes such as 'On Teleology' (1867/68) and 'Philosophy in the Tragic Age of the Greeks' are sketchy, there are, nevertheless, some suggestions that the source of Nietzsche's dissatisfaction resides in what he sees as Kant's appeal to a form of 'optimistic' physico-theology inferring the existence of a creator directly from observations of empirical order.[29] Nietzsche questions Kant's denial, contrary to the arguments of Lucretius and his predecessors Epicurus, Leucippus and Democritus[30] that the evolution of complex systems is subject to 'chance' in favour of the view that this is the best of all possible worlds.[31] The reason for Nietzsche's preference for 'chance' rather than God as an explanation is that he regards the latter as a superfluous doctrinaire teleology, adding nothing of explanatory value to the notion of intrinsic natures and ultimately undermining the initial appeal to intrinsic natures by rendering them the products of an extrinsic divine intention.[32] According to Nietzsche, Kant's project in *Universal Natural History*, if faithfully executed, should conclude that the fundamental constituents of reality are intrinsic but not products of divine creation. In his mature writings Kant adopts a critical stance towards physico-theology, claiming that it amounts to a dogmatic assumption of divine intention from the outset. Contrary to such dogmatic claims to immediate knowledge, the mature Kant argues that whilst a theoretical proof for the existence of God is impossible, the regulative idea of the world as a product of design facilitates the non-dogmatic discovery of natural purposes and the representation of nature as a systematic unity.[33] Nietzsche is also concerned to avoid dogmatism as a result of his view that explanation of the empirical world requires that we refuse to take the senses at face value without, however, claiming privileged knowledge of inner natures.[34] Despite Nietzsche's praise for Kant's appeal to regulative belief as an attempt to overcome the dogmatist presupposition of immediate insight into things, he remains discontented, arguing that Kant's critical writings, rather than solving the difficulty of how to cater for intrinsic natures at the level of empirical reality, in fact sow the seeds of their dissociation. In the next section we shall see that the seeds of destruction, according to Nietzsche, reside in Kant's 'transcendental' engagement in a proliferation of explanatory levels designed to avoid dogmatism in metaphysics but ultimately serving to separate the relational character of empirical reality from the intrinsic but non-relational character of things-in-themselves. In response, Nietzsche appropriates what he perceives as the merits of Kant's project in *Universal Natural History* but in a way that both pays due respect to the anti-dogmatic intentions of his Copernican turn whilst, however, avoiding its pitfalls.

NIETZSCHE'S ENGAGEMENT WITH KANT'S CRITICAL PROJECT

The centrepiece of Kant's critical philosophy, the Copernican turn, attempts to overcome the twin dangers of dogmatism and scepticism by reconfiguring the relationship between the knower and the known. Rather than the knower conforming to an independent object, the object must now conform to the conditions of our knowledge.[35] However, as a consequence of taking the turn, Kant's response to the issue of force undergoes considerable alteration in his mature writings resulting in his relegation of intrinsic natures to the realm of unknowable things-in-themselves. Nietzsche argues that the ultimate outcome of Kant's Copernican turn is the dissociation of relational force from its intrinsic nature as a result of Kant's claim that whilst our knowledge is restricted to that of the mechanical operations of empirical reality constituted by us we can have regulative belief in but not knowledge of intrinsic natures. As items of regulative belief, Kant contends that we are unavoidably disposed to think of there being intrinsic natures but that these natures are objects of thought that cannot be known by us to obtain at the level of empirical reality. Nietzsche contends that this conclusion, signalling the collapse of Kant's aim to reconcile intrinsicality and relationality is evident in both *Critique of Pure Reason* (1781/1787) and *Critique of Judgment* (1790). Kant predominantly addresses the unknowability of intrinsic natures in *Critique of Pure Reason* and the possibility of their being objects of regulative or reflective belief in *Critique of Judgment*.[36] Although Nietzsche wants to avoid the separation of relational force from its intrinsic nature, he is nonetheless as concerned as Kant to avoid the philosophical dogmatist's appeal to direct insight into reality.[37] For this reason Nietzsche contends that any attempt to overcome the dissociation of relational force from its intrinsic nature must do so by engaging with the terms of Kant's Copernican turn as manifested in both books.

In the 'Amphiboly' section of *Critique of Pure Reason* Kant parts with his pre-critical self when he argues that empirical substance constituted by force is exhaustively relational and that we cannot know its intrinsic nature. In *Metaphysical Foundations of Natural Science* (1786), which he describes as giving specific content to the arguments of *Critique of Pure Reason*, Kant writes that matter is the 'movable in space' that fills a space by means of a special moving force and that 'all matter is divisible to infinity, and indeed into parts each of which is again matter'.[38]

Whereas in some writings of the pre-critical period Kant had associated the Newtonian force of inertia with the internal or intrinsic nature of fundamentally simple substance, in his critical writings he argues that the force of inertia is an 'external cause'.[39] He argues that all forces act externally from material points of an infinitely divisible matter and that the defining conception of matter and force is that it is capable of spatial-temporal representation. Kant therefore rejects the empirical feasibility of intrinsic natures in his critical writings on the basis that intrinsic natures cannot be so represented.[40] He contends, in the context of his rejection of the Leibnizean monadological view of substance in the 'Amphiboly', that we cannot know the inner determinations of substance, arguing that we can know only its external spatial relations through the empirical rather than pure employment of the Understanding. The inner determinations of substance, if they obtain at all, Kant maintains, must reside in the non-empirical thing-in-itself. To claim knowledge of such inner natures, however, is to engage in what Kant calls a 'transcendental amphiboly', defined as 'a confounding of an object of pure understanding with appearance'.[41] It involves, Kant claims, confusing appearances with representations of things-in-themselves by failing to recognise the role of sensible intuition in the constitution of empirical objects of our knowledge. Thus, in opposition to Leibniz's non-relational noumenal substance, Kant contends 'substantia phaenomenon in space' is 'nothing but relations, and it itself is entirely made up of mere relations.' He writes:

> We are acquainted with substance in space only through forces which are active in this and that space, either bringing objects to it (attraction), or preventing them penetrating into it (repulsion and impenetrability). We are not acquainted with any other properties constituting the concept of the substance which appears in space and which we call matter.[42]

Here Kant denies we have access to the inner nature of things, arguing that we can only justifiably claim knowledge of the relational character of empirical substance. Thus force for the mature Kant admits only of outer external relations.[43]

Although Nietzsche is generally in favour of Kant's treatment of the concept of force at the level of empirical relations, he finds Kant's critical project ultimately unsatisfactory as a result of its failure to capture at the level of these empirical relations the intrinsic nature of force. He is critical of Kant's transcendental treatment of force, claiming it reduces it to the status of a mental 'projection' that captures only the 'form' of causality rather than its intrinsic nature.[44] This is due, according to Nietzsche, to Kant's treatment of force as an item of constitutive knowledge. By this he seems to have in mind Kant's appeal in *Critique of Pure Reason* to the transcendental subject as the source of *a priori* rules whereby the relations of appearances are determined in time according to the concepts of substance and causality. This is suggested by Nietzsche's claim that 'analysis revealed that even force was only projected into them, and likewise – substance'.[45] Constitutive knowledge for Kant entails the application through synthesis of *a priori* concepts of the Understanding to sensible intuition. However, Nietzsche suggests that Kant's constitutive account, in its attempt to explain the harmony between our non-empirical concepts and nature as it is available to our knowledge, reduces the natural world to our epistemology. According to Kant, to the extent that empirical reality is knowable by us it must conform to mechanical principles supplied by the human mind. Nietzsche argues that this idea makes it impossible to capture the intrinsic nature of force. For Kant's claim that the natural world as it is known by us is constituted by and reducible to our categories results, in Nietzsche's view, in the separation of the empirical world of our acquaintance and how things are in themselves. This has the result that empirical force in *Critique of Pure Reason* is divorced from its inner determinations in the thing-in-itself and reduced instead to the idea of rule-governed succession. Accordingly, one event is said to be causally connected to another if one event follows another according to a rule. Nietzsche argues that Kant's account of causality as a relation between successive events fails to capture the causal efficacy informing the relation as a corollary of Kant's failure to establish the metaphysical reality of empirical powers, something that can be achieved, according to Nietzsche, only by reconciling empirical force with its intrinsic nature. Kant's inability to forge such a union, Nietzsche argues, renders him unable to make adequate contentful sense of the idea of causal relations.[46]

> *Causalism.* – It is obvious that things-in-themselves cannot be related to one another as cause and effect, nor can appearance be so related to appearance; from which it follows that in a philosophy that believes in things-in-themselves and appearances the concept 'cause and effect' *cannot be applied*. Kant's mistakes – [47]

Nietzsche contends that the combination of Kant's restriction of our knowledge to the realm of empirical phenomena constituted by us in *Critique of Pure Reason* and his reference to things-in-themselves calls into question the 'validity of the knowledge attained by the natural sciences and altogether everything that can be known *causaliter*'. He is critical of what he sees as the implication of Kant's analysis that 'whatever is know*able* immediately seems to us less valuable on that account'.[48] Furthermore, Nietzsche suggests this difficulty is not only evident in *Critique of Pure Reason* but also permeates *Critique of Judgment*. Motivating Nietzsche's claim here is that the concept of intrinsic natures becomes split in Kant's critical period and metamorphoses into the 'internal nature' of non-empirical substance on the one hand, and the idea of the biological-teleological on the other.[49] Whilst Kant addresses the issue of internal natures at the level of things-in-themselves in the 'Amphiboly' section of *Critique of Pure Reason*, he addresses the issue of mechanism versus biological life in *Critique of Judgment*.

In 'On Teleology' (1868), a collection of early notes for a planned but ultimately unexecuted dissertation to be entitled 'On the Concept of the Organic Since Kant', Nietzsche argues that Kant's appeal in *Critique of Judgment* to a supersensible ground of the appearance of design in organisms and the systematic organisation of nature as a whole results in two distinct levels of explanation: mechanical explanation of the external relations between empirical phenomena available to our knowledge and a teleological account of inner natures grounded in things-in-themselves. Nietzsche contends that as a result of this distinction Kant introduces a schism between the 'moving forces' of mechanism and inner purposes.[50] He writes that Kant's limitation of our knowledge to mechanical relations, entailing explanation 'out of external causes', was introduced 'in order afterwards to set the inner (causes) against it'.[51] Nietzsche argues that Kant has an agenda in limiting our knowledge to that of mechanical relations, which is to allow in through the back door the traditional belief in God without offering a theoretical argument for its justifiability.[52] The problem is that Kant treats intrinsic natures in the same way, which means they must be denied the status of knowledge and must be grounded in things-in-themselves rather than at the level of empirical relations knowable by us.

The seeds of the schism between mechanism and teleology are sown in the 'Dialectic of Teleological Judgment' section of *Critique of Judgment* (Division II of 'Critique of Teleological Judgment') when Kant argues that as beings with a constitutive discursive mode of cognition that must subsume intuitive particulars under universal concepts, our knowledge is restricted to that of mechanical relations. This leads to a particular difficulty for Kant, however, because empirical observation teaches us that all natural phenomena cannot be explained in terms of mechanical causes. Some things in nature, organisms, are so organised that we can intelligibly think of them only as the intentional products of a designer. Mechanical explanation for Kant entails appealing to external relations between forces. Teleological explanation, however, appeals to inner natures, arguing that the law-like behaviour of organisms cannot be explained by external relations but rather requires that we appeal to an inner, design-like character of things as their intrinsic natures.[53] The problem with this is that teleological explanation, as explanation according to ends, appeals to final causes rather than mechanical ones, whereas our specifically human cognitive constitution is incapable of cognising things in terms of final causes.

Kant responds to this difficulty in the 'Dialectic' where he articulates his task as that of showing how beings with our specifically human cognitive constitution can at one and the same time judge of objects in terms of mechanical causes and final causes. The question is: how can we describe the realm of appearances knowable by us only in terms of mechanical laws as purposively designed? Moreover, Kant is concerned to justify our appeal to both mechanical and teleological accounts of empirical nature (the realm of appearances rather than things-in-themselves) in such a way that we avoid the dangers of dogmatism and transcending the legitimate empirical boundaries of our knowledge established in the Analytic section of *Critique of Pure Reason*.

There arises an antinomy of judgement, such as the abovementioned one between mechanism and teleology, according to Kant, in cases where there is a conflict between principles that are equally necessary and where both principles 'have their basis in our cognitive powers' such that the conflict is deemed to be a 'natural one, an unavoidable illusion that we must expose and resolve' through a transcendental critique.[54] The antinomy of teleological judgement rests on a conflict between two maxims. The thesis reads that 'All production of material things is possible in terms of merely mechanical laws' whilst the antithesis reads that 'Some production of material things is not possible in terms of merely mechanical laws'.[55] Kant argues the antinomy arises when these two principles are taken to be constitutive, confronting us with a contradiction whereby one of the principles must be false. That is, Kant contends that the two principles are contradictory if both are taken to be conditions of ontological or epistemic possibility, as either conditions of how the world is or as conditions under which we come to know it. In such a case the contradiction is deemed to be real. However, Kant's claim that both mechanical and teleological principles are reflective rather than constitutive principles sets in place the first step to overcoming the antinomy. Kant writes: 'Hence all semblance of an antinomy between the maxims of strictly physical (mechanical) and teleological (technical) explanation rests on our confusing a principle of reflective judgment with one of determinative judgment . . . .'[56] Understood as reflective rather than constitutive principles, mechanism and teleology undergo a shift in meaning, transforming into methodological directives rather than constitutive conditions of ontological or epistemic possibility. These principles, according to Kant, are not objective but rather subjective maxims of research. He writes: 'this principle is not objective and cannot provide an objectively adequate basis for cognizing the object, it has to serve as a merely subjective principle governing the purposive use of our cognitive powers – i.e. our reflection on a [certain] kind of objects.'[57] When mechanical and teleological principles are viewed purely methodologically, Kant contends that it is impossible for beings with our specifically human and sensible mode of cognition to hold that either principle is true or false as an explanation of organisms. He writes:

> We are quite unable to prove that organized natural products cannot be produced through the mere mechanism of nature. For we have no insight into the first inner basis [responsible] for the endless diversity of the particular natural laws, because they are contingent for us since we cognize them only empirically; and so we cannot possibly reach the inner and completely sufficient principle of the possibility of nature (this principle lies in the supersensible).[58]

On the face of it there seems to be an inconsistency here as Kant had argued in *Critique of Pure Reason* that mechanical principles are constitutive. That is, in that book they are presented as necessary conditions for the possibility of science and objective human experience in general. In *Critique of Judgment*, however, Kant argues these principles are reflective subjective maxims of research rather than objective constitutive forms of knowledge. However, Kant's claim that mechanical principles are reflective applies to their 'expansive' use.[59] Mechanical principles are constitutive with regard to the form of our objective experience such that, for instance, we know that all events must have a cause. They are reflective with regard to the diversity of empirical content (the discovery of particular causal laws) or the explanation of the possibility of organisms. That is, whilst it is the task of the Understanding to subsume under the *a priori* categories that which is 'given' in experience, Kant contends, for example, that it is possible that nature is so varied that the categories apply only to singular instances rather than allowing us to formulate empirical laws that apply to many similar instances.[60] Reflective judgement, however, addresses the contingency and particularity of empirical data, adopting an *a priori* principle that 'presupposes and assumes' that such empirical data can be understood as part of a systematic whole.[61] Mechanical judgements are employed reflectively in *Critique of*

Judgment, then, only when one is confronted with empirical phenomena that defy obvious mechanical explanation, in cases where one is unable to determine whether a mechanical explanation is true or false. However, Kant contends that since mechanical principles are conditions of the possibility of human cognition we should seek to employ mechanical principles as far as we can:

> I am only pointing out that I *ought* always to *reflect* on these events and forms *in terms of the principle* of the mere mechanism of nature, and hence ought to investigate this principle as far as I can, because unless we presuppose it in our investigation [of nature] we can have no cognition of nature at all in the proper sense of the term.[62]

That the methodological reflective employment of both mechanical and teleological principles is a first step, however, and not the conclusion and resolution to the antinomy as some have suggested can be discerned from the fact that the claim is made at the beginning of Kant's discussion in sections which he describes as a 'presentation' (*Vorstellung*) of the antinomy and a 'preparation' (*Vorbereitung*) of its resolution.[63] Rather, Kant's claim that teleological and mechanical judgements are reflective when applied to the explanation of organisms and the systematic unity of nature is intended to draw attention to our cognitive limitations with the consequence that in response to the question of how we can justifiably appeal to both mechanical and teleological principles to explain one and the same object (the empirical sphere of appearances), his answer is that *we* cannot but that a being with a different form of cognition to us *possibly* could. We cannot ultimately ascertain either the truth or falsity of mechanical or teleological explanation when applied to empirical diversity or organisms. Kant tells us that from our specifically human point of view and as applied to one and the same thing mechanism and teleology cannot be reconciled:

> As applied to one and the same natural thing, we cannot link or reconcile the mechanical and the teleological principle [if we regard them] as principles for explaining (deducing) one thing from another, i.e., [regard them] as dogmatic and constitutive principles [of] determinative judgment for [gaining] insight into nature. For example, if I assume that a maggot should be regarded as a product of the mere mechanism of nature (i.e., of the restructuring that matter does on its own, once its elements are set free by putrefaction), I cannot then go on to derive the same product from the same matter [now regarded] as a causality that acts in terms of purposes. Conversely, if I assume that the maggot is a natural purpose, then I cannot count on there being a mechanical way of producing it and cannot assume

this as a constitutive principle for judging how the maggot is possible. . . .
For the two kinds of explanation exclude each other . . .[64]

His solution is to appeal to the logical possibility (but not objective
reality) of a supersensible designer who can conceivably employ the
mechanical causes of nature to serve teleological ends. Here we see Kant
shift the argument of *Universal Natural History* to the reflective level.
However, although avoiding dogmatism, he continues to address the
idea of intrinsic natures as the purposeful intention of a supersensible
designer.

Central to Kant's solution to the antinomy, then, is his emphasis on
the species-specific character of human knowledge, which introduces
the idea of a non-human knower. Kant contends the antinomy would
not arise for a being with intellectual intuition because for such a being
there is no distinction between the actual and the possible. A being with
intellectual intuition has insight into the inner intrinsic nature of things
due to the absence of any distinction between appearance and reality for
this non-human intellect. In contrast, restricted as we are to knowledge
of appearances conforming to the principles of our Understanding, Kant
contends that beings with our specifically human cognitive constitution
must cognise empirical reality in terms of mechanical conditions or relations. In order for us 'to acquire so much as an empirical cognition of
the intrinsic character' of organisms we must think of them as products
of an intentional designer.[65] So, in order for us to comprehend the possibility of organisms we must think of them as purposes. However, for a
being whose mode of intuition is intellectual, a 'mechanical' explanation
of organisms is conceivable.

The bifurcation of explanatory levels entailed by Kant's transcendental critique is made particularly evident here. He tells us that although
we must think of nature as purposive in order to think of it as necessary rather than contingent, the basis for this purposiveness cannot be
found within empirical nature itself but rather the idea of purposiveness
points to a supersensible substrate outside nature. According to Kant, we
can conceive intrinsic natures only as the intentions of a supersensible
designer, the appeal to which, as a result of Kant's transcendental critique, is a subjective principle. It is not an objective claim about empirical
nature or about the existence of such a designer but rather a reflection of
the limitations of our human cognitive constitution. Nevertheless, Kant's
critical response to the antinomy of teleological judgement is inescapably
linked to theology and the idea of a supersensible ground of empirical
reality knowable by us.[66]

> [Yet] it also seems that for external objects as appearances we cannot possibly find an adequate basis that refers to purposes, but it seems instead that, even though this basis also lies in nature, we must still search for it only in nature's supersensible substrate, even though all possible insight into that substrate is cut off from us: hence it seems that there is absolutely no possibility for us to obtain, from nature itself, bases with which to explain combinations in terms of purposes; rather, the character of the human cognitive power forces us to seek the supreme basis for such combinations in an original understanding, as cause of the world.[67]

Kant's proliferation of explanatory levels and his views regarding the limits of our knowledge, in addition to his treatment of intrinsic natures as the purposive intentions of a supersensible designer, are the sources of Nietzsche's dissatisfaction with Kant's critical project. Nietzsche argues that Kant's plea of ignorance of intrinsic natures is a ruse to facilitate his theological leanings.[68] However, it is, in Nietzsche's view, a ruse that backfires, serving ultimately to undermine the completion of Kant's critical project in *Critique of Pure Reason* to restrict the applicability of causality to the realm of empirical reality. Here we witness Nietzsche's assessment of the full metaphysical implications of Kant's Copernican turn in general. By reducing the knowable empirical world to the forms of our epistemology in *Critique of Pure Reason* whilst allowing reflective belief in but not knowledge of intrinsic natures in both *Critique of Pure Reason* and *Critique of Judgment* Kant puts pay, according to Nietzsche, to any possibility of the reconciliation of intrinsic natures with empirical relations. Moreover, he argues that Kant's reference to a supersensible ground of things in both books is a disingenuous attempt to transgress the legitimate jurisdiction of possible knowledge set out in the terms of the Copernican turn. It is for this reason that Nietzsche regards Kant's efforts to capture the intrinsic nature of empirical reality by appealing to a supersensible designer in *Critique of Judgment* as an attempt to explain the known in terms of the unknown:

> He appeals to the whole in order to judge the world. To that however belongs a knowledge that is no longer piecemeal. To infer from the whole to the fragments is the same as to go from the unknown to the known (Fischer).[69]

In contrast, Nietzsche aims to explain the unfamiliar in terms of the familiar, arguing that we can contentfully conceive the intrinsic nature of force only analogously to the human. Using this method to capture the inner constitution of things Nietzsche claims in his later writings that a 'force we cannot imagine is an empty word', proposing in turn that the 'victorious concept "force" . . . still needs to be completed: an inner will must be ascribed to it, which I designate as "will to power"'.[70] However, he contends that although the specifically human forms of our cognition guide our understanding of reality, that reality is nonetheless neither reducible to nor constituted by the forms of our cognition. He writes: 'Man recognizes things which both coincide with and differ from human analogy and asks after the explanation.'[71] By attempting to explain nature analogously but non-reductively to the forms of our knowledge Nietzsche sees himself as operating in the true spirit of Kant's Copernican revolution. The cornerstone of that revolution for Nietzsche is its emphasis on the human character of our knowledge. Nietzsche thinks Kant's reference to a supersensible designer, albeit reflectively, betrays the true spirit of the Copernican turn. The full implementation of Kant's incomplete project of restricting causality to the empirical sphere entails, according to Nietzsche, the reconciliation of empirical relations with intrinsic natures as objects of knowledge for us rather than merely for a being with a non-human mode of cognition.

Central to both Nietzsche's response to Kant and his proposal of the will to power is his rejection of Kant's constitutive account of knowledge and his assimilation of it to the status of reflective belief. Nietzsche's assimilation of the constitutive to the reflective, moreover, is not a partial assimilation as it is for Kant in *Critique of Judgment*; rather, it is a complete assimilation and so applies to Kant's arguments in both this book and *Critique of Pure Reason*. That is, Nietzsche abandons Kant's view that the forms of our knowledge are constitutive of the nature of objects knowable by us. In so doing he suggests that empirical nature is irreducible to our epistemology but that the concepts of our epistemology reflect our interests and act as directives to our research into nature. Nietzsche's dismissal of Kant's constitutive account of knowledge is articulated in 'On Teleology', where he puts forward the view that force is an object of reflective rather than constitutive judgement:

> One can only comprehend the mathematical completely (that is the formal view). In all else man stands before the unknown. In order to overcome this man invents concepts, which only gather together a sum of appearing characteristics, which, however, do not get hold of the thing. Therein belong force, matter, individual, law, organism, atom, final cause. These are not constitutive (*constitutiven*) but only reflective (*reflektirende*) judgements.[72]

Despite initial appearances, Nietzsche's claim in this passage that we stand before the unknown seems not to be a reference to the unknowable thing-in-itself that he attributes to Kant, but rather a reference to the non-reducibility of reality to the forms of constitutive judgement. Kant's constitutive judgements, according to Nietzsche, deliver only 'coarse perceptions' of things, capturing the 'form' that we impose on them and not the complexity of their inner constitution.[73] In contrast, Nietzsche argues that the forms of our knowledge are reflective maxims that guide our inquiry into nature. They do not, however, constitute that nature.

In his early notes Nietzsche describes his project, in opposition to Kant's critical one, as entailing 'mechanism joined with causality'.[74] Here Nietzsche depicts his aim as that of bringing together the relational character of empirical force with its intrinsic nature. The execution of this task is made possible by Nietzsche's assimilation of the constitutive to the reflective, which opens up an avenue for him to appeal to the intrinsic nature of force at the level of empirical reality without relegating the status of those hypothetical claims to the realm of the cognitively impotent thing-in-itself. Nietzsche suggests Kant's view of the non-cognitive character of reflective belief derives from the fact that Kant understands the scope and capacity of reflective belief as parasitic on the idea of constitutive knowledge such that anything that is non-constitutive must be non-cognitive and unable to yield epistemic objectivity. Nietzsche's dismissal of Kant's constitutive account of knowledge, coupled with his rejection of the unknowable thing-in-itself witnessed by us in earlier chapters, ensures, however, that there is only one reality and that this reality is neither reducible to our knowledge nor inaccessible to it in principle. Thus in 'On Teleology' Nietzsche writes of Kant's appeal to the possible mechanical origin of organisms from efficient causes on the one hand, and his denial of 'the possibility of knowing it' on the other, that 'If then the possibility of mechanism is present, then the possibility of knowing it should also be there.'[75] According to Nietzsche, once the epistemic accessibility of reality is in principle established we are justified in ascribing an intrinsic nature to empirical force if this view is supported by our best human reasons and has comprehensive explanatory scope.[76] As a result Nietzsche considers that he has avoided a non-empirical metaphysics of the Schopenhauerian or Kantian kind where the inner determinations of reality reside in a non-empirical thing-in-itself, claiming the latter idea is 'meaningless', capable only of a 'negative' definition.[77] Rather, Nietzsche embraces a concept of '*natural* causality', which in its fully developed form is articulated as the will to power and described as 'The world as it is seen from the inside, the world defined and described by its "intelligible character"'.[78]

The ultimate consequence, then, of Nietzsche's attempt to implement in full the Kantian project of restricting the applicability of the concept of causality to the empirical sphere is the emergence of his particular metaphysics, incorporating within the realm of empirical relations an emphasis on the intrinsic nature of these relations. However, Nietzsche denies he is guilty of re-enchanting the world with mysterious occult qualities. Rather, his appeal to the inner intrinsic nature of a thing is that aspect of it which it has independently of its relations with other things but which informs its relationality. Relationality for Nietzsche is not grounded in or otherwise reducible to the non-relational. Intrinsicality is not opposed to relationality. Rather, for Nietzsche, fundamental powers are, at one and the same time, intrinsic and relational. According to Kant, as we have seen, intrinsic and relational qualities are inherently opposed to the extent that intrinsicality obtains at the level of the thing-in-itself whilst the empirical sphere is relational. Nietzsche argues that only by overcoming this traditional metaphysical opposition can we succeed in capturing the intrinsic nature and hence metaphysical reality of empirical causal powers. Abandoning the metaphysics of opposites, Nietzsche considers his will to power thesis to have completed Kant's causal project by allowing for the real causal efficacy of empirical powers as a result of his view that intrinsic natures obtain at the level of empirical reality rather than things-in-themselves.

However, as indicated earlier, Nietzsche's proposal with regard to his will to power thesis is a contentious one, not just in its historical context as a response to Kant, but as a philosophical thesis in general. Consequently, Nietzsche's metaphysics has met with a particular objection that claims his attempt to reconcile relationality and intrinsicality is doomed to failure on the basis of the view that intrinsic and relational natures are mutually exclusive. In the next chapter we shall consider this objection in detail, arguing that Nietzsche has at his disposal the necessary conceptual tools to overcome it. Thus in our next chapter we shall attempt to show how Nietzsche's project of reconciling relational and intrinsic natures is a cogent though still controversial position.

NOTES

1. Friedrich Nietzsche, *Beyond Good and Evil*, translated by Marion Faber (Oxford: Oxford University Press, 1998 [1886]), 36. Henceforth cited as *BGE*.
2. Arthur Schopenhauer, *The World as Will and Representation*, Volume II, translated by E. F. J. Payne (New York: Dover 1966 [1844]), p. 44. Henceforth cited as *WWR*, II. For Schopenhauer's argument that natural force is a direct objectification of the Will as thing-in-itself, see Arthur Schopenhauer, *The World as Will and Representation*, Volume I, translated by E. F. J. Payne (New York: Dover, 1966 [1819]), pp. 133–4. Henceforth cited as *WWR*, I.

3. Friedrich Nietzsche, *The Will to Power*, edited by R. J. Hollingdale, translated by Walter Kaufmann (New York: Vintage Books, 1968 [1901]), 95. Henceforth cited as *WP*.

4. Friedrich Nietzsche, *The Gay Science*, translated by Walter Kaufmann (New York: Vintage Books, 1974 [1882/1887]), 357. Henceforth cited as *GS*. Nietzsche has often been interpreted as a proponent of Hume's criticism of the objective applicability of the concept of causality. Advocates of this interpretation tend to appeal for support to Nietzsche's comments on the Will as cause and to his suggestion that the concept of causality is a useful fiction and not a representation of real causal relations in passages such as *BGE*, 21 and *Twilight of the Idols*, 'The Four Great Errors', 3. Friedrich Nietzsche, *Twilight of the Idols*, included in *Twilight of the Idols/The Anti-Christ*, translated by R. J. Hollingdale (London: Penguin, 1990 [1889]). Henceforth cited as *TI*. However, if one examines Nietzsche's comments on the topic of causality and the Will in detail we find that it is only a particular view of causality and the Will that he rejects. That is, Nietzsche abandons the mechanist account of causality as succession, what he calls 'the *most common* explanations' (Nietzsche, *TI*, 'The Four Great Errors', 5), and he rejects a 'simplistic' understanding of the Will as something unitary and modelled on the idea of a substantial subject rather than causal efficacy *per se* (Nietzsche, *BGE*, 19). See chapter 4 for further discussion of these issues.

5. See Friedrich Nietzsche, *Sämtliche Werke. Kritische Studienausgabe*, edited by Giorgio Colli and Mazzino Montinari (Berlin and München: de Gruyter and dtv, 1980), 1, pp. 799ff. Henceforth cited as *KSA*. I have consulted Marianne Cowan's translation, *Philosophy in the Tragic Age of the Greeks* (Washington: Regnery Publishing 1998). Henceforth cited as *PTG*.

6. Gottfried Wilhelm Leibniz, *Die mathematischen Schriften*, 7 volumes, edited by C. I. Gerhardt (Berlin: verlag von A. Asher, 1849–63), Volume 6.

7. René Descartes, *Principles of Philosophy* (1644), translated by John Cottingham, Robert Stoothoff and Dugald Murdoch, in *The Philosophical Writings of Descartes*, Volume I (Cambridge: Cambridge University Press, 1990), Part two, section 25, p. 233.

8. See 'A Letter from M. Leibniz to the Editor, Containing an Explanation of the Difficulties which M. Bayle found with the New System of the Union of the Soul and Body' (1698), in *G. W. Leibniz. Philosophical Texts*, translated by R. S. Woolhouse and Richard Francks (Oxford: Oxford University Press, 1998), p. 207.

9. G. W. Leibniz, *Specimen Dynamicum* (1695), in *G. W. Leibniz. Philosophical Texts*, sections 37–40, pp. 168ff.

10. Sections 1–11 and 114–15 of *Thoughts on the True Estimation of Living Forces* (1749) are translated by John Handyside in *Kant's Inaugural Dissertation and Early Writings on Space* (Westport, CT: Hyperion Press, 1929). The entire text is to be found in Volume 1 of the Academy edition of Kant's works, *Gesammelte Schriften*, edited by Akademie der Wissenschaften (Berlin: Reimer, later DeGruyter, 1910). Henceforth cited as *LF*.

11. I draw on the following discussions of Kant's philosophical development: Lewis White Beck, *Early German Philosophy. Kant and His Predecessors* (Bristol: Thoemmes Press, 1996 [1969]); Gerd Buchdahl, *Metaphysics and the Philosophy of Science* (Cambridge, MA: Basil Blackwell, 1969); Michael Friedman, *Kant and the Exact Sciences* (Cambridge, MA: Harvard University Press, 1994 [1992]); Martin Schönfeld, *The Philosophy of the Young Kant: The Precritical Project* (Oxford: Oxford University Press, 2000).

12. Kant, *LF*, 15–18.

13. Ibid., 15–17.

14. Ibid., 1.
15. Kant contends in Part II of *LF*, despite some initial and unsuccessful attempts to argue for the mv2 quantification of its effects, that mathematics cannot prove the mv2 Leibnizean estimation of the magnitude of internal force. In response to arguments that in *LF* Kant aims to prove Descartes' approach to the question of force correct and Leibniz's mistaken, Martin Schönfeld contends that Kant aimed to reconcile the oppositions of Cartesianism and Leibnizeanism (Schönfeld, *The Philosophy of the Young Kant*, chapter 2). Nietzsche views Kant's pre-critical arguments as attempts at reconciliation. However, Kant's efforts in *LF* fall short of Nietzsche's envisaged reconciliation as a result of Kant's distinction between the metaphysical and physical reality of force.
16. Kant's calculations in *LF* were, however, in error. See Schönfeld, *The Philosophy of the Young Kant*, p. 53 for a discussion of this issue.
17. Kant illustrates his thesis regarding the self-organising character of matter in *Universal Natural History* with his nebular hypothesis, which was later described by Schopenhauer as the 'Kant–Laplace' hypothesis due to the fact that Pierre-Simon de Laplace had published a similar hypothesis in 1796 (Schopenhauer, *WWR*, I, p. 148). According to Kant, the formation of the solar system is similar to the formation of the cosmos. He argues that a 'single universal rule' informs and guides the evolution of the cosmos from primitive matter endowed initially with attractive force and later repulsive force. In addition to formulating the nebular hypothesis of the origin of the solar system, Kant explains the appearance of the Milky Way and argues for an infinite number of galaxies like our own, the existence of a planet between Mars and Saturn and others beyond Saturn.
18. Immanuel Kant, *Universal Natural History and Theory of the Heavens*, translated by Stanley L. Jaki (Edinburgh: Scottish Academic Press, 1981 [1755]), p. 91. Henceforth cited as *UNH*.
19. Ibid., p. 82.
20. Ibid., p. 84.
21. Ibid., p. 88. Lewis White Beck claims that in *UNH* Kant 'out-Newtoned Newton'. See his *Early German Philosophy: Kant and His Predecessors*, p. 431.
22. Kant, *UNH*, p. 85.
23. Ibid., p. 86.
24. Ibid., p. 86. Kant's attempt to bring together in one ontological domain the quantitative character of sensible matter with the qualitative character of intelligent life is evident in his view that the development of intelligent life is the ultimate telos of the planets. He argues that the mechanical operations of matter will give rise to intelligent and rational life where the composition of the material parts due to their distance from the sun will determine the level of rationality in a living organism.
25. Nietzsche, *PTG*, pp. 109–10. Nietzsche attributes this view to both Anaxagoras and Kant.
26. Nietzsche, *WP*, 563–5.
27. G. W. Leibniz, *Monadology* (1714), 50, in *G. W. Leibniz. Philosophical Texts*, p. 274.
28. Nietzsche, *WP*, 688.
29. Friedrich Nietzsche, 'Zur Teleologie', in *Werke und Briefe. Historisch–Kritische Gesamtausgabe* (München: C. H. Beck'sche Verlagsbuchhandlung, 1933–42), 3: 371–94. These notes are translated by Claudia Crawford and included under the heading 'On Teleology' as an Appendix to her *The Beginning of Nietzsche's Theory of Language* (Berlin: de Gruyter, 1988), p. 252. Henceforth cited as *OT*.

30. Kant, *UNH*, pp. 85–6.
31. Nietzsche, *OT*, p. 248. 'Chance' is not opposed to 'necessity', for Nietzsche, but rather it is opposed to the idea that the empirical world is ordered, however immanently, according to a divine intention such that this is the best of all possible worlds.
32. For his rejection of superfluous teleology, see Nietzsche, *BGE*, 13. One might argue that Nietzsche's will to power thesis is teleological. However, it is not, in Nietzsche's view, superfluously so, because it does not appeal to a final state of things, nor does he suggest that this is the best of all possible worlds. Nietzsche entertains the possibility that reality might be configured differently if the fundamental constituents of reality, powers, configured their relations to other powers differently. See his view that the world, constituted by force, 'transforms' itself in Nietzsche, *WP*, 1067. Nietzsche thinks that his appeal to chance, a 'storm that throws things about' (Nietzsche, *OT*, p. 248), allows for such alternative arrangements, whilst Kant's appeal to perfection precludes it. Nietzsche's emphasis on chance, rejecting that this is the best of all possible worlds, is another point of difference between him and Leibniz.
33. Immanuel Kant, *Critique of Pure Reason*, translated by Norman Kemp Smith (London: Macmillan 1929 [1781/1787]), A685–8/B713–16. Henceforth cited as *CPR*. See *CPR*, A691/B719 for both Kant's description of physico-theology as dogmatic and his non-dogmatic regulative proposal. Nietzsche indicates in *OT* that he is not ultimately happy with Kant's pre-critical efforts, contending that the project is overly 'optimistic' in its emphasis on a 'plan' rather than 'chance' (Nietzsche, *OT*, p. 252). That the source of his criticism resides in Kant's physico-theology is suggested in his naming Kant's 'The Only Possible Argument in Support of a Demonstration of the Existence of God' (1763) alongside *UNH* in *OT* (Nietzsche, *OT*, p. 252). Section 2 of the latter text is an abbreviation of Kant's argument in *UNH*. Kant contends his argument in section 2 is a probabilistic one, not strictly qualifying as a proof, whilst the ontological argument outlined in the first section does properly constitute a demonstration. Immanuel Kant, 'The Only Possible Argument in Support of a Demonstration of the Existence of God' (1763), in Immanuel Kant, *The Cambridge Edition of the Works of Immanuel Kant. Theoretical Philosophy 1755–1770*, translated by David Walford (Cambridge: Cambridge University Press, 1992), 2: 161–2.
34. Nietzsche, *BGE*, 12, 14.
35. Kant, *CPR*, Bxvi.
36. Kant also addresses the possibility of regulative belief in the systematic unity of empirical nature in his 'Appendix to the Transcendental Dialectic', in *CPR*. In *CPR* Kant attributes the regulative ideal of systematicity in empirical knowledge to the faculty of theoretical reason, whilst in *Critique of Judgment* he attributes this task to the faculty of reflective judgement. Since I am primarily concerned with the function and role of regulative principles rather than the faculty to which they should be assigned, I shall refrain from investigating why Kant makes this change, using the terms 'regulative' and 'reflective' indiscriminately.
37. Nietzsche, *BGE*, Preface.
38. Immanuel Kant, *Metaphysical Foundations of Natural Science*, translated by James Ellington (Indianapolis, IN: Bobbs-Merrill, 1970 [1786]), 503. Henceforth cited as *MF*. Kant's Principle of the 'Anticipations of Perception' is: 'In all appearances, the real, which is an object of sensation has intensive magnitude, that is, a degree' (Kant, *CPR*, B207). Here Kant argues that empirical realities must be intensive magnitudes. His dynamic view of matter in *MF* is intended to provide empirical content to the principle of the 'Anticipations' (Kant, *MF*, 478).

39. Kant, *MF*, 543. We have seen how in *UNH* Kant attempted to reconcile the relational character of force with its intrinsic nature. In another work belonging to the same period entitled the 'Physical Monadology' (1756), Kant addresses this issue in terms of explaining how the Leibnizean view that the ultimate constituents of matter are absolutely simple can be reconciled with the geometrical infinite divisibility of space. Kant's solution to the difficulty is to argue that monads are themselves indivisible extensionless points whose sphere of activity is infinitely divisible. (The text is included in Kant, *The Cambridge Edition of the Works of Immanuel Kant. Theoretical Philosophy 1755–1770*, pp. 47–66.) However, Kant's critical writings abandon all attempts to reconcile the simplicity of Leibnizean substances with spatial divisibility, contending that the attempt to combine these two elements derives from a transcendental realist viewpoint that mistakes appearances for things-in-themselves. Consequently he argues in the 'Dynamics' chapter of *MF* that material substance is, like space, infinitely divisible. In the 'Second Antinomy' of *CPR* he also argues that empirical substance is infinitely divisible, although we never actually experience it as infinitely divided. These arguments lead to his rejection of the simplicity of empirical substance. What this ultimately amounts to is the view that empirical substance is relational through and through and that simplicity can obtain only at the level of things-in-themselves.
40. See Buchdahl, *Metaphysics and the Philosophy of Science*, p. 556 for discussion of this issue in the context of Kant's notion of 'construction'.
41. Kant, *CPR*, A270/B236.
42. Ibid., A265/B321.
43. This has the consequence for Kant that 'matter has no absolutely internal determinations and grounds of determination' (Kant, *MF*, 543).
44. Nietzsche, *WP*, 562.
45. Ibid., 562.
46. At *CPR*, A171/B213 Kant construes force as causally efficacious and as something known empirically, denying that the relational character of force requires intrinsic natures. However, according to Nietzsche, the empirical nature of force for Kant is reducible to *a priori* conditions of epistemic and ontological possibility supplied by the human mind. As a result, Kant fails to establish the metaphysical reality of empirical powers. Nietzsche maintains that causal powers can be considered real and causally efficacious only if they are both relational and intrinsic.
47. Nietzsche, *WP*, 554. Nietzsche does not seem to recognise Kant's appeal to reciprocal causality in the 'Third Analogy' in *CPR* as a feasible solution. The reason seems to be that Kant, according to Nietzsche, treats reciprocal causality as a formal imposition (Nietzsche, *BGE*, 21). Nietzsche may also have been influenced by Schopenhauer's claim that Kant's appeal to reciprocal causality is incoherent on the basis that if causes are events, then mutual interaction would entail a two-way causal relation between two events (Schopenhauer, *WWR*, I, pp. 459ff.). For a more favourable and recent account of Kant's Third Analogy, see Eric Watkins, *Kant and the Metaphysics of Causality* (Cambridge: Cambridge University Press, 2005).
48. Nietzsche, *GS*, 357.
49. See Buchdahl, *Metaphysics and the Philosophy of Science*, p. 556 for discussion of this issue.
50. Immanuel Kant, *Critique of Judgment*, translated by Werner S. Pluhar (Indianapolis, IN and Cambridge: Hackett, 1987 [1790]), 65. Henceforth cited as *CJ*. In *MF* Kant tells us that 'life means the capacity of a substance to determine itself to change, and of a material substance to determine itself to motion

or rest as change of its state.' (Kant, *MF*, 544). In his critical writings Kant rejects his earlier pre-critical view outlined in *LF* that there is a positive striving on the part of matter to maintain its state having taken on board Newton's view that inertia like rest is a state and that force is required only to induce an alteration in this state and not to maintain it. In so doing, he abandons what he calls 'hylozoism' as incompatible with the very concept of matter and empirical substance constituted by force. He writes in his 'Observation' to the proof of the second law of mechanics in *MF* that 'The inertia of matter is and signifies nothing but its lifelessness, as matter in itself' (Kant, *MF*, 544). In *CJ* he writes that 'we cannot even think of living matter [as postulated by one form of hylozoism] as possible. (The [very] concept of it involves a contradiction, since the essential character of matter is lifelessness, [in Latin] *inertia*)' (Kant, *CJ*, 73). He contends that we can conceive self-determining powers only in terms of an intelligent cause such as God that acts intentionally (Kant, *CJ*, 84).

51. Nietzsche, *OT*, p. 246. An issue arises, however, with regard to whether Kant understands mechanism in the same way in both *CPR* and *CJ*. Some commentators argue that Kant's understanding of mechanism in *CPR*, entailing the notion of succession in time, is different from his account of mechanism in *CJ*, entailing the determination of the whole by its parts. See, for example, Henry Allison, 'Kant's Antinomy of Teleological Judgment', in Paul Guyer (ed.), *Kant's Critique of the Power of Judgment: Critical Essays* (New York: Rowman and Littlefield, 2003), pp. 219–36 esp. pp. 221–2. Despite interpretive difficulties, Nietzsche seems to think that the two accounts are continuous in that they both restrict human knowledge to external relations. According to Kant, knowledge of the intrinsic character of things, whether construed as the 'internal nature' of non-empirical substance as in *CPR* or biological life as in *CJ*, is beyond the remit of the possibility of objective knowledge 'for us'. In *OT*, Nietzsche, citing Kuno Fischer's explanation of Kant, defines mechanism in terms of the efficient forces of physical science, applying these definitions to Kant's account of mechanism in *CJ*. He writes that 'mechanically to explain means to explain from external causes' or that 'What reason knows of nature through its concepts is nothing other than the effect of moving force, that is, mechanism' (Nietzsche, *OT* p. 242). That Nietzsche associates Kant's appeal to mechanical causality with his constitutive account of knowledge of *CPR* can be seen again from his citing Fischer's explanation of Kant: 'Matter is only external appearance' (Nietzsche, *OT*, p. 242). Consequently, Nietzsche's understanding of mechanism in Kant applies generally to Kant's project in both *CPR* and *CJ* and construes Kant's understanding of mechanical relations as external ones constituted by the human mind.

52. Nietzsche, *WP*, 253.

53. See Hannah Ginsborg, 'Kant on Understanding Organisms as Natural Purposes', in Eric Watkins (ed.), *Kant and the Sciences* (Oxford: Oxford University Press, 2001), pp. 231–58 for the characterisation of organisms in terms of normativity.

54. Kant, *CJ*, 69.

55. Ibid., 70. When mechanical and teleological judgements are considered reflective the thesis reads that 'All production of material things and their forms must be judged to be possible in terms of merely mechanical laws' whilst the antithesis reads that 'Some products of material nature cannot be judged to be possible in terms of merely mechanical laws. (Judging them requires a quite different causal law – viz., that of final causes).' As reflective principles we hold that although we must estimate nature in terms of mechanical laws it is nonetheless possible that other forms of causality obtain.

56. Ibid., 71.
57. Ibid., 69.
58. Ibid., 71.
59. Ibid., 70.
60. The possibility that the diversity of empirical nature may surpass the application of the categories suggests that nature for Kant, contrary to Nietzsche's argument, is irreducible to our epistemology. However, Nietzsche thinks, to the extent that reality is irreducible to our epistemology for Kant, it relies on intrinsic natures grounded in something unknowable, non-empirical and non-relational. Nietzsche wants to bring intrinsic natures to bear at the empirical and relational levels.
61. Kant, *CJ*, First Introduction, V, pp. 399–404. Kant contends that our specifically human cognitive constitution can cognise nature only in terms of mechanical laws. However, he argues that such cognition is contingent. The reason for this is that our cognition is sensible and requires the subsumption of empirically given data under the universal concepts of the Understanding. According to Kant, there is a gap between our mode of cognition and the possible diversity of empirical data such that we cannot be assured of the necessary empirical lawlikeness (the whole) of nature in its particularity (the parts) (Kant, *CJ*, 77). That is, although we can cognise particular instances, we cannot be assured that these instances form a system or whole connected necessarily.

    Kant argues that the only way this contingency can be overcome is by regulatively appealing to the logical possibility of a being whose mode of cognition is active rather than passive like ours and from whose point of view there is a necessary harmony between particular natural laws and our judgement. This entails that we think of the diversity of particular empirical laws as a system that has been purposively designed for our cognition (ibid., 77). Such contingency would not apply to a being whose mode of intuition is intellectual because its mode of cognition 'is not discursive but intuitive, and hence proceeds from the *synthetically universal* (the intuition of the whole as a whole) to the particular, i.e. from the whole to the parts. Hence such an understanding, as well as its presentation of the whole, has no *contingency* in the combination of the parts in order to make a determinate form of the whole possible' (ibid., 77).
62. Kant, *CJ*, 70. See also *CJ*, 78.
63. Ibid., 70–1. This means that the suggestions of some commentators, such as H. W. Cassirer and S. Körner, that Kant resolves the antinomy by rendering both mechanical principles and teleological principles regulative cannot be the whole solution. See J. D. McFarland, *Kant's Concept of Teleology* (Edinburgh: Edinburgh University Press, 1970), pp. 120–1 for a record and discussion of this literature. See also Henry Allison's 'Kant's Antinomy of Teleological Judgment', pp. 219–36.
64. Kant, *CJ*, 78.
65. Ibid., 75.
66. Ibid., 75. Kant writes that 'teleology cannot find final [*Vollendung*] answers to its inquiries except in a theology'.
67. Ibid., 77.
68. Nietzsche, *WP*, 253. Nietzsche's appeal to a primordial intellect in his early writings is obviously problematic here. Although there are some suggestions that the early Nietzsche thinks his own appeal to a primordial intellect avoids the charge of proliferation of explanatory levels on the basis that the experiences of the primordial intellect and those of the human instinctive intellect are identical, he nonetheless rejects the notion in his mature thought. See chapter 3 for discussion of this issue.

69. Nietzsche, *OT*, p. 252.
70. Nietzsche, *WP*, 621, 619. Kant also appeals to analogy, arguing that we can conceive the possibility of a natural purpose as a 'regulative concept for reflective judgment, allowing us to use a remote analogy with our own causality in terms of purposes generally' (Kant, *CJ*, 65). However, Nietzsche is dissatisfied with the fact that Kant's teleological explanation 'analogous to the causality of an understanding' (ibid., 75) appeals to a supersensible understanding. For a further discussion of Nietzsche's argument from analogy, see chapters 4 and 6.
71. Nietzsche, *OT*, p. 251.
72. Ibid., p. 246. I have modified Crawford's translation of this passage slightly to include Nietzsche's reference to constitutive judgements, which is omitted from Crawford's translation.
73. Nietzsche, *OT*, p. 249.
74. Ibid., p. 243. Nietzsche argues that Kant's account leads to a 'false antithesis' between the organic and the inorganic. Contrary to Kant, Nietzsche contends, 'it is admissible that the same principle exists within organic nature in the relationship of organisms to one another as in "inorganic nature"' (ibid., p. 248). This principle is that of 'chance' rather than design, rendering primary the constituent parts of the whole, which, possessed of an intrinsic nature, according to Nietzsche, may enter into various possible formations with one another. To the extent that the constituent powers contribute to such a whole, they are expedient, but only in an extrinsic sense. This is because, Nietzsche argues, the whole is a product of chance encounters between the parts. Nietzsche writes that 'Chance rules unconditionally, that means the opposite of expedience in nature. The storm which throws things about is chance. That is knowable' (ibid., p. 248). Consequently, Nietzsche draws the following conclusion:

> In the organic being the parts are expedient to its existence, that means it would not live, if the parts were inexpedient. With that nothing is decided about the single part. The part is a form of expedience: but it cannot be discerned, that it is the only possible form. The whole does not condition the parts, while the parts necessarily condition the whole. (ibid., p. 248)

75. Nietzsche, *OT*, p. 251.
76. See chapters 2 and 4.
77. Friedrich Nietzsche, 'On Schopenhauer' (1868), pp. 260–1, in Christopher Janaway, *Willing and Nothingness. Schopenhauer as Nietzsche's Educator* (Oxford: Clarendon Press, 1998). See also Friedrich Nietzsche, *Human, All Too Human*, translated by R. J. Hollingdale (Cambridge: Cambridge University Press, 1996 [1878–86]), Volume I, 'Of First and Last Things', 9. Henceforth cited as *HAH*.
78. For Nietzsche's appeal to natural causality, see Nietzsche, *HAH*, Volume I, 'The Religious Life', 111; Nietzsche, *BGE*, 36.

Chapter 6

Relationality and Intrinsicality in Nietzsche's Metaphysics

In our last chapter we saw that Nietzsche's metaphysics can be understood as a response to deficiencies in the Kantian system. According to Nietzsche, Kant fails to capture the nature of real causal efficacy, and central to Nietzsche's response to Kant is his proposal of the will to power thesis, which holds that empirical powers are causally efficacious because they are metaphysically real. Controversially proposing a metaphysics that understands the ultimate constituents of empirical reality as both relational and intrinsic, the will to power thesis represents the final step in Nietzsche's overcoming the metaphysics of opposites with which we began our investigation in chapter 1, particularly the opposition between self and world Nietzsche detects in Kant. Pivotal to Kant's separation of self and world, according to Nietzsche, is the disconnection between relational empirical reality and intrinsic natures obtaining at the level of things-in-themselves. Therefore, the ultimate success of Nietzsche's overcoming the opposition of self and world rests on the philosophical coherency of his aim to house intrinsic natures within the relational sphere of the empirical world.

In light of the importance of Nietzsche's metaphysics, this chapter extends our analysis of the will to power beyond the confines of its Kantian context in order to consider the philosophical cogency of Nietzsche's argument in favour of the reality of causal powers, a proposal that has been subject to a fundamental objection. The objection claims that the will to power thesis contains two incompatible aspects. On the one hand, Nietzsche wants to develop a relational metaphysics, describing the will to power as 'a kind of instinctual life in which all the organic functions . . . are synthetically linked to one another'.[1] He writes that the idea of a non-relational 'in-itself' is an 'absurd conception' and a 'nonsense'.[2] On the other hand, he appeals to the will to power as a thesis about the ultimate and intrinsic constitution of reality, describing it as 'The world as it is seen from the inside, the world defined and described by its "intelligible character"'.[3] It is objected that these two aspects of Nietzsche's metaphysics are incompatible on the basis of the understanding that relational properties and intrinsic properties are mutually exclusive.

First, we shall consider the roots of the objection to Nietzsche's proposal that the ultimate constituents of reality are both intrinsic and relational. The objection is founded on the view that Nietzsche's dismissal of both traditional substance metaphysics and the Kantian thing-in-itself necessitates the rejection of intrinsic natures and the consequent development of a relational metaphysics. Intrinsicality, equated with non-relational substances in which properties inhere, is thus construed as antithetical to relationality. This is the predominant view that claims that a relational property cannot also be an intrinsic one.

Second, we shall assess how Nietzsche can overcome this objection by putting forward a metaphysics of dispositional powers that rejects the idea of a non-dispositional substance base and not the idea of intrinsic natures *per se*. Nietzsche abandons the dichotomy between grounding relational properties in a non-relational substrate, on the one hand, and 'bare' dispositions, on the other. Informing this dichotomy is the idea that relational properties are real only if they are grounded in a non-relational substrate. In contrast, Nietzsche argues that relational properties are not bare in this sense but rather are intrinsic. The suggestion here is that part and parcel of Nietzsche's rejection of the metaphysics of opposites is his thesis that relationality and intrinsicality are not mutually exclusive.

OBJECTIONS TO NIETZSCHE ON THE ISSUE OF INTRINSIC AND RELATIONAL PROPERTIES

Our aim in this section is to inquire into what constitutes a relational property that is also intrinsic for Nietzsche. In this way we can come to understand how Nietzsche's claim that intrinsic and relational properties are not mutually exclusive opposites informs his thesis regarding the reality of powers. However, as indicated, in order to successfully implement this task we shall initially need to consider possible objections to the proposal that Nietzsche puts forward the idea of intrinsic properties at all. There are two significant but interrelated objections raised by Nietzsche commentators. The first objection is raised by Peter Poellner; the second by Hales and Welshon in response to Poellner.

Peter Poellner argues that Nietzsche puts forward a relational metaphysics that rejects the very idea of intrinsic properties. Moreover,

Poellner suggests that this relational metaphysics collapses into incoherence due to its dismissal of such intrinsic properties. Poellner's analysis is informed by two theses. The first claims that a relational property cannot be an intrinsic one. The second puts forward the view that relational properties must be grounded in something intrinsic and non-relational if they are to be real. Thus, according to Poellner, Nietzsche's proposal of a relational metaphysics is ultimately incoherent because it holds that all properties are relational or subject-implying whilst disallowing the possibility of essential properties. Citing Nietzsche, Poellner defines Nietzsche's anti-essentialism as the view that 'the properties of a thing are effects on *other* "things" . . . i.e. there is no thing without other things'.[4] On the basis of passages such as this one Poellner, asking us to consider a highly simplified Nietzschean universe comprising just two forces, assesses Nietzsche's position as follows:

> If indeed 'the essence of a thing is only an opinion about the "thing"' (WM 556), then the 'essence' of the quantum of force *a* would consist in whatever is the content of *b's* interpretation, which would therefore not really be an interpretation of anything ontologically independent of it, since *a's esse* would consist in its being perceived (or 'interpreted') by *b* as an entity of a certain kind affecting it (i.e. *b*). If we follow this strand of Nietzsche's thinking, *a* would have no existence other than *qua* perceptual or 'interpretive' content *vorgestellt* by *b*. But what are we to make of *b*, the second entity in this imaginary Nietzschean universe? Since his analysis of the essence of any entity as 'its' relations to (i.e. effects upon) other entities is universal in its scope, it has to apply to *b* as well. This means that, in our model, *b* is not identifiable separately from its effects on *a*; it *is* this effect, namely a certain perceptual content of *a's*. Nietzsche's claims thus seem to force us to say that *a* exists only *qua* perception ('interpretation') of *b*, while *b* exists only as a perception of *a* – yet both are also required to be separate in some sense, since otherwise there would not be a plurality of quanta of force at all.[5]

Poellner thus interprets Nietzsche's anti-essentialism along the lines of a Berkeleian idealism which suggests a quantum of force is reducible to sensations (perceptions/interpretations) in another quantum of force. The incoherence sets in, Poellner contends, when Nietzsche claims that the other quantum of force (the 'second entity' in the particular relation evoked here) also lacks a constitution in itself. However, Poellner argues that Nietzsche is ultimately inconsistent in his anti-essentialism because 'he does assert a number of things about the intrinsic nature of beliefs, emotions, desires, and intentions – in particular, that all desires are variations of the desire for the experience of power and that the nature of our emotions, intentions, and even of our beliefs is at any time specified by the particular form which this desire takes, i.e. by the form of the will to power an instance of which we *are* at that time.' Poellner suggests, however, that Nietzsche has within his means a plausible solution to the incoherency charge. He contends that Nietzsche would need to argue that (a) there are beings that have no intrinsic nature or existence independently of their being 'my' interpretation and (b) that 'I' have an intrinsic nature which is correctly described as the will to power.[6] However, Poellner claims Nietzsche deprives himself of this solution by transferring his perspectival or relational analysis of objective reality to the sphere of the subjective:[7]

> For Nietzsche, it makes no sense to speak of the intrinsic nature, the constitution in itself, of objects *qua* objects, independently of their being objects of awareness and concern for some 'subject'. Many of his reflections in the notebooks show that he universalizes his account of objects so as to apply also to any kind of mental content. Rather like Schopenhauer in some passages, he is thus led to the position that every content of awareness – every instantiation of phenomenal qualities having a certain perspectival what-it-is-likeness – is what it is not intrinsically, but only *for* what perforce has to be a transcendental subject which, logically, cannot have any intrinsic properties. Consequently, there can be nothing which has intrinsic, non-relational properties, i.e. a 'constitution in itself'.[8]

According to Poellner, Nietzsche would have avoided the charge of incoherence if he had made all qualities of objects subject-dependent qualities of an independent and intrinsically constituted subject. He suggests that Nietzsche should have appealed to an intrinsically constituted subject upon which all relational properties existentially depend.[9] Implicit here is the idea that relationality is existentially committed and intrinsicality is not. Poellner holds that, for Nietzsche, a relational 'thing' is bare, implying other things on which it depends for its existence, whilst an intrinsic thing is a non-relational thing that is not existentially dependent. A relational property, according to such an analysis, implies accompaniment whilst an intrinsic property is one the having of which does not imply or depend on other existents. By definition, the argument goes, a relational thing cannot also be an intrinsic thing because a relational thing is existentially committed to the existence of other things whilst an intrinsic thing is not existentially committed in this way even though it is compatible with other things depending on it.[10] Intrinsicality is thus thought to be non-relational whilst relationality is thought to be non-intrinsic.

Steven D. Hales and Rex Welshon argue, in response, that Poellner has misidentified essential properties with intrinsic properties and that

Nietzsche can, contrary to Poellner's view, successfully combine the idea of relational properties with the idea of essential properties. Thus Hales and Welshon contend that, for example, having a and b as my parents is essential to me although the property of having a and b as my parents is a relational extrinsic property because 'my instantiation of it requires the existence of two entities distinct from me in order to be instantiated'.[11] Moreover, Hales and Welshon contend that the issue of essentialism and anti-essentialism are only bit players in Poellner's articulation of Nietzsche's argument, which 'goes from the claim that there are only relational properties and no intrinsic properties to the contradictory conclusion that there is and there is not a plurality of entities'. Hales and Welshon define the problem as follows:

> he cannot affirm both that all of an entity's properties are relational properties and that there is a plurality of entities. Since he does affirm both claims, it looks like Nietzsche's perspectivist ontology is internally inconsistent.[12]

However, Hales and Welshon argue, contrary to Poellner, that if all of an entity's properties are relational, then there must be a plurality of entities:

> After all, a relational property F of x entails the existence of a $y \neq x$ in order that F be instantiated by x. Hence, if there is anything at all that has a property, then there are at least two things. So, the Parmenidean worry is overturned: it is consistent to affirm both that all of an entity's properties are relational properties and that there is a plurality of entities. In particular, it is consistent for Nietzsche to affirm that all of an entity's properties are perspectives by another entity and that there is a plurality of such perspective-constituted entities.[13]

Nonetheless, Hales and Welshon, like Poellner, argue that Nietzsche rejects the idea of intrinsic properties. The reasoning informing Hales' and Welshon's argument is similar to that informing Poellner's. Both arguments imply that intrinsic properties are incompatible with relationality because intrinsic properties are existentially uncommitted. Thus Hales and Welshon contend that Nietzsche can justifiably appeal to essential properties that are extrinsic and relational because such properties are existentially committed. A relational property, they maintain, implies the existence of another perspectivally constituted entity on which its existence depends. Yet Nietzsche cannot, according to their argument, combine relationality and intrinsicality because this would be to attempt to reconcile existential committedness with existential uncommittedness. Relationality and intrinsicality, according to this view, are mutually exclusive.

However, there are both specifically textual reasons and generally philosophical ones that warrant understanding relationality and intrinsicality as compatible rather than mutually exclusive. First, the appeal to relational intrinsic properties facilitates both Nietzsche's rejection of the metaphysics of opposites and his Kantian-inspired argument in favour of the fundamental reality of causal powers. Both Poellner's and Hales' and Welshon's identification of the relational with the non-intrinsic fails to make adequate sense of Nietzsche's obvious appeal to inner determinations of things, a factor of which Poellner is aware in his discussion of Nietzsche's supplementation of force with an 'inner will'.[14] Second, the idea of intrinsic relational properties is arguably a coherent and legitimate idea on a particular understanding of what constitutes intrinsicality and relationality.

Nevertheless, before we proceed to demonstrate the compatibility of intrinsicality and relationality, it is important to note that Poellner's concerns are not without foundation. For passages abound in Nietzsche's writings, where he suggests relationality implies that individual power-wills are reducible to perspectives taken on them from without and consequently that relational properties are existentially committed in just this sense. For example, Nietzsche writes:

> There are no 'facts-in-themselves', for a sense must always be projected into them before there can be 'facts'.
>
> The question 'what is that?' is an imposition of meaning from some other viewpoint. 'Essence', the 'essential nature,' is something perspective and already presupposes a multiplicity. At bottom of it there always lies 'what is it for *me*?' (for us, for all that lives etc.)
>
> A thing would be defined once all creatures had asked 'what is that?' and had answered their question. Supposing one single creature, with its own relationships and perspectives for all things, were missing, then the thing would not yet be 'defined'.
>
> In short: the essence of a thing is only an *opinion* about the 'thing'. Or rather: 'it is considered' is the real 'it is', the sole 'this is'.[15]

Nietzsche also writes: 'There is no "essence-in-itself" (it is only relations that constitute an essence)', thus suggesting that all relational properties are existentially committed.[16] That is, the properties of a thing are reducible to a perspective taken on it by another thing. We cannot explain away such passages. But perhaps we may understand them in terms of Nietzsche's reluctance to explicitly distinguish intrinsically constituted force from its effects on other things lest it be said he distinguishes between non-relational substances and their inherent properties. Nevertheless, if the above passages constituted Nietzsche's only statement on the matter, he would indeed be guilty of Poellner's charge. However, in other places such as *Beyond Good and Evil*, 36, Nietzsche appeals to the intrinsic nature of force whilst also ascribing relationality to force. Thus, although there are evident tensions in his position, tensions that arguably stem from his insufficient understanding of the type of metaphysics that he was proposing, Nietzsche nonetheless on occasion gives us reason to believe that his ascription of both relationality and intrinsicality to the ultimate constituents of reality is philosophically cogent. The task of explaining how powers can be relational whilst also intrinsic or existentially uncommitted entails, therefore, glossing over the tensions in Nietzsche's writings, focusing on those aspects that lend support to and make sense of the thesis that relationality and intrinsicality are not mutually exclusive.

Nietzsche assists such efforts when he argues, contrary to Poellner's suggestion that relationality can be combined with intrinsicality only by succumbing to subjective idealism or phenomenalism, that relational properties are existentially uncommitted to the actual existence of a human subject with intrinsic properties. Nietzsche makes relational properties non-subject-implying in this sense by making it clear in *Beyond Good and Evil* that it is something like Lockean tertiary qualities rather than secondary qualities that he has in mind. Tertiary qualities, like secondary qualities, are relational and dispositional but, unlike secondary qualities, are perceiver-independent. The property of being soluble in water, for example, is a tertiary quality whilst colour is a perceiver-dependent secondary quality. That it is tertiary qualities that Nietzsche has in mind can be seen from his statement: 'I do not mean the material world as a delusion, as "appearance" or "representation" (in the Berkeleian or Schopenhauerian sense), but rather . . . as a kind of instinctual life in which all the organic functions . . . are synthetically linked to one another . . .'[17] These tertiary qualities are subject-independent but relational. They relate to things other than a human perceiver. Thus the instantiation of these properties is independent of there being a human perceiver.[18] However, the fact that the relational properties of the will to power metaphysics are not reducible to or grounded in a human subject with an intrinsic nature does not save Nietzsche completely from Poellner's charge. Nietzsche must also be able to show that relational properties are not subject-implying in the other sense of being existentially dependent on one another. For Nietzsche claims reality itself is perspectival and that the individual power-wills that make up this reality view the world from a particular point of view. Poellner's charge of incoherency suggests that perspectivally oriented tertiary qualities are existentially dependent on the actual existence of other tertiary qualities. If Nietzsche is to overcome the charge, he must demonstrate that power-wills are both independent entities possessed of an intrinsic nature and relational. Nietzsche's views on this issue are complex. He wants to appeal to intrinsic natures but without re-instantiating the substance/attribute distinction of traditional metaphysics. He needs some way to reconcile these demands. He can do this by demonstrating that power-wills are irreducible to its effects or interpretations imposed from without by another perspectivally constituted power-will. That Nietzsche allows that powers are irreducible and thus intrinsic is evident from how he construes the relations between individual power-wills, an examination of which affords us significant insight into how he understands relationality and intrinsicality.

Nietzsche contends that power-wills can be understood as either 'active' or 'reactive' and that this characterisation of their natures explains the manner in which they relate to one another. Active or strong powers are motivated by a certain spontaneity to express their natures.[19] That is, they are motivated from within to perform their distinguishing activity.[20] He writes of the 'fundamental instinct of life which aims at *the expansion of power*'[21] and 'the essential pre-eminence of the spontaneous, attacking, infringing, reinterpreting, reordering, and formative forces'.[22] Although active because they are also wills to power, powers of a weaker constitution express themselves in reaction to the activity of stronger powers. Nietzsche describes the characteristic behaviour of weaker powers as 'an activity of second rank', thus suggesting that powers, both weak and strong, desire to manifest fully, either actively or reactively, their specific natures.[23] However, powers must take due heed of certain impediments to their manifestation. Due to the activity of strong powers, weaker powers must resist their possible vanquishing in a desire to preserve themselves whilst the stronger power must attempt to overcome this resistance. As a result, power-wills are drawn into a hierarchical relation with other powers. This is the origin of object-formation, according to Nietzsche, whereby a 'thing' is constituted by powers coming together to form a collection of qualities or dispositions. He adopts two positions with regard to the relations between powers that constitute an 'object'. Although the first position supports Poellner's interpretation, Nietzsche also endorses a second position that supports the possibility of rendering compatible intrinsic and relational properties. Consequently, although on some occasions he appears to subscribe to a subjectivist account of object-formation, on other occasions he abandons this view, arguing that powers form 'things' by grouping together with other powers according to their natures.

Subjectivism is the view that the properties of a 'thing' are interpretations of that 'thing' by an external interpreter. It suggests that stronger powers overcome resistances to their manifestation by entirely appropriating and vanquishing their weaker counterparts.[24] The incoherence detected by Poellner above, however, arises from the fact that for Nietzsche this external observer, the stronger power, is also perspectivally constituted and so is, in turn, dependent on an external observer. As a result, subjectivist objects do not form aggregates according to their natures but rather their union is extrinsic to their natures. On such a view, what passes for an object in one perspective may be very different from what passes for an object in another perspective. In this case the 'nature' of the appropriated power is defined by the stronger power whilst the nature of the stronger power is, in turn, reducible to its interpretation by yet another power. However, it is not clear that Nietzsche ever fully endorsed the idea that a 'thing' is constituted by a perspective taken on it by an external observer. For Nietzsche argues by way of criticism of the subjectivist view that objects are individuated according to the intrinsic natures of its component parts. He writes, for example:

> Where a certain unity obtains in the grouping of things, one has always posited *spirit* as the cause of this coordination: for which notion there is no ground whatever . . . there is no ground whatever for ascribing to spirit the properties of organization and systematization.[25]

On the basis of this criticism Nietzsche adopts an associationist theory of object-formation over the subjectivist model. According to the associationist view, quanta of force interact and collaborate according to their respective natures:

> Perspectivism is only a complex form of specificity. My idea is that every specific body strives to become master over all space and to extend its force (– its will to power) and to thrust back all that resists its extension (*und Alles das zurückzustoßen, was seiner Ausdehnung widerstrebt*). But it continually encounters similar efforts on the part of other bodies and ends by coming to an arrangement ('union') with those of them that are sufficiently related to it: thus they then conspire together for power. And the process goes on –[26]

Nietzsche suggests that although strong powers seek to express their natures through spontaneous activity they encounter resistance on the part of other powers. The associationist view of object-formation holds that dispositions come together by way of a compromise to mutually facilitate the optimal expression of their intrinsic natures. Consequently, Nietzsche argues that powers 'conspire together', suggesting that they have an intrinsic nature that cannot be reduced to or entirely vanquished by another. He writes:

> To what extent resistance is present even in obedience; individual power is by no means surrendered. In the same way, there is in commanding an admission that the absolute power of the opponent has not been vanquished, incorporated, disintegrated. 'Obedience' and 'commanding' are forms of struggle.[27]

Here Nietzsche suggests that informing the relations between powers is the insatiable desire on the part of power-wills, both constitutionally 'strong' and 'weak' wills, to express their natures. A strong power does so by seeking to incorporate within itself the weaker power.[28] However, such attempts at appropriation are met with resistance, which must be overcome. The conspiratorial relations into which it enters with the weaker power are a means of addressing the *de facto* resistance which the strong power encounters to its efforts, and these arrangements lead, according to Nietzsche, not to the vanquishing of the weaker by the stronger whereby the weak is reduced to the strong but rather to the qualitative expansion of the 'greater' power.[29]

Against the background of this particular model of the relations between powers, Nietzsche contends that greater powers 'appropriate' lesser powers whereby 'the latter operates as a function of the greater power'.[30] However, the incorporated 'lesser' power, Nietzsche contends, retains its intrinsic nature and is not a mere instrument of the greater power's will. Nietzsche suggests as much when he writes: 'It is a matter of a struggle between two elements of unequal power: a new arrangement of forces is reached according to the measure of power of each of them.'[31] Nietzsche argues that by entering into relations the greater power 'grows' in a qualitative sense; its perspective becomes broader and more comprehensive as it incorporates the viewpoints of the other powers with which it has made an 'arrangement'. It does not relinquish its own viewpoint but rather expands it by incorporating within it the viewpoint of the other power in such a way that this extended viewpoint enhances the attainment of its specific end.[32] Nietzsche writes of the manner in which a strong power enters into relations with others that its intention is to assimilate new 'experiences', whilst enhancing its feeling of growth and increasing its power.[33] However, although lesser powers do not expand in the same way but rather seek to preserve themselves by expressing their natures in the context of the stronger power, both greater and lesser powers retain their intrinsic natures and are ultimately irreducible to one another. According to Nietzsche, the activity of an individual power is informed by an 'inner will' as its intrinsic nature, suggesting that its specific point of view is irreducible to the point of view of other power-wills. Consequently, a power's nature is existentially independent of perspectives taken on it from an external vantage-point.

Nietzsche responds here to a challenge concerning the ultimate reality of force-dispositions. Locke denies full metaphysical status to both secondary and tertiary qualities. Relational properties, he contends, are 'not contained in the real existence of things', but are 'something extraneous and superinduced'.[34] According to Locke, both secondary and tertiary qualities are powers in the object to induce effects either in a subject or another object. Only primary qualities, which are non-relational and non-dispositional, he claims, are fully real. Poellner sees Nietzsche as also denying the fundamental reality of powers when he argues that powers for Nietzsche are reducible to interpretations imposed on them from without by perspectivally constituted entities and that Nietzsche should have grounded power-wills in an intrinsically constituted subject. In contrast, however, Nietzsche appeals to the inner or intrinsic nature of force, rendering force existentially independent of other forces. The intrinsic nature of force is manifested, according to Nietzsche, in the specific quantum of power which that force is. He appeals to objective degrees of power, which in turn indicate the measure of the power's causal efficacy.[35] The degree of causal efficacy dictates a power's capacity to express its nature by overcoming resistances or by preserving itself against the encroaching attempts of other powers. As a result, force-dispositions are real and informed by an intrinsic nature.

However, if power-wills are real and their engagements with other powers do not entail their existential dependency on those other power-wills, how are we to understand their relational character? We need to identify how Nietzsche construes relationality if not in the subject-implying sense suggested by Poellner's analysis. Answering this question will also shed further light on what the existential independence or intrinsicality of powers entails. Throughout his writings Nietzsche indicates that he rejects an event model of causality in favour of a model based on causal powers.[36] According to the event model, relations can obtain only between actually existent relata. Consequently, both cause and effect must exist if a relation is to be instantiated. Moreover, according to Hume's event model of causality, cause and effect relate to one another in terms of temporal succession.[37] In contrast, on some versions of Nietzsche's power model the proper relata of a power is its manifestation, which may or may not exist at any particular time.[38] Nietzsche suggests that the power is intrinsically connected to its effect understood as the manifestation of its 'inherent' nature and that when manifested this relata is simultaneous rather than successive.[39] Thus Nietzsche rejects what he calls the 'doing separated from that which it does'.[40] Some commentators have interpreted Nietzsche as claiming here that a power is reducible to its effect where its effect is understood to be its reception or interpretation by another perspectivally constituted entity. In fact, it is precisely this view that gives rise to Poellner's incoherency charge.[41] However, if understood in terms of his rejection of an event model of causation as succession in time, we can see that Nietzsche is proposing a power model where cause and effect are simultaneous rather than reducible to one another and where the effect is the manifestation of the power's nature rather than its interpretation by another power. A power manifests itself, we have seen, by adopting either the role of 'dominator' or 'dominated' in its associations with other powers. As a result, although a power manifests its nature in the context of entering into arrangements with other powers, neither its nature nor its manifestation is reducible to its interpretation by those other powers. According to Nietzsche's associationist model of object-formation powers retain their intrinsic natures when engaging with other powers rather than being vanquished by them. Consequently, by understanding the proper relata of a power to be its manifestation Nietzsche draws our attention to the spontaneity and activity of powers in addition to affording us insight into what properly constitutes the intrinsic character of power-wills. For if the proper relata of a power-will is its manifestation, then the intrinsicality of the power entails the power's conceivable independence of its manifestation. One way of demonstrating such independence would be to show that powers can retain their natures even when they are not manifested. That Nietzsche can allow for this possibility is suggested by his reference to the 'weakness of the weak' as 'his *essence*, his effecting, his whole unique, unavoidable, undetachable reality'.[42] It remains for us now to show how relationality and intrinsicality, understood in these specific senses, are compatible rather than mutually exclusive. Assessing the coherency of the idea that a power does not cease to be even when it is not manifested, we must investigate the cogency of claiming that relationality can also be intrinsic.

THE COMPATIBILITY OF RELATIONALITY AND INTRINSICALITY

The usual view of relations claims that for a relation to hold, both terms in the relation must actually exist.[43] The usual view, then, maintains that dispositional powers cannot be intrinsic because unmanifested dispositions do not exist. They exist only when their relata actually obtain, that is, when they are manifested. The usual view of relations when applied to the metaphysics of dispositions would claim, for example, that a pianist when not engaged in the activity of playing the piano does not have the power to play the piano. Nietzsche's view, formulated on the basis of his rejection of an event model of causality, that the proper relata of a power is its manifestation rather than another power that interprets it and that a power is conceivably independent of its manifestation, leads to his denial of the usual understanding of relations. In this section I shall examine two responses to the question of how Nietzsche's dismissal of the usual view of relations and his consequent claim that power-wills are both relational and intrinsic might be a coherent philosophical position. Of the two responses, which include the conditional analysis and an argument from analogy, only the latter is properly suited to Nietzsche's purposes. Moreover, I shall contend that Nietzsche's position bears significant resemblances to a contemporary alternative to the conditional analysis of powers, an examination of which sheds light on how Nietzsche can overcome some of the most difficult objections that have been levied at the power thesis in general.

The conditional analysis is the most notable attempt to explain how a thing can have a disposition or power even when the disposition or power is not being manifested.[44] That is, the conditional analysis attempts to explain how a disposition can be intrinsic. The conditional analysis in its simplest form attempts to save the intrinsicality of dispositions by arguing that an object can have a power without manifesting it if the manifestation of the power is dependent or conditional on an external stimulus.[45] However, a conditional analysis is unsuitable to Nietzsche's project for two reasons. First, the conditional analysis, unless supplemented with the notion of a causal base conceptually distinct from the power, threatens the intrinsicality of dispositions. Second, Nietzsche's appeal to the active spontaneity and independence of dispositions suggests, contrary to such conditional analyses, that the manifestation of a dispositional power is not dependent on a stimulus to activate the disposition. Moreover, the conditional analysis of dispositions is a purely conceptual argument that is inadequate to Nietzsche's project of capturing the real causal efficacy of powers. The conditional analysis is initially formulated in its simplest form as:

An object x is disposed at time t to give response r to stimulus s iff, if x were to undergo stimulus s at time t then x would give response r.

However, this initial formulation of the conditional analysis succumbs to a number of difficulties, which pose a threat to intrinsicality. The conditional analysis does not appeal to the nature of the object to explain why the response follows from the stimulus. Consequently, the conditional analysis as it is articulated in the simple version allows for the possibility that x does not itself have the power to manifest r, and that the only powers manifested are Malebranche dispositions that belong to something extrinsic to the object rather than to the object itself.[46] According to Malebranche, bodies are conserved through the eternal and continuous creative power of God. This is an occasionalist thesis, which appeals to an extrinsic determining force of events in time. The simple conditional analysis gives rise to occasionalism thus threatening the intrinsicality of dispositions.[47] However, this is not the only difficulty arising from the simple conditional analysis. A further threat to the intrinsicality of dispositions confronts the simple conditional analysis in the form of the problem of finkish dispositions, as diagnosed by C. B. Martin.[48]

The simple conditional analysis explains counterfactually how an object can have a power or disposition even when it is not being manifested. According to this analysis a thing would manifest a disposition should certain conditions, stimulus s, for example, obtain. However, the problem of finkishness suggests that the very condition to which the simple conditional analysis appeals to save the intrinsicality of a disposition may in fact give rise not to the expected result but rather to the acquisition or loss of a disposition.

In order to demonstrate how the problem of finkishness can lead to the loss of a disposition, let us suppose that an object x is disposed to give response r to stimulus s. The problem of finkish dispositions arises when the stimulus s is the condition under which object x loses the disposition to give response r. In such a case x retains the disposition for as long as s does not occur. That is, although x is disposed to give response r to stimulus s, the disposition is not manifested. In which case, the analysandum is true (it is true that an object x is disposed at time t to give response r to stimulus s) but the analysans is false (it is false that if x were to undergo stimulus s at time t then x would give response r). Martin gives the example of a wire, which has the dispositional property of conducting electricity (thus being live – response r) when touched by a conductor (stimulus s). According to the simple conditional analysis, the wire would conduct electricity (give response r) if touched by the conductor (stimulus s). However, Martin argues that the disposition could be lost in such a case where the wire is connected to an external device, an electrofink, which sensing that the wire is to be touched by the conductor, renders the wire dead by causing the wire to lose the dispositional property of conducting electricity.

The problem of finkishness also pertains to the acquisition of dispositions. To illustrate this, let us suppose that an object x is not yet disposed to give response r to stimulus s. However, Martin points out that x might gain this disposition and that stimulus s might be the condition under which x so acquires it. In such a case the analysandum is false (it is false that x is disposed to respond r to stimulus s because x has not yet acquired this disposition) whilst the counterfactual analysans is true (it is true that if x were to undergo stimulus s at time t then x would give response r). In Martin's example, a wire that is dead and thus lacking the disposition to conduct electricity when touched by a conductor would, however, due to the electrofink, conduct electricity when subject to the conductor stimulus.

David Lewis argues that the problem of finkish dispositions arises in the context of finkish causal bases. Lewis agrees with an argument put forward by Prior, Pargetter and Jackson that every disposition necessarily has a causal base. A causal base, according to their analysis, is 'a causally sufficient antecedent condition' operative in, say, the breaking of a glass.[49] A causal base is said to explain why an object manifests a disposition. The causal base, according to Lewis, comprises some property B of the object that joins with a stimulus s to jointly cause the object to manifest a disposition. The causal base of a non-finkishly fragile glass would be this property B which joins with striking to cause breaking.[50] A finkish causal base is one where the finkishly fragile glass has property B that would join with striking to cause breaking and yet the glass does not break because the moment the glass is struck it loses property B. Lewis illustrates the problem of finkish dispositions by giving the example of two glasses on a production line which are possessed of the disposition of fragility. The glasses are identical and would be expected to break when struck. However, a sorcerer having taken a particular interest in one of the glasses intervenes at the point when it is to be struck and renders it immune to breaking and thus no longer fragile. The sorcerer in the example plays the role of an extrinsic causal base. Extrinsic causal bases are finkish and pose a threat to the intrinsicality of dispositions. Conversely, according to Lewis's illustration a glass that finkishly lacks a causal basis for fragility would break when struck because it would immediately gain some property B as a causal basis for fragility. Lewis contends that the problem of finkish causal bases arises when those bases are extrinsic properties of the object. He illustrates the problem of extrinsic causal bases with 'the case of Willie':

Willie is a dangerous man to mess with. Why so? Willie is a weakling and a pacifist. But Willie has a big brother – a very big brother – who is neither a weakling nor a pacifist. Willie has the extrinsic property of being protected by such a brother; and it is Willie's having this extrinsic property that would cause anyone who messed about with Willie to come to grief. If we allowed extrinsic properties to serve as causal bases of dispositions, we would have to say that Willie's *own* disposition makes him a dangerous man to mess about with. But we very much do not want to say that. We want to say instead that the disposition that protects Willie is a disposition of Willie's brother. And the reason why is that the disposition's causal basis is an intrinsic property of Willie's brother.[51]

If the causal bases of dispositions are extrinsic, then we would have to say that the dead wire in Martin's example, by virtue of its connection to the electrofink as extrinsic causal base, is not dead but live. We would have to say that Willie, by virtue of having a big brother, is not a weakling but a dangerous man to mess with. Or, to return to the glass example, that the glass on the production line, by virtue of having the sorcerer as an extrinsic causal base, is not fragile. Lewis attempts to save the conditional analysis from the problem of finkish dispositions by offering what he calls a 'reformed conditional analysis' that presupposes the problem of finkishness and writes this presupposition into the analysis itself. It does this by appealing to the notion of a partial cause in an attempt to ground dispositions in something that is independent of factors that are extrinsic to x. With regard to the glass example, Lewis argues that we need to say more than that the glass would break when struck. To say that the glass would break when struck fails to capture the dispositional character of the glass to break under these circumstances. That is, we need to say what it is in the object that causes it to break when struck. We can succeed in doing this by appealing to some intrinsic property of the object that together with striking causes the glass to break. In so doing, Lewis argues that the having of a disposition is dependent on a causal base that is intrinsic to a thing. This involves appealing to a partial rather than complete cause of the manifestation of a disposition. Taking the property B as the intrinsic causal base, Lewis argues that the stimulus 's and x's having of B would jointly cause x to give response r'.[52] If x is to be disposed to give response r to stimulus s by virtue of its intrinsic causal base, B, then x must retain B for as long as it takes to give response r. Lewis argues that s and B jointly constitute a partial or 'x-complete cause' to ensure that the relevant causal factors are intrinsic rather than extrinsic to the object. Such a partial cause comprises an intrinsic property of the object, B, and the stimulus s. Lewis articulates the reformed conditional analysis thus:

> Something x is disposed at time t to give response r to stimulus s iff, for some intrinsic property B that x has at t, for some time t' after t, if x were to undergo stimulus s at time t and retain some property B until t', s and x's having of B would jointly be an x-complete cause of x's giving response r.[53]

The result of Lewis's response to Martin's example is that the dead wire is correctly predicted not to be disposed to conduct electricity when touched by the conductor. Although the dead wire would conduct electricity when touched by the conductor in Martin's example, it is not due to the intrinsic nature of the wire but rather to something extrinsic to the wire (the external device, the electrofink). Conversely, in the case where the live wire does not conduct electricity this is due not to its intrinsic nature but rather to the extrinsic fink. Consequently, the reformed conditional analysis correctly predicts, on the basis that the wire has an intrinsic property, that if the wire were to retain that property, it would conduct electricity in response to being touched by the conductor and having the property of being live.

By identifying the causal base with a partial rather than complete cause of the manifestation pertaining only to that part of the cause that is intrinsic to the object, Lewis extricates the causal base from all elements that are extrinsic to the object. Lewis claims that this manages to save the intrinsicality of dispositions. However, despite these modifications Lewis's reformed conditional analysis is unable to meet our requirements to show that relationality and intrinsicality can be successfully combined in a metaphysics of powers. The reason for this is that the appeal to a causal base stipulates that powers require grounding in other properties. The concept of a ground for a power requires that the ground be conceptually distinct from the power itself and that the ground confers power on its bearer. The appeal to a causal base of dispositions thus argues that the having of a power entails the having of two properties. Lewis contends that when we say that a disposition has a causal base, we are referring to both a first-order and second-order property of the object and that we need not say which of the two properties is dispositional:

> When a glass is fragile, it has two properties. It has some first-order property which is a causal basis for fragility; it also has the second-order property of having some causal basis for fragility or other. We need not say which of these two properties of the glass is its fragility.[54]

Lewis refuses to be drawn on the issue of whether the causal base comprises dispositional or non-dispositional 'categorical' properties.[55] Nevertheless, the causal base and the disposition are conceptually distinct. These properties are, as articulated by George Molnar, function (function of causing under certain conditions) and executor of function (the property that carries out the causal role). As a result, the appeal to a causal base of dispositions runs into particular difficulties. These difficulties centre on the issue of distinguishing which of the two properties is the power and which the cause of the manifestation. If we say that both properties cause the manifestation, then we have overdetermination of every event that manifests a power.[56] In order to avoid such overdetermination we are forced to make a choice between the two properties. If we opt to say that the base alone is the cause of the manifestation, and the power is to be identified with the causal function executed by the base, then the power does not cause the manifestation. This renders powers causally impotent. As our primary concern here, however, is to assess the philosophical cogency of Nietzsche's development of a metaphysics that appeals to qualities that are both relational and intrinsic, we need to stress the implications of the conditional analysis for Nietzsche's project.

It should be clear that the simple conditional analysis cannot achieve Nietzsche's aims because it fails to capture what it is in the nature of an object that gives rise to the manifestation of a disposition. This is obviously at odds with Nietzsche's aim to capture the nature of real causal efficacy. The reformed conditional analysis is equally unsatisfactory in this regard. As a result of its oscillation between overdetermination and causal impotency it too threatens to deprive powers of causal efficacy, thus precluding Nietzsche from adopting the distinction between causal bases and powers that informs its analysis. Moreover, the very conditionality of the analysis and its appeal to a conditioning stimulus is evidently incompatible with Nietzsche's appeal to the spontaneity and activity of causal powers. He describes powers as quanta of 'dammed-up energy' that are 'waiting to be used up somehow', not at the bidding of an external stimulus but rather in response to the intrinsic spontaneity of their natures.[57] He contends that explosive powder, for example, is intrinsically possessed of the power to explode and that the lighting of a match in its vicinity, whilst causing the powder to manifest its nature in a particular way, is not primarily responsible for the manifestation of its explosive nature. Consequently, Nietzsche warns us against taking the 'helmsman for the steam', arguing that we must distinguish the 'cause of acting' from the 'cause of acting in a particular way' and that we must give primacy to the intrinsic causal nature of the power rather than to extrinsic stimuli.[58] However, all is not lost just because the conditional analysis is unsuitable to Nietzsche's project. For Nietzsche proposes an alternative account of powers that arguably renders his aim of combining relationality and intrinsicality, as he understands these concepts, an intelligible possibility. Consequently, Nietzsche offers an account of powers that is analogous to our human experience of desire and mental activity. On the basis of such an analogy, he ascribes to both the realm of the organic and the inorganic, human and non-human, a certain intentional directedness. Nietzsche suggests, by employing 'man as an analogy' to our understanding of the world,[59] that there is a fundamental isomorphism between the organic and the inorganic sphere:

> Assuming that nothing real is 'given' to us apart from our world of desires and passions, assuming that we cannot ascend or descend to any 'reality' other than the reality of our instincts (for thinking is merely an interrelation of these instincts, one to the other), may we not be allowed to perform an experiment and ask whether this 'given' also provides a *sufficient* explanation for the so-called mechanistic (or 'material') world?[60]

The justifiability of Nietzsche's making such an analogy has been an issue for heated debate in Nietzsche commentaries and has even led some commentators to argue that the will to power thesis is an implausible and unjustifiable metaphysical extravagance if taken to apply to anything other than the human sphere of psychology.[61] However, the significance of Nietzsche's argument from analogy has been overlooked. The reason for this is that it is regarded as a return to a philosophical position that Nietzsche criticises. The position he rejects is the characteristic one of modern, epistemologically centred philosophy that takes human consciousness to be the constitutive centre of things. Nietzsche writes: 'Critique of modern philosophy: erroneous starting point, as if there existed "facts of consciousness" . . . .'[62] It is objected that Nietzsche's argument from analogy succumbs to the idea of taking 'inner facts' as a foundational basis on which to understand the world. However, if we probe a little deeper, we see that Nietzsche's approach and aim differ considerably from the traditional view he criticises. For his proposal that '*This world is the will to power – and nothing besides! And you yourselves are also this will to power – and nothing besides!*'[63] undermines the view that the human subject is a constitutive centre and poses significant challenges to 'our belief in the "ego" as a substance, as the sole reality from which we ascribe reality to things in general'.[64] According to Nietzsche, although our investigations are confined to our human point of view, our proposals are not 'facts' but rather conjectures that shall be deemed warranted only if they are supported by our best reasons and capable of providing us with convincing explanations of the nature of things. Moreover, Nietzsche's argument from analogy is significant to his project of preserving the reality of powers. The claim that the relationship between the human and the non-human is analogous suggests that the two spheres, although similar, are neither identical nor reducible to one another. Powers cannot therefore be grounded in a non-relational subject-substance. Furthermore, Nietzsche's argument from analogy plays an important role in his rejection of the metaphysics of opposites and in his espousal of the compatibility of relational and intrinsic properties in the will to power thesis. Understood analogously to our human experience of desire, Nietzsche draws our attention to the intentional character of empirical powers. That Nietzsche's appeal to the intentional character of powers supports the compatibility of relationality and intrinsicality can be discerned by turning to an account of powers put forward by George Molnar. By drawing out the implications of intentional directedness and what properly constitutes the intentional object of powers, Molnar enables us to see how Nietzsche's claim that relational and intrinsic properties are compatible rather than mutually exclusive is a plausible one.

Molnar offers an alternative to the conditional analysis of dispositions by appealing to the intentionality of physical powers. He rejects Brentano's thesis that intentionality is the mark of the mental, arguing that physical powers are also characterised by directedness. Molnar contends that both psychological states and physical properties (powers) are directed to something beyond themselves. He claims that physical powers such as solubility or electromagnetic charge have a direction towards something outside themselves that is also typical of psychological attributes. On the basis of this parallel between the intentionality of psychological states and the intentionality of powers, Molnar holds that 'a physical power is essentially an *executable* property', arguing that the 'intentional object of a physical power is its proper manifestation'.[65] This is the only form of relation, according to Molnar, in which a power can manifest its nature. Thus the nexus between a power and its manifestation, he claims, is non-contingent because the manifestation expresses the nature of the power. However, although the intentionality of physical powers is tantamount to their relationality, Molnar contends that physical powers are not relational through and through. That is, he argues that physical powers are also intrinsic properties. Molnar argues for this position by stressing the intentional character of powers and distinguishing the relation between a power and its manifestation from a causal relation between events. Whereas an event model of causality requires that all the relata actually exist, he contends that in the relation between a causal power and its manifestation, the manifestation of the power may be possible rather than actually realised. However, appealing to the parallel between psychological and physical intentionality, he argues that the power is real and independent of its manifestation. He claims that the intentional object of mental states can be existent or nonexistent, writing, 'We can be looking for, seek or want something that may or may not exist. We can have beliefs about non-existent objects, attribute fictitious properties to things that exist as well as to things that do not.'[66] Similarly, we can claim that intentional physical powers exist even when their intentional object, their manifestation, does not exist. Molnar thus concludes that powers are intrinsic because they exist independently of their manifestation whilst their relationality resides in their possible or potential manifestation. By way of illustration, Molnar contends that a purely physical object can be soluble without ever dissolving, or fragile without ever breaking. Physical powers, according to this analysis, are relational but they are also intrinsic.

Nietzsche's rejection of an event model of causality in favour of a power model, coupled with his argument from analogy, ascribing intentionality to both the human and non-human world, complies with this characterisation of dispositional properties as both relational and intrinsic. It is also consistent with Nietzsche's description of a power as an 'undetachable reality' that the power is real and does not cease to exist even when it is not being manifested.[67]

However, Nietzsche's characterisation of powers on the model of intentionality is subject to a particular difficulty that, unless overcome, threatens his thesis that intrinsically constituted powers are empirically instantiated. That is, if the relation between a causal power and its manifestation is not to be understood in the sense of an event model of causality where both the cause and the effect must actually obtain in order for the power to be understood as relational, then it may succumb to what Molnar refers to as the 'always packing never traveling' objection. This objection claims that causal powers are mere potentialities whose empirical instantiation is just a promissory note. John Foster is one such writer who levies this objection against the power thesis by raising the problem of the location of powers. He argues that to be capable of empirical investigation powers must be spatially located. Yet, something is capable of occupying space, according to Foster, only if it is a substantial object, which he describes as something 'with an intrinsic nature independent of its causal powers and dispositions'.[68] Thus, according to Foster, powers must be grounded in a non-relational substrate with a non-power nature if they are to be spatially located. If Foster's objection is secure and if we refuse to ground powers in a non-dispositional substrate, as Nietzsche declines to do, then we can intelligibly speak of powers only in terms of their potential effects rather than their actual empirical instantiation. However, Molnar provides the power thesis with a defence strategy to such objections. His proposed defence is consistent with Nietzsche's project.

In response to Foster's challenge to the coherency of the power thesis Molnar probes Foster's understanding of what constitutes a substantial object. He claims that according to folk physics a substantial object is one that has *bulk* or *volume*. For something to be voluminous it must have size and shape. However, Molnar contends that such voluminous objects fill rather than occupy space. Moreover, space filling entails that there is something in that volume of space and that it is this something that *has* size and shape. Molnar concedes that this ordinary notion understands substance to be something that has an intrinsic nature. However, he contends that common sense is noncommittal as to whether this intrinsic nature is independent of causal powers.[69] It is in the context of this line of reasoning that Molnar offers a solution to Foster's objection. The solution involves rejecting what Molnar calls 'pan-dispositionalism' in favour of 'moderate dispositionalism'. Pan-dispositionalism claims that all properties of an object are powers. Moderate dispositionalism claims that the intrinsic properties of an object are powers but that not all its properties are powers. According to Molnar's moderate dispositional-ism, an object also has extrinsic properties such as spatial location that are not powers. In response to Foster's objection, Molnar contends that 'Foster has not given a sound argument to the conclusion that space occupants must have a non-power nature'. According to Molnar the notion of space-occupancy properly applies to sub-microscopic rather than to ordinary voluminous objects. He argues that simple objects 'have no volume and do not *fill* a space' but rather are in space just by having a spatial address, by being '*at* a point-location'. Molnar explains that 'If the fundamental particles that make up the physical world are (spatially) simple, as we have some empirical reason to believe, they are space occu-pants without being substantial (voluminous) objects.'[70] Here Molnar contends that powers can have spatial location without being grounded in non-dispositional substrates. Powers can have a spatial address, he argues, without being grounded in something that is not itself a power. Consequently, Foster's objection can be overcome, according to Molnar, by considering that an object has both extrinsic and intrinsic properties. Its extrinsic properties provide the necessary location of the object whilst its intrinsic nature is constituted by powers.

This appeal to space-occupying points of force is compatible with Nietzsche's suggestion that forces are located at points and emanate from these points from which space is everywhere filled with the effects of force. Nietzsche describes the world on the model of the will to power as

> a firm, iron magnitude of force that does not grow bigger or smaller, that does not expend itself but only transforms itself; as a whole, of unalterable size, a household without expenses or losses, but likewise without increase or income; enclosed by 'nothingness' as by a boundary; not something blurry or wasted, not something endlessly extended, *but set in a definite space as a definite force (sondern als bestimmte Kraft einem bestimmten Raum eingelegt)*, and not a space that might be 'empty' here or there, but rather as force throughout, as a play of forces and waves of forces, at the same time one and many, increasing here and decreasing there . . . (my emphasis)[71]

Nietzsche's appeal to points of force adopts a view similar to Molnar's moderate dispositionalism whereby a thing has both extrinsic and intrinsic properties. As an extrinsic property, spatial location is a contingent factor of an object, which can be altered without changing its intrinsic dispositional character. Nietzsche describes powers as fixed quanta and argues that the difference between quantities is a quality suggesting that what is intrinsic to a thing is its qualitative nature.[72] Implicit in his statement here is the idea that powers cannot be reduced to a Pythagorean ontology of numbers and quantities. Rather, Nietzsche suggests these numbers must be measurements *of* something that have qualitative content.[73] Similarly, Nietzsche's view of spatial location as an extrinsic property suggests there must be *something*, some primitive non-voluminous quality, that occupies the position. The quality rather than its location is intrinsic according to Nietzsche.

Nietzsche's will to power metaphysics is thus equipped with the necessary resources to silence Foster's concerns about the empirical instantiation of powers, leaving Nietzsche free to hold as a result of his argument from analogy that the fundamental constituents of empirical reality are both relational and intrinsic. We recall that it was the issue of existential commitment that made relational properties incompatible with intrinsic properties in Poellner's analysis; the claim that relational powers are existentially committed to other powers leads to the view that relational and intrinsic properties are mutually exclusive. However, since Nietzsche's appeal to empirically instantiated properties that are both relational and intrinsic is a cogent philosophical position because such properties are understood as non-subject-implying and extrinsically located powers whose proper relata is their manifestation, Nietzsche has, in his view, secured the ultimate intelligibility of his metaphysical thesis as a suitable vehicle to overcome the metaphysics of opposites.

CONCLUDING REMARKS

Nietzsche's argument that the fundamental constituents of reality are both intrinsic and relational is the hallmark of his overcoming the Kantian opposition between self and world. The empirical world, Nietzsche concludes, contrary to Kant, is available, but metaphysically irreducible, to human knowledge. Nietzsche's appeal to powers that are intrinsic and relational is crucial to securing this conclusion, allowing that the fundamental constituents of reality are metaphysically real and capable of empirical investigation. Nietzsche's response to Kant on the issue of self and world culminates, then, in the will to power thesis.

An alternative interpretation proposing the existential dependency of powers and drawing on the fact that Nietzsche sometimes adopts this approach, argues that a relational metaphysics devoid of intrinsic natures can still give Nietzsche what he wants.[74] It suggests that Nietzsche can construe the empirical world as real 'for us' without appealing to intrinsic natures. Informing this submission is the idea that the empirical world, although independent of human minds, is nonetheless constituted by relations of existential dependency between powers. The problem with this suggestion, however, is that in addition to ignoring Nietzsche's engagement with and response to Kant on the issue of intrinsic natures, it also brings Nietzsche's will to power thesis to the brink of incoherency due to the fact that each power would be reducible to its interpretation by another power lacking an intrinsic nature, rendering the second power, in turn, reducible to another power's interpretation, and so on. Consequently, the suggestion that powers are existentially dependent on one another disallows the possibility that powers are real, even for us, because succumbing to Poellner's charge of a vicious regress they cannot be described as real in any meaningful sense at all. Thus although Nietzsche thinks powers interact, it is important for his response to Kant that these relations are not those of dependency. Rather, the relations between powers must be extrinsic and derivative of the fundamental desire on the part of individual powers to manifest their intrinsic natures, their proper relata residing in this manifestation. To successfully dismount from Kant's opposition between self and world, allowing that the knowable empirical world is metaphysically independent of us, Nietzsche's relational powers must also be intrinsic.

Nietzsche's argument in favour of the reality of powers represents, as he sees it, the completion of Kant's unfulfilled promise to secure the objectivity of our knowledge. The will to power thesis is a comprehensive perspective that, in putting forward a metaphysics that is both relational and intrinsic, brings the Kantian project to full fruition by restricting the justifiable applicability of the concept of causality to the empirical world. This entails for Nietzsche that causal relations are informed by intrinsic natures that obtain in the empirical world available in principle to our knowledge rather than at the level of the non-empirical, non-relational and unknowable thing-in-itself. According to Nietzsche, the empirical world is relational and intrinsic; it is available to our knowledge but metaphysically independent of it. The position that causal powers are existentially independent is an integral component to Nietzsche's execution of this argument. Nietzsche's 'world in view', therefore, is one that operates according to an intrinsic and natural necessity. He writes, contrary to Kant,

> 'Regularity' in succession is only a metaphorical expression, *as if* a rule were being followed here; not a fact. In the same way, 'conformity with a law.' . . . That something always happens thus and thus is here interpreted as if a creature always acted thus and thus as a result of obedience to a law or a lawgiver, while it would be free to act otherwise were it not for the 'law'. But precisely this thus-and-not-otherwise might be *inherent in the creature*, which might behave thus and thus, not in response to a law, but because it is *constituted thus and thus*. All it would mean is: something cannot also be something else, cannot do now this and now something else, is neither free nor unfree but simply thus and thus.[75]

It is evident that Nietzsche's engagement with Kant results in his proposal of a metaphysics that, supported by reasons and justified from within our perspectival immersion in the world, is of both historical and general philosophical significance. However, reluctant to participate in a project that is of theoretical significance only, Nietzsche's metaphysics carries with it further ramifications. In the Introduction it was suggested that Nietzsche's historical and theoretical arguments are inextricably linked to his more practical concerns. This has now come to pass. The repercussions of Nietzsche's conclusion that the empirical world is intrinsically constituted from within and irreducible to human minds extends beyond historical or theoretical significance, permeating his philosophy of value and informing his 'fatalism'. Nietzsche contends that the human self as an organisation of intentionally directed drives, which he describes as 'our spiritual *Fatum*' and 'our *unteachable* essence',[76] is part of a larger 'totality' that also operates according to an inner necessity.[77] This necessity does not entail a 'superfluous teleology', postulating a determined and irreversible end-point to the development of things, but rather recognises that there is no norm or imperative external to the world governing how it 'should' be.[78] A thing is necessary because it cannot be other than it *is* and because it *must* be what it is intrinsically. Contrary to the nihilist's hankering for a world as it 'ought' to be, Nietzsche proposes 'Amor fati' or the 'ability to see as beautiful what is necessary in things'.[79] Moreover, acknowledgement that 'Everything is necessity' brings freedom, according to Nietzsche, from the idea that the world could or should be other than it is.[80] Unlike Kant, who introduces the noumenal realm to cater for the freedom precluded by mechanical laws of nature in the empirical world, Nietzsche argues, true to his aim of overcoming metaphysical oppositions, that freedom entails affirmation of necessary natures. Although an investigation of the full existential implications of Nietzsche's views on the nature of affirmation and freedom are beyond the scope of the present study, it is nonetheless clear that examination of the specifically philosophical and theoretical side of Nietzsche has practical implications, acting as 'preparatory work for the philosopher's task of the future' to 'solve the *problem of value*' and 'determine the *order of rank among values*'.[81] Nietzsche's epistemology and metaphysics, in conclusion, are important for life.

NOTES

1. Friedrich Nietzsche, *Beyond Good and Evil*, translated by Marion Faber (Oxford: Oxford University Press, 1998 [1886]), 36. Henceforth cited as *BGE*.
2. Friedrich Nietzsche, *The Will to Power*, edited by R. J. Hollingdale, translated by Walter Kaufmann (New York: Vintage Books, 1968 [1901]), 583A. Henceforth cited as *WP*.
3. Nietzsche, *BGE*, 36.
4. Nietzsche, *WP*, 557.
5. Peter Poellner, *Nietzsche and Metaphysics* (Oxford: Oxford University Press, 1995), p. 283.
6. Ibid., pp. 285–6.
7. Though, of course, both parties to this relation are, strictly speaking, 'subjects' for Nietzsche in the sense that they are intentionally directed. For a discussion of this issue that reaches different conclusions from mine, see James I. Porter, 'Nietzsche's Theory of the Will to Power', *A Companion to Nietzsche*, edited by Keith Ansell Pearson (Oxford: Blackwell, 2006), pp. 548–64.
8. Poellner, *Nietzsche and Metaphysics*, p. 287.

9. Ibid., p. 287.
10. For this characterisation I draw on R. Langton and D. Lewis, 'Defining Intrinsic', *Philosophy and Phenomenological Research*, Vol. 58, No. 2, 1998, pp. 333–45. See also George Molnar, *Powers: A Study in Metaphysics*, edited by Stephen Mumford (Oxford: Oxford University Press), pp. 39–41.
11. Steven D. Hales and Rex Welshon, *Nietzsche's Perspectivism* (Urbana and Chicago, IL: University of Illinois Press, 2000), p. 83.
12. Ibid., p. 83.
13. Ibid., p. 84.
14. Poellner, *Nietzsche and Metaphysics*, p. 268.
15. Nietzsche, *WP*, 556. See also *WP*, 583A.
16. Ibid., 625.
17. Nietzsche, *BGE*, 36.
18. I use the term 'property' here in the same sense as George Molnar when he writes that causal powers are properties as tropes where 'Tropes are genuine, mind-independent properties, but they are non-repeatedly particular' (Molnar, *Powers: A Study in Metaphysics*, p. 23). Molnar distinguishes properties from predicates where 'A predicate is a language-dependent thing, whereas a property (i.e. on the present account, a trope) is a feature of reality that is, in typical cases, independent of language or of thought' (ibid., p. 25).
19. Nietzsche defines activity as a 'reaching out for power'. He defines reactivity in terms of resistance to anything that hinders one's moving forward. It is to be noticed that Nietzsche thinks even reactivity entails a certain degree of activity (Nietzsche, *WP*, 657). See also Friedrich Nietzsche, *On the Genealogy of Morality*, translated by Maudemarie Clark and Alan J. Swensen (Indianapolis, IN: Hackett, 1998 [1887]), II, 10–12. Henceforth cited as *GM*.
20. Nietzsche argues that specific dispositions or drives, the disposition to explode or the desire for food, for example, are instances of the will to power. Their will to power resides in their desire to manifest their individual natures (Nietzsche, *WP*, 675). Thus the will to power operates on both the general and particular level. For a discussion of this issue, see Bernard Reginster, *The Affirmation of Life: Nietzsche on Overcoming Nihilism* (Cambridge, MA: Harvard University Press, 2006), pp. 126ff.; and John Richardson, *Nietzsche's System* (Oxford: Oxford University Press, 1996), pp. 28–35.
21. Friedrich Nietzsche, *The Gay Science*, translated by Walter Kaufmann (New York: Vintage Books, 1974 [1882/1887]), 349. Henceforth cited as *GS*. Nietzsche's distinction between stronger and weaker powers is related to his distinction between 'activity' and 'reactivity' in the sphere of values. An active individual embraces the task of the revaluation of values, whilst a reactive individual proves unequal to the challenge. For a discussion of the ontological and evaluative implications of Nietzsche's distinction between activity and reactivity, see Gilles Deleuze, *Nietzsche and Philosophy*, translated by Hugh Tomlinson (London: Athlone Press, 1992 [1962]), chapter 2. Although Deleuze's examination of these issues in the context of the will to power thesis seems to me to be correct, his argument that Nietzsche ultimately aims towards the elimination of the reactive seems at odds with Nietzsche's doctrine of 'Amor fati'.
22. Nietzsche, *GM*, II, 12.
23. Ibid., II, 12.
24. Nietzsche, *WP*, 520, 560, 656. See Hales and Welshon, *Nietzsche's Perspectivism*, pp. 68ff.; and Richardson, *Nietzsche's System*, pp. 28–35 for a discussion of this issue. I draw on their arguments here.
25. Nietzsche, *WP*, 526.
26. Ibid., 636.

27. Ibid., 642.
28. If one takes the view that a power overcomes resistance as a *de facto* impediment to its manifestation, then we are entitled to claim that the manifestation of a power is not existentially dependent on other powers. According to such a view, an active power would seek to manifest its nature whether other powers accompanied it or not. However, if one adopts the view, which Nietzsche sometimes does, that the overcoming of resistance is an integral component of what it means for a power to manifest its nature, then clearly we would not be entitled to this claim. *WP*, 636 finds in favour of my interpretation whilst *WP*, 656 finds against it. *WP*, 636 suggests powers seek compliance on the part of other powers. *WP*, 656 suggests powers seek resistance. However, as indicated earlier, my aim in this chapter is not to suggest that Nietzsche had these issues entirely worked out but merely that he has at his disposal the key ingredients necessary to make plausible a metaphysics that proposes that the ultimate constituents of reality are both relational and intrinsic.
29. For a discussion of this issue that draws an alternative conclusion to mine, see Reginster, *The Affirmation of Life: Nietzsche on Overcoming Nihilism*, pp. 126–33. Reginster argues that the nature of power, for Nietzsche, entails the seeking of resistance. In response to John Richardson's argument that the will to power tells us something about the manner in which individual drives pursue their specific ends and that the overcoming of resistance is merely instrumental in the achievement of these ends, Reginster contends overcoming resistance is an intrinsic component in what constitutes power. However, when understood as a metaphysical thesis in the way that I have suggested, resistance is not a logical component of the idea of force but rather a *de facto* condition that strong powers must overcome in their desire to expand their sphere of influence. This condition derives from Nietzsche's view that weaker powers also have an intrinsic nature and so seek to preserve themselves against the appropriating efforts of stronger powers.
30. Nietzsche, *WP*, 552; Nietzsche, *BGE*, 230. According to Nietzsche, the weaker power is drafted in to serve the aims of the greater power. However, he suggests that both the strong and weak power co-operate with one another due to the fact that they are sufficiently alike. Nietzsche contends powers group with others as a result of their respective natures. It is not the case, then, that the weaker power is entirely vanquished by its stronger counterpart. The relation into which the powers enter with one another is a mutual and reciprocal one.
31. Nietzsche, *WP*, 633. See also *WP*, 855 and 634.
32. That individual powers are distinct is suggested by Nietzsche's claim that 'One and the same force cannot also be another force' (Nietzsche, *WP*, 631).
33. Nietzsche, *BGE*, 230.
34. John Locke, *An Essay Concerning Human Understanding*, edited by P. Nidditch (Oxford: Clarendon Press, 1975 [1689]), Book II, chapter xxv, section 8.
35. Nietzsche, *GM*, I, 13; Nietzsche, *WP*, 710. The behaviour of a power-will, according to Nietzsche, is closely linked to its degree/quantum of power, rendering it active or reactive.
36. Nietzsche, *GM*, I, 13; Nietzsche, *WP*, 631, 633. See also Nietzsche, *GS*, 112.
37. David Hume, *A Treatise of Human Nature* (Oxford: Clarendon Press, 1992 [1888]), Book I, part III, section xiv.
38. As I have already indicated, Nietzsche's thoughts on the nature of powers are not always as clear as we might like, particularly when trying to make sense of the complicated metaphysical suggestion that powers can be both relational and intrinsic. When it comes to the manifestation of a power, Nietzsche on occasion suggests that powers are continuously manifested. On these occasions he

appears to think that this is necessary if he is to overcome substance metaphysics where powers inhere in non-relational substrata. However, the suggestion that powers are continuously manifested is compatible with the idea that powers are independent of their manifestations and that manifestations are simultaneous rather than successive.

Nevertheless, whilst Nietzsche's rejection of substance metaphysics in *GM*, I, 13 may suggest, on an initial reading, that powers are continuously manifested, there are suggestions later in the text that powers, rather than continuously manifesting their natures to their fullest degree, in fact seek out optimal conditions for their manifestation. At *GM*, III, 7 Nietzsche writes:

> Every animal . . . instinctively strives for an optimum of favourable conditions under which it can vent its power completely and attain its maximum in the feeling of power; just as instinctively . . . every animal abhors troublemakers and obstacles of every kind that do or could lay themselves across its path to the optimum . . . .

Here Nietzsche suggests that conditions and context matter to the manifestation of a power. This also complies with the associationist model of object-formation where the associations between powers are not arbitrary but rather are determined by the respective natures of the powers. That Nietzsche allows for the possibility that some powers are continuously manifested whilst others are not is suggested by his dual definition of the will to power 'as an insatiable desire to manifest power', on the one hand, and 'as the employment and exercise of power', on the other (Nietzsche, *WP*, 619).

39. For his appeal to 'inherent' natures, see Nietzsche, *WP*, 632. For the view that the manifestation of a power's nature is simultaneous, see Nietzsche, *GM*, I, 13. Read in a particular way, one might interpret this latter passage as claiming that a power cannot be differentiated from its manifestation. For example, Nietzsche writes: 'A quantum of power is just such a quantum of drive, will, effect . . .'. However, it is important to bear in mind that Nietzsche's target in this passage is substance metaphysics where the 'doer' that is separated from the 'doing' is an 'indifferent' and non-relational substratum in which powers are said to inhere. See also Nietzsche, *WP*, 631.

40. Nietzsche, *WP*, 634.

41. It may be objected that in *BGE*, 36 Nietzsche identifies effects with effects on other wills. He writes: 'one must dare to hypothesize, in short, that wherever "effects" are identified, a will is having an effect upon another will –' Obviously, if Nietzsche is suggesting that the necessary effect of a power-will is another power-will, as he sometimes does elsewhere, it is incompatible with his attempt to articulate a metaphysics combining intrinsicality and relationality. However, it is to be noted that Nietzsche is contrasting his will to power thesis with mechanism in this passage, highlighting the contrast by employing the terms of reference of the mechanical event model of causality. Moreover, it is not inconsistent for Nietzsche to claim that the proper relata of a power is the manifestation of its intrinsic nature whilst also holding that powers interact and influence one another. Rather, what this combination amounts to is the idea that powers, in their efforts to manifest their intrinsic natures, come into contact with other powers with which they interact in a real, though extrinsic and derivative, fashion.

42. Nietzsche, *GM*, I, 13.

43. Armstrong is a proponent of the usual view. See D. M. Armstrong, *A World of States of Affairs* (Cambridge: Cambridge University Press, 1997), p. 70. See also Molnar, *Powers: A Study in Metaphysics*, p. 83 for a discussion of this issue.

44. R. Kevin Hill denies the will to power is a dispositional concept arguing that such concepts, due to their counterfactual status, fail to capture the notion of power as an active ability. Hill argues that Nietzschean powers are not just causal properties but rather are normative to the extent that abilities are activities that have better or worse ways of playing things out. He argues that the disposition to explode, for example, is quite different from the bacterium's ability to digest food.

However, in GS, 360 Nietzsche argues, by distinguishing the intrinsic causal efficacy of a power (such as explosive powder) from external stimuli, that powers or dispositions are essentially active. Their apparent passivity stems not from their essential natures but rather from their activity which strives but sometimes fails to overcome the active resistance of other powers. Consequently, dispositions, as Nietzsche understands them, are fundamentally active and only appear passive when subject to the constraining efforts of other powers. See R. Kevin Hill, Nietzsche: A Guide for the Perplexed (London: Continuum, 2007), pp. 66ff.

45. The simple conditional analysis has been endorsed by Gilbert Ryle, The Concept of Mind (London: Hutchinson, 1949); Nelson Goodman, Fact, Fiction and Forecast (Cambridge, MA: Harvard University Press, 1954); and W. V. Quine, Word and Object (Cambridge, MA: MIT Press, 1960).

46. Molnar, Powers: A Study in Metaphysics, pp. 84–5.

47. George Molnar, 'Are Dispositions Reducible?', The Philosophical Quarterly, Vol. 49, No. 194, 1999, pp. 1–2.

48. C. B. Martin, 'Dispositions and Conditionals', The Philosophical Quarterly, Vol. 44, No. 174, 1994, pp. 1–8.

49. E. W. Prior, R. Pargetter and F. Jackson, 'Three Theses about Dispositions', American Philosophical Quarterly, Vol. 19, No. 3, 1982, p. 252.

50. David Lewis, 'Finkish Dispositions', The Philosophical Quarterly, Vol. 47, No. 187, 1997, p. 149.

51. Ibid., p. 155.

52. Ibid., p. 156.

53. Ibid., p. 157.

54. Ibid., p. 152. Molnar argues that if it is to be properly reductionist, the causal base must be non-dispositional. See Molnar, 'Are Dispositions Reducible?', p. 8.

55. The appeal to non-dispositional categorical properties suggests that powers cannot be categorically ascribed to objects whilst it is considered a categorical fact that objects have properties that are not powers. See Molnar, Powers: A Study in Metaphysics, p. 158.

56. Ibid., p. 130. See also Lewis, 'Finkish Dispositions', pp. 151–2.

57. Nietzsche, GS, 360.

58. Ibid., 360.

59. Nietzsche, WP, 619.

60. Nietzsche, BGE, 36. See also Friedrich Nietzsche, Sämtliche Werke. Kritische Studienausgabe, edited by Giorgio Colli and Mazzino Montinari (Berlin and München: Walter de Gruyter and dtv, 1980), 12, I [30]. Henceforth cited as KSA.

61. See, for example, Maudemarie Clark, Nietzsche on Truth and Philosophy (Cambridge: Cambridge University Press, 1990), chapter 7. See also Reginster's further development of Clark's argument in The Affirmation of Life: Nietzsche on Overcoming Nihilism, chapter 3. This issue has given rise to a protracted debate on the topic of anthropomorphism in Nietzsche. See the contributions of Elaine P. Miller, Daniel W. Conway, James I. Porter and Henry Staten, in Ansell Pearson (ed.), A Companion to Nietzsche.

62. Nietzsche, *WP*, 475.
63. Ibid., 1067.
64. Ibid., 487. See chapter 4 for a further discussion of this issue.
65. Molnar, *Powers: A Study in Metaphysics*, p. 63. Note that there is no inconsistency between my description of Nietzsche's will to power thesis as a metaphysical thesis and Molnar's reference to physical powers. Although the will to power obtains at the level of empirical reality, I describe it as a metaphysical thesis in order to capture both its origins as a regulative research maxim and its appeal to intrinsic natures. Molnar's appeal to physical powers may also be described as metaphysical. What Nietzsche's and Molnar's arguments have in common is their desire to capture the reality of powers.
66. Molnar, *Powers: A Study in Metaphysics*, p. 62. Molnar's claim that the relation between a disposition and its manifestation (its intentional object) is not a genuine relation is not intended to downplay the relational status of dispositions but rather to contrast the relational character of dispositions from the type of relations that obtain between events.
67. Nietzsche, *GM*, I, 13.
68. John Foster, *The Case for Idealism* (London: Routledge & Kegan Paul, 1982), pp. 67–9.
69. Molnar, *Powers: A Study in Metaphysics*, p. 175.
70. Ibid., p. 176. Molnar points out that there are in fact very few pan-dispositionalists. A pan-dispositionalist holds that all properties, both intrinsic and extrinsic, are powers. Moreover, Molnar contends that Boscovich was not a pan-dispositionalist, writing that 'His position is the more common one of treating all intrinsic properties of objects as powers, but allowing the extrinsic positional properties to be non-powers' (ibid., p. 179).
71. Nietzsche, *WP*, 1067. Nietzsche contends that our ordinary perceptual view of space rests on the erroneous idea of substantial voluminous objects in empty space (Nietzsche, *WP*, 520). He indicates that the erroneousness of our perceptual view of space does not preclude the spatial location of force as an extrinsic property when he writes, 'I believe in absolute space as the substratum of force' whilst denying that space exists 'in itself' (Nietzsche, *WP*, 545). According to Nietzsche, the spatial location of powers is a derivative property of its extrinsic, though nonetheless real, relations with other powers.

    It is to be noted that the notion of spatial location as an extrinsic property does not commit Nietzsche to Leibnizean metaphysics. This is because extrinsic relations, for Nietzsche, do not constitute a pre-established harmony that renders their status ideal. Rather, according to Nietzsche, these relations, founded on *agon* and strife as fundamental powers seek to overcome resistance to the manifestation of their natures, are real though not intrinsic.
72. Nietzsche, *WP*, 563. In line with his view that force is not to be properly understood as a quantifiable unit expressible only in mathematical equations, Nietzsche refers to points of force as points of will. He claims that a purely mathematical account is concerned with quantity to the detriment of quality or the actual causal efficacy of force (Nietzsche, *KSA*, 13, 11 [73]). For a further discussion of this issue see Robin Small, *Nietzsche in Context* (Aldershot: Ashgate, 2001), pp. 161–2.
73. Deleuze argues that the qualitative aspect of force constitutes its essence and informs its relationality, writing that 'Difference in quantity is the essence of force, and the relation of force to force' (Deleuze, *Nietzsche and Philosophy*, pp. 43–4). It is to be noted, however, that although Deleuze's analysis of force and the will to power point to the need for intrinsic relational properties, this is not explicitly articulated by Deleuze. This is arguably because Deleuze's primary

interest is in the relational character of force and the manner in which the will to power acts as a synthetic principle responsible for the hierarchical relations between forces. Therefore, according to Deleuze, the 'will to power is manifested as a capacity for being affected' (ibid., p. 62).

74. R. Kevin Hill puts forward such an argument. See his *Nietzsche's Critiques: The Kantian Foundations of His Thought* (Oxford: Clarendon Press, 2003), pp. 138–40.

75. Nietzsche, *WP*, 632.

76. Nietzsche, *BGE*, 231.

77. Friedrich Nietzsche, *Twilight of the Idols*, included in *Twilight of the Idols/The Anti-Christ*, translated by R. J. Hollingdale (London: Penguin, 1990 [1889]), 'Expeditions of an Untimely Man', 49. Henceforth cited as *TI*.

78. Nietzsche, *BGE*, 13; Nietzsche, *TI*, 'Morality as Anti-Nature', 6. Nietzsche argues that although we cannot be other than we are, we can commit ourselves to a course of action in accordance with our natures. Despite the necessity of our being will to power, we can make promises (Nietzsche, *GM*, II, 2). See John Richardson, *Nietzsche's System* (Oxford: Oxford University Press, 1996), pp. 207–16 for a similar view.

79. For Nietzsche's characterisation of nihilism, see Nietzsche, *WP*, 585. For his notion of 'Amor fati', see Nietzsche, *GS*, 276.

80. Friedrich Nietzsche, *Human, All Too Human*, translated by R. J. Hollingdale (Cambridge: Cambridge University Press, 1996 [1878–86]), Volume I, 'On the History of the Moral Sensations', 107.

81. Nietzsche, *GM*, I, 17.

Index